A KIST OF SORROWS

A KIST OF SORROWS

A novel

by

DAVID KERR CAMERON

LONDON
VICTOR GOLLANCZ LTD
1987

First published in Great Britain 1987
by Victor Gollancz Ltd,
14 Henrietta Street, London WC2E 8QJ

© David Kerr Cameron 1987

British Library Cataloguing in Publication Data
Cameron, David Kerr
  A kist of sorrows: a novel.
  I. Title
  823'.914[F]   PR6053.A4/

ISBN 0-575-03952-3

Typeset in Great Britain by Centracet
and printed by St Edmundsbury Press Ltd
Bury St Edmunds, Suffolk

A KIST OF SORROWS

LAST NIGHT I took the old roads and heard the old speak. I listened again to the still voices and felt the sting of the wind on my cheek. And it was good, like a home-coming. The old track is grass-grown, almost obliterated by the years, and I am a stranger now where the old wind wanders, where it reeshles the dry broom and tugs at the tufted grass. The hill is quiet, shorn of voices. There is neither a whimper nor the snarl of a dog borne on the wind, only the silent throb of the centuries and the distant grey growl of the sea. The small echoes of history linger where the tumbled, moss-green stones mark the site of a dwelling, the line of an old hill dyke that once margined a poor man's kingdom, and in the stunted tree that guards the lonely gable. Unroofed, the hearth looks at the northern sky, lone and forlorn.

Time has mellowed the stones, as it has sutured the hurts of the heart; hallowed them as the last reminder of the folk who once had their life and their being here. They rest, stilled forever in their coffin'd sleep, and now on the hill nature has reclaimed her own. Below, in the broad haughlands of the farmtouns, the fields are bleak and spare but orderly still under the plough in an unbroken continuity with the past as they run for the plain and the sea. As the cold autumn light fails it is a land, suddenly, that chills the soul. Once its bare parks and its damp, poor-lit bothies bound a proud folk prisoner, sapping their will to leave it, slowly taking the heart out of them; circumscribed in it they lived out their sorrows and their chance encounters and endured the rote of their days, fulfilling bleak destinies till the kirkyard claimed them.

They were not, those folk of the old hill crofts and the mud-girt farmtouns, raillers against the terrible futility of their lives; nor were they sad lamenters. Their time was not heavy with regretting, though their guarded despair slipped out, like rabbit-guts from a rotten bag, in the worn rough poetry of their guttural speak and now and then in the words of a plaintive song that caught their sadness. Even the land itself begrudged

7

them, endlessly denying them, for their hairsts were late and haggard and rarely abundant. In its poor yield the soil quietly mocked them . . .

The wind teases the memory, restoring to it the fragments from another life, the images of another eye. Here in the crofting uplands where the heather has encroached it conjures into the mind the interlacing fall of the small croft fields, the fall of the track, now overgrown and bereft of footsteps, into the farmlands below. It was never a hospitable place. It broke men in body and will and with a strange kind of bankruptcy that haunted their gaunt faces. Theirs was a slow dance to the music of eternity, a minuet to the movement of the seasons. Few escaped unscathed. I cannot tell you now how it was with all of them, only a few. In my blood runs their blood. Once, slow down that stony track tumbling its way through the patterns of the past stumbled a lass with a winsome smile, and an impish sense of mischief that shone still in the eyes of the old woman I knew by the chimney corner. Strange and intangible the thing that bound us then, that continuity of race and creed that united the tenuous thread of her yesterdays with my own tomorrows. It is from the old woman that I have the memory of it and how it was.

Slow through the still of the fields she had come as night folded down and slipped blue-hazed into the hollows of the land. It thickened the hedgerows and crouched like a thief by the dykesides and already it had begun to take the Croft Hill by stealth, creeping upward in a mounting gloaming tide that blurred the patchwork of its small and pitiful fields. From his study window under the eaves of the manse, Patrick Pringle watched the solitary figure descend the track and take the road that led round the skirt of the hill, a speck that moved slow-motioned in the empty evening landscape. Dusk did not conceal the errand or the identity from the man who had long held God's embassy in the parish, for he was already aware of them. He watched until the thickening mirk of the November night took the figure from his sight, merging it with its own darkness, before sitting down at the desk behind him. There he lit the lamp and waiting, watched as its yellow light spilled slowly over the open bare page of his day-book. Brooding over its blankness a sadness gathered in him. Strange to him still the ways of men, and of God.

'So be it.'

His sigh was neither rebuke nor acceptance, only a recognition of the imponderables of life, of the tortured destinies that blew folk through it like windlestraes. That weighed heavily; there were times when Patrick Pringle wondered about God. Then, dipping his quill, he began to write quickly, as though the hand were already impatient with the tale it would unfold.

November 28, 1878:

This nicht, as the licht failed, saw James MacCaskill's lass go home on the moss road to her new place, the Campbell toun of Mossgair. God pity the poor bairn that it must be so for I misdoubt that she will find much of the milk of charity or human kindliness there. It is a sore heart that awaits her and I would it were not so—that the Hill folk did not have to sell their children into slavery for the avoidance of another mouth to feed. But such is their penury, the grind of their want, they must have recourse to it. May God protect the bairn who yet must be a woman ere she has left her childhood behind her.

Pringle rose from his desk. A restlessness gripped him, as now it so often did. What was it, this desolation of the soul that so possessed him? Beyond the cold panes he looked out on the night, on the pale cluster of lights in the village below him. Dark had come suddenly as he wrote so that now only the black mound of the Hill loomed against the lighter shading of the sky. He pulled the curtains. Folk, he knew, would wonder at MacCaskill, feeing his lass to the likes of the Campbells.

'So be it,' he murmured again and the pity moved in his bowels as he stepped again to the desk to shut the diary page from his sight, the past from his heart, closing the large leather-bound volume that was his only confidant, in a way his only friend. It was long years now since Hannah had died; so long that he was no longer sure of the sound of her voice in his inner ear or that the image of the face conjured by remembrance on the membranes of the mind was really hers. He felt a deep sense of loss that it had become so. There were nights when Pringle grieved for the wasteland his life had become, for the emotional desert of his days and for the lonely bed that was now his living tomb. That desolation had deeply lined the strong, heavy features of a face that might have been handsome once. The thick wiry grey of his crisply cropped hair ran down to side-whiskers and the thrust of a cropped, steely grey beard. His garb was the evangelical uniform of his calling worn without grace or distinction, as though it sat on a ploughman, and without the need to excuse it for the hands that held the quill might as capably have handled the stilts and would not have deigned to do so. It was Pringle's strength that he had never found it difficult to equate the things of the earth and the fields with the will of Heaven.

Now in the quiet room of Kilbirnie's Free Kirk manse, its silences broken only by the spit and crackle of the larch log in the grate, he minded the start of him there, the cloth but new to him yet, and his first coming among them. The Free Kirk folk of Kilbirnie had been ill to please with their ministers. When their new-biggit kirk's pulpit had fallen suddenly vacant—when old MacBain, their hero of the Disruption, had finally started to haver and speak stite and had been pressed into an unwanted retirement—it had taken them an unconscionable time to vote in his successor. The first they had tried had been a begeck to them all, a sickly, simpering laddie from the refined streets of west Aberdeen who would not have kenned one end of a black stirk from the other: he had fair scunnered them with his fine, English-like accent and his pained reasonableness and his hash was soon enough settled when he was bidden to come to his denner by Tait of Littleshin who was an elder and elder statesman of the parish and held great sway with the session. He had gone home the laddie, after the sermon, and almost at once had put Littleshin fair out of humour with his dainty-like steppies and the unctuous way he wiled a path through the glaur of the Littlins close—'just like a lassie near,' old Tait had said later, 'as though he had nivver in's life seen coo's skitter afore!' And forbye, he had been tactless enough to kicher and hoast once or twice on Mistress Tait's Sunday boiled beef (she was terribly put-out), so it wasn't that long before Littlins was convoying him from the place, good riddance to him, and that was the last and hinderend the Kilbirnie folk saw of him.

The next nominee promised better, coming from somewhere round Echt: he was a fine and decent old man who once had written long-heided books till the years began to overtake him and he spoke right civilly to them in a quiet, fatherly way. But they were feared of him all the same, old like he was, in case he gaed the way of MacBain.

So syne Pringle was sent for and came from his kirk away down in Dundee. Young he had been then, his old father a crofter man still in the upcountry of Rhynie. He had pleased them fine.

'Fine and standyont,' they said, one to the other. 'He will have nae truck wi' thae Moderates.'

He had great muckle hands on him they saw like a plough-man's and that had reassured them, and the way he had taken hold of the edge of the pulpit had garred the timmer crack and they had kenned for sure he was the very man they were looking for. And right enough he had girned and glowered at them and indicted and damned them and they had likit that fine (not a blink of a nod could they take, his eye aye upon them) and when it had come time to go home with Littleshin to his Sunday bite of denner he had taken through the sharn of the toun without breaking his stride or giving a care to the shine of his patent leather boots and that had so pleased old Tait that he had taken the liberty as well of offering a dram and had it willingly, no-nonsense accepted. And when he had pushed the soup plate from him to make way for the second course at Mistress Tait's table he had gobbled the great unsavoury dollops of her boiled beef a damned sight faster than any fee'd laddie they had ever had about the place. Forbye that, the thick black hair of him wagging above vigorously masticating jaws, he had speired knowledgeably between mouthfuls about Littlin's beasts and his seed corn and the upshot of it was that Tait and him were real chief afore it came time for him to take his leave. And instead of that, he had been bidden to stay to his supper and syne to his bed and when he had left in the morning he had known he had the pulpit. But before then he'd had time to take a keek under his brows at Tait's youngest daughter—the fine oval of her sun-kissed face and the wild tumble of her deep brown hair—and her at him, the look between them something strange and questioning like she had known him always. Queer she thought it, brooding long after.

'Fegs,' she told her sister, drawing the blankets up over them after the bedtime prayer, 'he doesnae look nane like a minister should look!'

'Wheesht!' her sister had said.

'He'd be a fair terror in yer bed.'

'Anna!'

But fine it would be—she had thought it all the same—to have his hands on your dowp.

So that had been the coming of Pringle, the young widower with his motherless bairn, guilty still in his grief. He had taken his god among them not knowing what the years would bring, a god in his own image: dour, straight and resolute.

Pringle cupped a hand over the glass to dowse the lamp's flame and came slow down the stair to the room that was kitchen and dining room both. There Miss Pringle was already boiling their supper eggs in the kettle slung low from the swey over the fire.

Night and silence brooded round the Campbell steading as Morag MacCaskill stepped into its shadows. There was no lantern alight as yet in the stable that housed the toun's Clydesdale pairs nor, that Term-night of the year, was there the ring of a tacketed boot on the cobbles of its close as a horseman took across it on some stable errand: to get a windling of straw for bedding to his beasts or a bag of bruised corn from the loft. On any other night of the year there would have been movement about the toun as it went about its tasks, the bob and sway of lanterns about it as men came home, lowsed from the plough, their shouts and banter as they threw hames and collars noisily on to the brackets on the lime-washed stable wall. Tonight, though, silence locked the toun: that Term-day of Martinmas, like that of Whitsunday, was a landmark in the farmtoun year when the folk of that countryside shed their past and began their lives anew as they moved on from one toun to the next, engaging themselves for a new six-month fee. The day before the loft bothy of Mossgair had released the toun's second horseman to a new stable and another Clydesdale pair and, its door dark by the stable gable, awaited its next incumbent who would look remarkably like the last. It was a place of habitation that would give little of life's comforts and make sure he moved on when he had completed his engagement.

The stillness settled on Morag, emphasizing her own footfalls as they echoed behind her. She came finally to the back door of the farm dwelling and, waiting, fought down her racing heartbeats. Her knock went through the house to gather its own echo and fade it slowly back to her, a lone cry in an endless cavern. Somewhere in the nightfall, maybe on the Croft Hill, a dog barked, riffling the calm of the countryside. Hesitatingly, quelling again the urge to flee the place and its threatening silences, she pounded the door and almost at once heard shuffling feet behind it. Inside a hand fumbled the latch and the door was flung open on a face vignetted in the glow of a guttering candle. From its deep sockets the eyes surveyed her, almost without interest.

'An' who micht ye be, quean?' The old man's voice was gruff, querulous.

'Gin it please ye, sir, I'm Mistress Campbell's new servant maid.'

The gaze was pitiless. 'Ye dinna tell me . . .' The head nodded, lolling sideways in the candlelight, taking in the small stature of the figure before it, and Morag realized now that the old Campbell had been drinking. The head nodded again, uncertain of its own equilibrium.

'Lord save us then . . .'

'If ye wid tell Mistress Campbell that I'm here——'

'Tell her yersel, lass. She's in the byre!' The door was swung shut in her face without ceremony and turning now in the way his nod had directed her she saw for the first time, a feeble glimmer—the only light about the farmtoun—that marked the cow byre. In a moment she had stooped under its low lintel into the fetid warmth of housed beasts and the commingling smells of sharn and urine. A mutched face lifted itself from the slow rise and fall of a cow's side as her step approached and she broke into the circle of lantern light. Its expression was one of obvious relief.

'Ye'll be Morag MacCaskill, bairn?'

13

'Aye, Ma'am.'

'Then haud ye tae the hoose and see to oor suppers, gin ye would. I'll be inbye presently, when I've seyed the milk.' The tone was firm but not unkindly. It halted Morag as she reached the byre-door.

'Can ye milk kye, lass?'

'Fine, Ma'am.'

'Of coorse, yer a crofter's bairn. I need hardly have speired.' It was as near to apology as she could make it. 'Godbethankit for that, for the last quean couldnae! The beasts jist widnat lat doon their milk tae her.'

Morag waited.

'Awa' wi' ye then, tae the hoose. And . . .' the words were tossed savagely after her '. . . get that lazy auld devil in there tae licht the lamp tae ye and throw a fresh peat or twa intae the fire.'

Inside the farmhouse a long stark corridor led to the open kitchen door. Campbell was slumped morosely in his seat by the fire, contemplating its feeble glow. Maybe he saw there the reflection of his own despair, of olden dreams. He let Morag stand for a moment, establishing their relationship, then indicated one of the wooden kitchen chairs.

'Sit ye doon.' The chair was hard, unyielding against her back. Campbell's gaze was drunkenly speculative.

'And yer foo aul' noo?'

'Nearly sixteen, sir.'

'Jist so, an' yer come of Hill folk?'

'Aye.' It was well he knew it. Strange she thought it for him to be letting on that he did not know of James MacCaskill, hill crofter and dyker, for all that he was beholden to him now and then for the day of a thresh or a haud-tae with the hairst or to rebuild a bit of Mossgair dyke that had succumbed to the frost. But all that was by the by; Campbell sly on it now, not wanting to be overly familiar with the crofting riff-raff, folk, so to speak, only on the very fringe of respectable society.

'And yer last place would be wi'——'

'With Miss Colquhoun. I was there four years.'

'A genteel body, Miss Cohoon, I wouldn't wonder?'

The tone was one of fine-judged curiosity and maybe the old man found it a disappointment that the lass's discretion was greater than her years. A strange lady, Miss Colquhoun; he'd heard rumours now and then, the passing whiff of obloquy.

'Would like everything verra proper, I daresay?'

'Verra proper, sir.' Morag bit her tongue too late.

'Aah, weel . . .' Campbell seemed disposed to savour a small triumph. 'Ah weel, ye'll maybe find things a bit different here.' The sweep of his hand took in the dismally bare comfort of the Mossgair kitchen, the bare functional accoutrements of dresser and press and deece and deal table and the chill of the cold stone floor. 'This'll be yer domain. Ye'll hae the fee'd man tae meat morning, noon and nicht, have his brose kettle boiling by the quarter-hoor of six ilka mornin' but the Sabbath and syne it'll be seven. Mistress Campbell will supervise oor ain mealtimes.'

'Aye, sir! Thank ye, sir!'

'Oho, but that's not all, lass. When ye've finished inbye there will be wark tae ye oot in the parks at the hairst and the hyow mebbe and at the hay. We'd expect ye tae pit tae a hand. Mistress Campbell's nae sae weel as she was.'

Well enough she knew what he meant for there was nothing remarkable in the long litany of jobs he had listed to her. It was the same for every lass in the kitchen of every farmtoun in the parish. Campbell paused, glowering under his brows.

'And ye'll clean the lad's bothy once in the week and when he's oot o' the wye, or else, mind ye—nae sweep it at a'!' Again she kenned fine what he meant.

'Ye need hae nae fears on that score, sir. I——'

Their interview was interrupted by the noisy lift of the door-sneck from its latch and the tall of a foot in the lobby as Mistress Campbell cried ben to them. 'Yer new horseman's here, Angus! Come ye and see tae him. He's inaboot but a meenit since and I've sent him up to his bothy. When he's sorted his horse tell him tae come tae the hoose for his supper. He's brocht his fiddle wi' him, I see'—her voice hardened, suddenly bitter—'we'll get a dance, Angus, you and me . . .'

So that was the start of you there, Old Woman, and I can see you now for the lass that you were, for long have I imbibed the memory of your days. It is often you told me of it: that nicht by your lone and at last in the great kitchen of Mossgair letting down your hair, the stoon of despair gripping you as you dressed down in the last glow of the peats to your inmost flannel petticoat. The tears had welled in you then and the sobs racked you as you pulled the box bed's blankets over your head and listened to the eerie night sounds of the steading; and the long dark history of the Campbells came back to you—you barely sixteen and all but a woman. I gather now the sum of your days and their fragile joys. I know how it was as the days slipped through December, the weather unseasonably mild and the month dragging by in a dreary procession of days one at the tail of the other and the heart of you like to break as you put them away with all the other grey days you had known; you'd be glad they were gone. And winter settling a grey sadness on the end-of-year fields; you had known it before, blithe and young though you were, this sorrow that clung to the land broken only by the cry of the raucous gulls as they trailed the winter ploughs, hopping and wheeling and squawking, God damn their gluttony. Fine you would remember it then, those days when it was only Miss Pringle's school that had claimed you, a prison though you thought it, John Lorimer whistling in the close of Corthyfold as you passed, coarse tink that he was he would tease and torment you so. *Aye, aye*, you would say and go on, letting fly with a stone at one of his beasts and then you'd feel fine (gype that he was, saying such things to you).

Quick down the hill and owre the parks you had come to the little school that stood back from the road away from the main clash and birl of Kilbirnie itself, screened behind its curtain of firs. Winter and summer, barefoot and booted, you had stumped down the hill, the six pennies pocketed in your starched petticoat going *thump* on your thigh. Cold on your thigh the pennies to pay for your schooling; you'd have sooner stayed home to twine straw ropes in the barn, for wasn't Miss Pringle just a fair deave to you with all her questions, so stern and prim, and you would wonder whiles why was it she hadn't a man like other womenfolk though again that hadn't surprised you, there was a something about her . . .

But you would forgive her all that soon enough when she told you of the clansmen and battles, stories that made your blood leap; tales of Harlaw and Flodden and Culloden in her soft voice that moved you with its harboured melancholy and you would know even then in the child's heart of you that maybe once Miss Pringle had loved a man and did so still in some secret corner of her being. You liked her fine, like a lass herself as she told you of Bonnie Prince Charlie: just a loon he had been with red hair and dreams in his heid. And after it all the clansmen had lain hackit and deid on the gore-soaked moor of Drummossie, butchered and bloody. There had been a tear in your eye at the thought of it, an inward rage in you at the cruel callousness of men, a hard bitter cry of disgust in you as you heard it.

And whiles there would be a funeral go past in the bright afternoon, slow down to the lochside, a last journey into the dark: you minded still when Liza Bailey cuttit her throat; you minded that fine for young and bonnie she had been, the flower of her father's old een; she had liked books and things and was clever but all the same poor man he'd had to send her home to be the kitchen maid at Lochhead. Nobody'd kenned why she had done it for she'd have had all the lads at her door. She had gone out with the supper things washed to the barn and lain doon . . . She had Lochy's cut-throat razor still in her hand when they found her, her bright een dulled already and a half-smile on her mouth. She had made, after all, a damned poor job of it; the sight of her had made Lochy spew-sick when he found her. He would never forget it he said till the day that he deid. She had long flaxen hair that spilled oot from her face like a golden moonbeam and hung bonnie down to her waist . . . You had all stood in your schoolroom places to watch the coffin go past in Geordie Taylor's old hearse with the mettle-some black shelts pulling on the reins and wanting to be home—it did not take that long for it was into the middle of hairst and folk could not take time from their reaping, they were late as it was and the weather like to break. So they'd sent her some flowers instead, sad that she'd done it, not knowing why; they lay on the coffin, white and sweet-smelling. She would have been pleased about that; she had always liked flowers. God in heaven, folk said, what was it possessed her?

So later you had gone ben to the lochside, Miss Pringle quiet and strange beside you. The grief of it gripped you for she had been young like yourself. You had wantit to live for it was cold and dank in the grave. It had feared you, death going by in the afternoon sunlight.

The Campbell toun was like the rest of its kind that sat in that dour Lowlands landscape: squat and foursquare to the winds that usually whistled and moaned round its sharp gables and whiles filled the night with an eerie foreboding. The wind spoke to you then in the night-quiet toun of old deeds and folk that were gone, a strange legion of souls who had passed with Liza Bailey to the kirkyard and oblivion. All the same, on a still nicht you could hear the rustle of souls and an uncanny whisper nuzzled at your ear.

Like the rest of the touns Mossgair spread its skirts, the quilted pattern of its fields, behind it from where it stood a little back from the moss road, a patchwork of slow-changing colour through the days of summer, lying quiet and still through the dreich days of winter as the ploughmen drew their lonely furrows across them, hunched heavy in their jackets against the chill of the wind and the showers of slanting sleet. A man grew morose in the plough, day after weary day.

Mossgair's was that dour quadrangular layout that grouped byre and stable, strawshed and cartshed around its heart, the reeking dung midden, in a self-perpetuating cycle of feeding and fertility. Within its close compass man and beast followed their respective destinies, strutting their brief sojourn there before moving on. Mossgair, more than most, was a tribute to the man who long ago had raised its first biggings on the edge of the moor and the dogged persistence of the breed that had come after him. There had always been Campbells in Mossgair, folk said, for as long as anybody could remember, a dark glowering brood of them as proud as stink and about as civil, hardly bothering even to *Hallo* you as you went past on the way to the moss to cut your peats. They had all of them sprung from the ageing loins of that first black Campbell who had claimed its grudging acres with a stubborn insistence from the silent, impassive waste and builded its first bleak house— just a but and ben he had brought his new wife to, those long years ago; brought her there from you never heard where and bedded her there in the boxed kitchen bed, just the two of them there in the chaff-warm bed of their new-fired house, the flichter of flame from the peats throwing shadows long up the walls, her bridal finery a heap on the floor. Faith, folk said still, he had been a black pagan brute of a man, at one with the earth and its seasons. An heir to Mossgair he had gotten soon enough on his bed-wearied bride, poor lass. She had died on him then. But the old Campbell, they said, had hardly noticed: he had sown first the close-lying parks, taking in as year followed year a bit more of the moor, his love of the soil some deep and spiritual thing that drove him. He had breathed in some mystical unison with nature, rejoicing each spring in the fresh green brairds that carpeted the brown earth of his parks. He had loved their dark earth-odours and their ever-changing light, his whole being sublimated to their needs. Maybe he had cared little for what folk said of him, rising by his lone, ilka Sabbath, storm or fair, to yoke his black shelt into the gig, the heids of both of them held heich as they sped past on the road to the kirk as though in contempt of the crops of his farming neighbours. Oh, he had been proud that first incomer Campbell and the howe had never accepted him. It was as though a blight had come down in his kind. He had not lived to see the poor lame great-grandson who would one day take up his inheritance, a man who could not stride like a king as his great-grandfather had done over the Mossgair acres, and who would hirple through life for all of his days. Maybe that was as well, folk said; it would have been a heartbreak to him.

So, December dragged past its procession of days, ticked off in the mind, the bare parks an inward cry in the heart of you. As day followed day the furrows fell before the winter ploughs of Mossgair, turning the old stubble in on itself in a ritual old and time-hallowed. Strange you thought it whiles, this cycle of nature—that growth, that ripeness, that sad final mould of decay—that recurred and repeated in the immutable pattern of nature and of transient man. Faded stubble rose on the plough breast, the last trace left of last harvest's bounty, and fell brown from the mouldboard in that old inversion that was at once death and rebirth. In the Mossgair's second plough that year the toun's new second horseman was neither blate nor behind-hand. He kept his Clydesdale pair respectfully at the heels of the first horseman Charlie Skene, neither too close nor too laggardly, from the morning yoking till the deep dusk drove them home from the fields, coming in for his denner bite to Morag's kitchen about noon when he had watered and fed his beasts. He would take his bonnet off as he stepped in, and speir to wash his hands in the kitchen's tin basin before he sat down. Quiet you thought him at first for he spoke little, just *fine* when he'd had enough hot water into his morning brose caup, or when you'd ladled his denner broth, just the two of you there, for Campbell took his meat through the house with his guidwife where the board was richer by loaf-bread and sometimes scones.

Ewan Carmichael was the lad's name; he was some kin to the Campbells, folk said. He had come, he told you one suppertime, from up Bogandie way. And Charlie Skene, coming in for his night flagon of milk, sang his praises; he fair liked the loon he said, quiet though he was.

'He is young as yet,' he said, 'but he is gaun tae be a guid hand i' the ploo, mark my word.'

'He will that,' folk said, for you could see the lad's work where the Campbell parks lay close by the road, the furrows fine and straight and even, nearly as good as Charlie's own in the adjoining rig. Whiles Charlie would leave his pair and his plough in the bout to walk round with the loon, a guiding hand on the stilts now and then.

'Mair yird noo, loon . . . Aye, aye!'

'Mair lan' fae ye, eh?' The eye sternly critical but the heart full at the sight of such promising work.

'He will maybe be a match champion yet, for all we ken,' Charlie said, for he was a generous man.

'Maybe aye, and then maybe no,' folk said, contented to wait.

Only the Sabbath interrupted the pattern of the winter ploughs; the beasts stayed snug in the stalls, blinking sleepy lids as the sound of the tounkeeper's boots interrupted the drowse of the stable; the fee'd loons of the countryside slept late in their bothy beds and the parks were still and empty of folk, their peace shattered only by the tyranny of bells that summoned folk from their farmtouns, their crofts and cottar houses, all the lone and forlorn corners of the countryside, to Pringle's Free Kirk and to the Stablished church of Kilbirnie.

Few folk there were who would not worship at one time or another at one or the other, for God's writ ran strong through the land still—which is not to say that the Devil's work did not flourish between-times as the spirit weakened and the flesh gave way at times to total and insatiable greeds. But that doomful toll of the bells straited folk in their respective weaknesses and, some come to themselves, drew them on to the kirk road. Early on, you could tell how heavy a kirking it would be as the folk converged on the village creesh-hankit in their braws. Fine weather brought them out: it was always easier to have the Word threepit down your throat with your feet dry. Pringle would watch them come slow down the Croft Hill, black golachs in their Sabbath best, the black brows of him drawn but pity in his heart . . .

So they came, to hear the word of God: folk with their troubles and their inward sorrows, seeking succour in life and through Him some favour with the laird.

Morag rose early to meat the folk of Mossgair, syne dressed for the kirk with Ewan and Campbell. Mistress Campbell was not well, nor ardent about God any more than she was about her man, and though she took her communions that was as much. But rain or fine, Campbell crippled his way to meet God. (*Ye have need of Him, to be sure*, his spouse would tell him unkindly.) And up on the Croft Hill Margit Glennie rose, too, the sweat of her Saturday-night sin still on her and shook the prostrate man in the bed beside her (*Damn else would he think of*) and said *Time ye wis up gin yer gaun tae the kirk the day an' takin' yer Free Kirk brats wi' ye* and put on her coat, her black coat, above her apron and dichtit the hen-dirt from her sheen with the corn-sack that lay by the door and sallied forth to the kirk, the Stablished kirk that had been her father's kirk and was her auld mother's kirk and what was good enough for them was good enough for her dammit and damn the Disruption. She had darkened the doors of John Glennie's kirk only the once in her life and that with a terrible ill-grace when it became evident to both of them that he would have to make an honest wife of her.

And down in the haugh at Corthyfold John Lorimer said to his wife *No* as he always did ilka Sabbath for (as he said) dammit, he came home always the more guilt-stricken than he

21

had gone and forbye he wasnae nane keen for dealing aye with the middleman and there was his damned dislike of being criticized. Said his wife, poor Sarah, sore putten oot, *Ye'll be damned if ye don't*. He was a kyard tink the Lorimer cheil, folk said, shocked by his cantrips whiles and the free speak of him. No religion had he, poor man, to speak of; you would hardly know what to make of him, or what might become of him. And it would be just about then that Miss Colquhoun would pour the bree off her luncheon tatties and set her wee broth pot on to simmer on the bink of the grate and sail out like a galleon resplendent on the ploitery sea of the minister's brae—below Pringle's manse her house lay—to hear the modulated Moderate tones of James Grant so that just about the time she was negotiating the Stablished's dour portals Campbell cleekit past, with Ewan and Morag, and Miss Colquhoun most graciously paused to acknowledge her former maidservant, a gentle bow of recognition before she passed in at the door.

And Hallerton, late as ever (Jeemes wouldnae dare start without him) and coated up to the lugs in his astrakhan collar, leaned back in his seat as his black-shelted gig drew out from the grounds of the Big Hoose on to the main kirktown road and trotted past Elrick his home-farm grieve and his young Charlie loon that was going to be a poet and, right enough, maybe the muse was already dinning in the young lad's heid for he clean forgot to lift his bonnet to his betters and black affrontit his father; he would have warmed the loon's ear with his hand so being it would not have been unseemly on the Sabbath.

At the Free Kirk's gate, James MacCaskill stood respectfully back, elder though he was, deferring to the crippled Campbell and his brief retinue. He nodded austerely, to the man and syne to his own daughter.

'Ye're weel, lass?'

'Fine, Father.' It was little they saw of each other now.

'Ye'll have settled tae the wark?'

'That I have,' she said, and passed into the kirk to sit now, as she must, in the Campbell pew with the two men. The Mossgair seat had a horsehair cushion that made her feel religion wasn't so bad with it between your dowp and the cold timmer.

Hard on their heels came Caroline MacFarquhar that sang terrible high soprano; she walked richt ben the kirk to the choir stall and mercy you micht have thought her the Queen of Sheba with all her airs and graces and a glance neither to the richt nor the left of her except at the young Davidson whose folk had siller. Real chief the two of them, it was said, clever and witty, their news and banter beyond all plain folk's understanding. But Caroline was a fine singer all the same, and you could not have said otherwise. And as strong in her principles as in her stays, folk said, for in defiance of her father she had cast her lot with the Frees when she came of age and left the Stablished in the lurch and without a jewel in its choral phalanx.

Last in came Chae Bonner who followed her to the choir dais and had a fine droll voice that gave the *Amens* a dolorous ring of foreboding . . .

There was a hushed silence then as they settled themselves, all seated, a tremor of expectation as they waited for Pringle to mount the pulpit stair. Fine it was then as you were bathed for a moment in the somnolent drone of the harmonium and by a sun-bar that lanced unexpected through the window and danced iridescent with the dust from dowp-compressed cushions. But only for a moment that was . . .

Pringle, strong in voice, grimmer each Sabbath than the last, gave them little ground for hope, still less for salvation, something that he extended finally and at the very last only to the halt and the bed-bound, for only then was a man safe from his own folly. He would watch them, looking for sin, uncannily privy to their inmost secrets, kenning already who it was had cowpit little Nellie Mutch and what had become of it; who it was that threesh his wife in the barn for entertaining the fee'd lad till more than his denner. In the most secret places of the soul he could seek out avarice and envy and the unfulfilled wish for uninhibited lechery. A bad day it would be when he could not find sin among them. Not likely that was. He threw the Devil at their heads: spat him like a curse over them, mocking them, the strong sound of his voice carrying round the bare lime-washed walls of the little kirk and ringing back in their ears. For full measure he would linger long on Hell and damnation, naming sin and requitement till the long-soiled flesh of the matrons quivered from the assault of it and the blood fair lowpit in their veins and young servant lasses too soon compromised choked tearful with the thought of it. That watchful eye spotted the stray tear that trickled too late down the repentant cheek, the quick beetroot flush of a bailie loon or a third horseman here and there that told of lonely bothies and cheerless touns and young folk driven by the remorselessness of work to the yielding moment of pleasure. Week after week he scoured them with his relentless gaze, seeing the servant lass's belly swell slowly and as yet without kirkly authority and wondered which of her toun's men it would be that would shuffle sheepishly into the evening silence of his study. He would rub the heel of his hand owre the silky veneer of the pulpit's edge as he had done that first day among them, catching a sensual delight—as his dark een indicted them, glimmering as he thumped the Book, leaving palm sweat on its opened pages, railing at them till the membranes of the mind twanged and shrieked and Miss Pringle at the harmonium was near sick with the thought of it. Hell yawned at her feet.

Deny yourself. Deny the flesh. Hell awaits the licentious, the adulterers. Quiet the kirk then, the breath nearly choking you and the road to Heaven a quivering tightrope for accomplished prayer artists and that to Hell the broadest of highways. The breath choking you and the sermon ending and the heads going thankfully down, shame hidden in prayer, a long silence in which the echoes of Pringle's voice still held sway. A reeshle of petticoats then, all round the pews, and the quick intake of breath as folk eased the saliva into the starved roofs of their mouths, relief flowing back. It was like a siege had been lifted. In that pause Pringle's rage, all the rage he felt in his heart, subsided; almost kindly he gave them the Benediction and let them home . . .

And just about then, ben at the Stablished, where sin had always caused less consternation—and indeed almost enjoyed a tacit acceptance—James Grant, having worked a holy sweat on to his brow with his exposition of greed as an understandable failing and nodded briefly down at Hallerton in his pumphel stall, was coming out at the end of his thesis on covetousness (his religion took its roots in strong Tory principle) and

24

struggling to tie up the unruly tails of his argument so reasonably that Hallerton all but slipped into a dwam of self-righteous-
ness and near choked on his pandrop. And Miss Colquhoun
who had one of the side pews and was not at the expense of a
cushion because (as she had said roguishly once to a shocked
James) she was well-upholstered there anyway, watched
his thin beardless face, innocent of all guile and treachery,
and wondered *How long will he keep us?* But sure enough,
James had seen their restlessness, and in no time at all had
tied the whole thing into a muddle and let them go with his
blessing . . .

And Margit Glennie took out and away up the Hill like a
futret to ready her man's bite of denner: a fine bit of beef she
had for him pot-roasted, lazy lump that he was. And Miss
Colquhoun, released, ploitered home the way she had come
bestowing smiles where they were merited and put her Bible
down on the hot bink to gobble a tepid potato and poke an
exploratory finger into the broth. All the folk walking home
then, relief in their faces, home to their tatties . . .

By the time they had won home and gotten meated the haze
of night was hanging in the Kynoch firs and it was time for the
milking. And when they came in from the byre it was dark so
that Margit Glennie lit the kitchen lamp and shooed her brood
to their beds ben the house and put out her man's supper, the
second helping of cream and kale brose he had gotten that
day, and they leuch quiet-like one to the other and rising,
unbuttoning her frock, Margit went slow round the table to
him and took his heid of black curls on to her breist and felt his
hand go round her . . .

I cannot tell how it was with you Old Woman, what thoughts
it was went through you as you slaved from morn till late-
nicht in that kitchen that was colder than charity and somehow,
for all the folk that had filled it, devoid of human kindliness;
how it was then with you and Ewan Carmichael for you did
not tell me. I wonder why, so little there was that we did not
sift in the sieves of memory. Was it poor Liza Bailey you
minded on when the door was finally snibbed on the cold
northern night and you crept late and lonely into the box-bed's
dark and shut the doors behind you? Minding then how few

and short are the days of folk? I cannot say one way or the other for you did not speak of it. Of Ewan's folk I can find no memory, not in the session records nor in the quiet stones of the kirkyard. There is no speak of Carmichaels in far Bogandie now, no trace that lingers, no toun of the parish where they say *The Carmichaels farmed here*. Little it matters now, though fine it would have been to know the beginnings of the lad whose voice it was that fascinated you so, whose laughter it was that would ensnare the young and lightsome heart of you.

In the amber light flung round the room from the brass-bellied paraffin lamp that many might have thought an extravagance but which was a necessary concession to his failing eyesight, Pringle glanced up from his desk to cock an ear to the cantering clop of hooves on the road. Presently, as he listened, they slowed to a walk and turned in off the turnpike on to the approach of the minister's brae. Moments later, putting down his quill, Patrick heard the manse's front door thrown unceremoniously open and Mungo Munro's cry go through the house.

'God's in his garret is he?'

Pringle went out to the top of the stairs. 'Well, his unworthy emissary is, anyway,' he retorted, unworried by an irreverence that from another would have drawn his brows with wrath. 'Gang ye ben Mungo—I'll be down.'

Doctor Munro did as he was bidden, walking through to the manse's kitchen where the stooping figure of Pringle's daughter was already absorbed in the preparation of their meal.

'Good evening to you, Margaret.'

'Mungo!' She acknowledged him with a quick tight smile, pained with apology. 'There'll be a bit of a gap, I'm afraid, between the cock-a-leekie and the grilled herrings.'

Munro smiled bravely, accommodatingly: he had the kind of round open face that would have given neither dissembling nor sycophancy safe harbour. He bowed now with mock gallantry, a charmer with easy graces that could take him from the cottar's ingle to a grand drawing-room without strain, feeling alienation in neither. 'No matter, Margaret—all the better to whet my appetite, eh?'

He bent to warm his hands from the fire, small pink hands

that had never grasped graip or spade in all seriousness but had in their time known licensed familiarity with nearly every woman in the parish. One hand smoothed the other in soothing embrace, caressing, clasping.

'I've tethered Hector and the gig round by your gable,' he said over his shoulder. 'He'll be out of the wind, poor beast. And I've put the nosebag on him. He's a biddable shelt but I'd as soon he were left in the shafts . . . I've left the tools of my trade on your hall table.'

'You're expecting a call then, Mungo?' Pringle had appeared in the kitchen doorway. His tone had a tinge of disappointment, as it always had when Munro's duties threatened their evening.

'Mistress Gray of Kilwhinny. I've told them to send for me here, should they need me. Needs must, Patrick, gin the Devil drives.'

'Just so.' Pringle nodded, his shrug an acceptance. 'Her first that will be?'

'Aye, John was a long time about it.' Munro chuckled. 'Maybe the Devil didn't drive hard enough!'

Contrite at once, aware that his humour was that of a man coarsened by a necessary closeness to life, he turned apologetically to the minister's daughter, catching her eye.

'Your pardon, Margaret.' He humbled himself gladly, knowing the penalty might be banishment from her excellent cooking. Silently they sat to the soup.

'An ambrosial dish, Margaret.' His extravagance and smile mocked them both but restored rapport.

The herrings were demolished with desultory talk that did not rob the mind of the pleasure they gave to the tongue; their speak was of the lateness of the farmtoun work, and the incomers the last Term Day had brought among them, now that their characters were beginning to be known. It was the talk of equals whose efforts had a common centre, the guidance and welfare of the community. They stood—all three of them— a little above and to the side of affairs, in but not of the farmtoun society nor yet, in their allegiance, firmly on the side of the laird.

The syllabub that followed was as airy as a feather and just as evanescent. Munro smiled his gratitude. 'Like all life's pleasures, Margaret, too transient.' His words brought an unexpected blush as Pringle, more purposeful than usual, took off his bright Paisleyed napkin and folded it neatly beside him.

'If yer to have little time, Mungo, we will go up now and mebbe get a turn with the chessmen afore John Gray has need of you.'

'Surely!' Munro, acquiescing, thanked his hostess with grave courtesy and, well-fed, fell in behind Pringle as they mounted the stair to his study. There the minister had already set out the board and its combatants and a chair for each of them at either side of the desk.

He watched with sly satisfaction the doctor's acceptance of his opening gambit and sidled his queen out on a diagonal with a suddenty that spread waves of alarm in Munro. It was seldom—never, in the doctor's experience—that the Free Kirk's minister showed such spirited recklessness, such contempt for danger.

'Bye the bye'—Pringle's gaze keened the board with a studied intensity—'I was up at Hallerton Hoose the-streen.'

'You'll have found the laird, I hope Patrick, as hale spiritually, I trust, as I left him physically the other day?' Munro moved a wary knight to watch over the movements of the minister's wild queen and dominate a corner of the board. He had heard of Pringle's visit but had owed it to their friendship to let the older man approach it in his own way. They were, with the minister's daughter, under Hallerton's patronage, indebted to him in the bygoing not only for occasional financial favour for the sick and the needy but for the gift of the pheasant or fat hare from the keepers' guns on which they dined together at times.

'Myself,' said Munro, 'I'm always glad to accept his invitation to dine at the House—that French chef of his does extraordinary tasty tricks with a partridge——'

'This was more of a summons.'

'Oh!—I see.' Munro, non-committal, silently pondered the positions of the men at hazard on the board, waiting for the minister to continue.

'Mungo, Hallerton I believe has it in his mind tae clear the Croft Hill——'

'Clear the folk, you mean?' The doctor feigned ignorance though the idea was not news to him.

'Clear them! Kit and caboodle!'

'He's determined then?' Munro gave himself away, his fore-knowledge now evident.

'You'd heard?' Pringle's een accused him.

'A hint, no more.' The doctor shrugged, admitting his deception.

Pringle sighed. 'Aye, weel, there's nae doubt of it—he's determined right enough.'

'But why? And where in God's name will they go?'

'Where the poor have always had tae go, Mungo—to the wall. Out of sight, out of mind, so that they don't offend the conscience. It's what I asked him mysel'.' Pringle paused. 'What said he, think you? "They can go to Hell," he says, "so long as I never set eyes on them again." "In that case," I says to him, "Ye'd better send them the ither way." He wasnae pleased——'

'I'm sure not!' Munro chuckled, imagining the confrontation.

'I argued for leniency, for reasonableness on the grounds of common humanity. I minded him on the bond atween laird and folk, and that I can tell ye pleased him even less—that in relation to the poor crofter folk his position was patriarchal, almost, in a country where not long since a man paid for his bit ground with that unwritten pledge that gin there was need of it his sword arm was the laird's.'

'And what said he?' Eagerness lit the doctor's round face.

'He bamboozled me with economics I can tell you I was no match for him there. Gid on then about the need to put the Hill into farming ground.'

'Is that possible?'

'Oh, perfectly, Mungo. Perfectly. The crofter folk these past forty, fifty years—since ever they started to settle on the Hill and cultivate its poor ground—they've poured their sweat into it, made it raise crops of a kind. All it needs, now that it is thoroughly broken in, is more lime and manure—what the croft folk can nivver afford to give it.'

'He will evict, you think?'

'I wouldn't wonder, gin it come to it, but the time is past for that kind of thing. The social conscience is stronger now than it was, even among the gentry themselves. He could run into trouble among his own kind . . . In the Parliament in London nowadays there's speak of the Highland crofter's rights and his need for protection against the waur excesses of landlordism.'

'So they're safe enough then?' Munro was suddenly puzzled by the older man's concern.

Pringle's grin was kindly, tinged only with the faintest disdain. 'Yer naive, Mungo man, naive.' He spoke slowly. 'There are ither ways. Ye can price a man off his land, break him with capitalism so to speak, and the world will not say a word to you. Indeed, it will applaud ye.'

Munro nodded, seeing it all clearly now, scanning the board to make sense of a game both their minds had long since abandoned. Slowly the other man's moral dilemma dawned on him. 'And they're your flock, Patrick?'

'Aye.' The minister sighed. 'That's exactly what Hallerton said tae me, more or less. He was suggesting, if I read him aricht, that I should be preparing them for it.'

'And will you?'

'Use the pulpit as a kind o' mercat cross, Mungo?' There was a bitterness in Pringle's tone. 'Could I let the laird use the kirk that way?'

'I don't——'

Munro's thoughts were jolted by the rattling rain of blows on the manse's door. He rose quickly, relieved. 'Gray, I'd say. He's in a panic already. I'll need to give him something to settle him down before I begin with his guidwife. No, don't bother——' his gesture kept the minister in his seat—'stay you by the fire Patrick, I know this house well enough by now to get my own way out of it. Guidnicht to you.'

Munro's foot was light on the stairs. In the hall he shrugged into his coat with an ease long born of such unsocial exigencies and pulled on the luggit bonnet that took him on his errands through the cold northern night. A congestion of talk broke into the house as the door opened and was quickly shut again behind him: John Gray was indeed in a state of high excitement.

Drawing back the study curtains, Pringle watched the doctor's gig trot into the night, the two men side by side on the seat and Hector's hooves fleet on the road. He wondered idly what pique of destiny it was that chose a man from the ruck of his fellows to stand lonely and above them yet alive to their joys and their commingling sorrows. He had thought on it before . . . coming there with his small daughter those long years ago, a coming home though it had been, it had been lonely still in a way. He remembered it now, looking out on the black outline of the Croft Hill, a recumbent blue breast against the lighter shade of the night. Dreich clouds like the angry brows of God scudded across the disc of a pale moon, throwing shadows that drifted over the crop-bare fields. The earth and its immutable seasons alone resisted change, impervious to the guile of men, an unchanging tapestry beneath the lives that moved across it and finally merged into it. So it had been since the Day of Creation; so it would be till the candle-ends of time. As he watched, the feeble lights of the low croft dwellings began to blink out as their folk took to their beds. Pity moved in him for their plight, for the long betrayal that was the story of their days.

Hallerton House was a mansion crusted with legend; history permeated to the marrow of its mellow old stones. In its earlier form of keep and stronghold it had been held for king and Jacobite, rebel and loyalist, plundered and fired. Down the tumultuous centuries, though, it had preserved a consciousness of its own dignity. That factor remained; it brooded on in an ambience of green and cloistered calm amid the verdant shelter of its wooded policies, a place where the commoner's foot was now less than welcome, a haven of graciousness made possible by the complacence of its surrounding countryside. On its broad walks, gentry kept a seemly separateness from the urgent affairs of the land, from the haste of harvest and the smell of the cow dung that indirectly fertilized its very own existence. It was a sanctuary for the sovereign and the elegance it could buy in the fashionable dress salons of London. Once it had harboured heroes—men prepared at times to put all to the chance—now its preoccupations were grubbier and on a less grander scale. Yet another element had remained constant: the family it housed had always been Macleods. Some had died in their beds, some by the sword (not always gloriously) and one of a tempestuous, ill-advised liaison and syphilis. That night it gave the shelter of its roof to a sinister guest, a grey stooped man almost without the strength to lift a whisky decanter. His name was Gurney and he was a man of trade unable to understand the honour the old house did him in receiving him, and incapable of imbibing the warrior spirit that imbued it. Gurney was in iron, a practical, prosaic and necessary commodity: it did not stir men to rash deeds or the wider extremity of epic poetry: it did nothing to burnish the soul. Indeed it had broken Gurney with the worry of it all, for when you had one penny you had the urgent need of yet another to keep it company and syne some more to buttress that. It got like a drug in your bloodstream. He'd had a wife once, poor man, who finally took away with a groom for she had wanted more than silver in her life.

John Gurney had been prised away from his furnaces and foundries and brought to the house by a lawyer from Aberdeen, Hallerton's own man of business, a young man singularly without the saving grace of distinction in appearance or character but who wore guile like an armour and used words like fine chisels (for weren't they but the sharp tools of his trade?) weighing and measuring each with careful thought, so carefully that any moderately-drunk Gael would have made him seem a miser. Their presence there that night was the first act in a tragedy that would long be remembered and even now is unforgiven.

With the years, there had come on Gurney the need for a recognition, some embellishment on his life that would be indicative of its considerable achievement, a tangible proof of his status; and the conversation round the Hallerton dinner table was tacitly exploratory in all its nuances, no more, a taking of temperatures, the sifting of airy thoughts so slight that their substance could not as yet be contemplated. For all that there was awareness on both sides. Ostensibly Gurney was there, as he was yearly, to bid anew for the shooting; in reality it was news of the soss of Hallerton's affairs and what might be the outcome, that had drawn him. That sad state of things the laird's factor and lawyer, the sharp Lander Gregg, had more than hinted at in bringing him there.

The two of them were alone with the laird in the dining-room for her ladyship, on Hallerton's recent return, had clung to London for a further week or two before exposing herself to the boredom of the inhospitable north. Amid the glistening glass of the lamps and the starched splendour of white napery, the ironmaster ate desultorily, the laird himself with the languid lack of interest of a man who had always known where his next mouthful was coming from. Only Lander Gregg showed a suitable relish, an unsuspected weakness that squared ill with his careful talk. He looked now upon the delicate tracery of the bacilli that veined the Stilton and thought sweetly of his housekeeper's blue-veined thighs.

'Well, gentlemen——' His lips smacked appreciatively over the taste of the cheese and he made a quick pass with the napkin to expunge the gastric vapours that had risen to his lips before continuing in his role as intermediary. What he had done was to bring a disposable wealth within the ambit of a possible purchase, a move that in its different ways could be profitable for both parties, that could be handled (by him) with discretion without harm to either. His concern, contrived, seemed plausible enough.

'Am I to understand it then, Mister Gurney, that you are some thinking of retiring soon from the industrial treadmill?'

The ironmaster toyed with the stem of his glass as though aware for the first time of its faceted beauty. He looked finally at the factor.

'I will not say it has not occurred to me. Time catches up with us all, Mister Gregg.' He turned quickly to Macleod. 'Would you not say so, sir?'

Gurney had not been in iron-making all these years without learning the cool code of business guile: the turning away of interest while still allowing it some play on the line. But equally, Lander Gregg was nobody's apprentice.

'It would be well-deserved, I've no doubt.' He was affable, polite, a man of infinite understanding, ready, quietly, with the casual dart: 'And, of course, there is always one's health to think on, isn't there?'

Gurney smiled, tightening his lips, his only giveaway. 'There is that, Mister Gregg, to be sure.' He would not be the one to close the door.

'You'll have a country place I fancy in England . . .?'

'Er, no . . . No.'

Gregg shrugged. 'I'd have thought now that a man of your standing, Mister Gurney,' there was a well-feigned deference now, 'would have needed somewhere—for entertaining maybe,

33

a place to take shipmasters, manufacturing customers and the like.'

Gurney nodded: it was neither agreement nor contradiction. 'There are times, certainly, Mister Gregg, when I have considered the need for it.'

Gregg hurried a mouthful of Stilton on its way and again made a peremptory pass with the napkin. 'Nivver mind the pairtricks then Mister Gurney! Maybe ye should be trying the laird to sell you the lot. Eh, sir?'

The lawyer spoke lightly, banteringly even, shifting his gaze to the head of the table as he did so, where Hallerton, surprised to find himself consulted, gulped on his claret. 'Just so, Gregg. Just so—— Though I do say to you, Mister Gurney, that estate business these days——'

'Is such that the landowner these days is in a far better case than for many years and land does not come on the market as often as once it did.' Gregg's interjection, ill-mannered, cut the laird off from whatever opinion it was he might inadvertently have expressed. 'The agricultural improvements, Mister Gurney, you know. These last thirty, forty years . . . A revolution you might say . . . the rents of the farms rising, food demand increasing from the folk of the industrial toons. Oh,' Gregg opened his hands eloquently, 'a changed outlook completely.'

Gurney smiled, the smile of a man for whom life has lost much of its savour but also in wry acknowledgement at a consummate performer. 'In that case, Mister Gregg, maybe I will have to commission you to find me a suitable seat somewhere in the country where the scenery and the shooting are agreeable.'

Gregg was gracious: his humble bow to the ironmaster accepted the gambit. 'If I can ivver be of service to you, Mister Gurney . . .'

It was far enough for one night. Hallerton seemed morose. Gurney pushed Stilton chimbles lackadaisically round his plate as though trying to find some message in their shifting patterns. Gregg helped himself to yet another slice and settled this time to its silent and uninterrupted enjoyment.

So they sat, each isolated by his own thoughts under the gloom of the dark panelling; sat on with the claret well into the night till Gurney had twice slipped out of his chair and was humming sad songs and Hallerton himself was paralytic (as he often was) and had to be helped to his bed by Margit Taylor, the head housemaid, who was said to comfort him whiles when her ladyship was from home and not likely to hear of it. The young lawyer though was near-enough sober, the plans milling already in his heid.

The work of the land was late that year for the wet had set in as the last flurries of snow fled the fields, a dismal persistent rain that clouded the spirit and kept the horsemen of the howe off the last of the ley ground that waited the plough. Campbell kept a brooding vigil at the kitchen window of Mossgair forever in Morag's way as he looked out on the rain-sodden parks, the curse unspoken on his lips, Free Kirker though he was. Sometimes he lifted his een from the sad prospect of his own land to survey the Croft Hill that rose dreich and cold and as implacable as time before him, blotting his view of the western horizon. A kind of compassion, strange even to himself, would stir in him at the sight of the croft dwellings and the clutter of their minuscule patches, for theirs was an even more precarious existence: they clung to the lower slopes as though by the connivance of God, forever it seemed on the brink of tumbling to oblivion on the moss below. Likely there would be a fine smirr of rain moving across the Hill as he watched, wisping round it like a gossamer-grey shawl, and a furl of mist on its summit. Lonely and God-forsaken it looked then, unless you were born to it, reared in its shadow and minded it for as long as you minded anything in this life. And that's how it was with the folk of the howe: they looked at it as they fell out of their beds in the morning and again before going cold back to them at night and said:

'It will rain, I'm some thinking.'

Or maybe, though not often: 'She will be fine in the morning, we will get the neeps sown.'

You would not wonder that the folk of Lower Don called it the Hill of Beyond. Beyond what, Campbell wondered: hope, pity and the reach of all human charity? The Hill had been a symbol in his soul, a part of him almost from his first cry in the cradle. Now its unforgiving bleakness echoed the desolation of his own days. At the Mossgair window he would turn from his vigil to cast a glower at the portrait that hung beside it, that of Preacher Spurgeon, a man in his own dolorous mould, and faith there were times when you would have thought it was all the Baptist mannie's fault that it did nothing but rain, rain, rain. But Spurgeon stared inexorably back, unrepentant and unchanging except that his mowser it seemed got more drookit with the passing days. Outside, the Mossgair hens stood morosely in the shelter of the cartshed or on one leg by the stable door, eyelids drooping over pink, glazed een and more disconsolately dumb than before. And down at Corthyfold, John Lorimer's Black Leghorn cock stood equally daft and bewildered in the rain keening over the soss of his sottered feathers and uttering guttural gurgles of misery. John himself was in little better case; with his byre work done he would lounge at the door looking out at the on-ding of wet, just like Campbell except that his oaths were more florid and indicting and whiles he wiled his wife to her bed in the mid-afternoon; it was strange doing that in the broad licht of day (they had never before), unChristian she thought it.

'But John, supposin' somebody should come in on's?'

'Damn the fear of it, lass,' he'd assure her, ramming the door-bolt into its socket.

So she had gone with him then through to the ben end; glad she was now she had gone, for every day it surprised her all the tenderness in him (she had not known it before)—it got so she would want him to ask her again, almost glad of the rain. They would lie there listening to it drum on the barn's tin roof, she near like a young bride again when she held him; he was strong like a lover still when she'd roused him.

'You'll have me bairned, Lorimer,' she would gasp, lying back, in her heart's glow the wish it were so.

From his eyrie under the eaves, Pringle too looked out on the silent misery of the parks, at the bleared skies and the driving rain that sheeted across the Croft Hill. Pity, as always, welled deep in him for the crofter men, for theirs was a lonely dream, an impossible dream. What was it, he asked himself, that drew them? The need for a bit of ground, in that land-hungry time, to call their own? For a kind of independence that after all was no kind of independence at all? Year after

36

year, they beguiled themselves, connived and contrived and persevered in cheating themselves, somehow finding enough seed corn and the mental strength to sow again their meagre one-acre shifts believing that what they sowed was at last the seed that would give root to their fragile dreams?

Their holdings, their groupings of patchwork fields, were microcosms of those of the Lowe's farmtouns but there similarity ended, for on their stony hillside the soil was thin and the yield niggardly. Yet, remorselessly, as though they could no longer help it, year after year, they broke in more of the ground, pouring their sweat into it. Theirs was a fearsome treadmill that gathered its own bitter harvest of disillusionment. Yet hope died hard; over the years of his ministry Pringle had seen the Hill colonized by men who had come whiles from you never heard where, folk and families dislodged by the fever of improvement as laird after laird threw his old farming hamlets into the substantial farmtouns of the new agriculture, casting folk adrift on the face of the landscape little caring, folk who feared cities, who would have been strangers there not able to endure it. Some had come from the West and their soft speak and Highland names betrayed it; they had clung to the crofting as the only thing they knew rather than tie themselves to the cottar's life.

From his window, down the years, Pringle had looked out on their dwellings and their movements. They could not prosper; all they asked was to survive, and to do that they had to follow another calling by day: that of cobbler or roadmender, weaver or tailor, mason or ditcher and hire themselves out at hairst to the highest bidder while their wives and bairns gathered in their own small harvests. So, from the first scattering of poor dwellings, he remembered, their colony had grown, its story repeated on every bare hillside of that northern countryside. The prosperity that had, these last thirty years, put the farmtouns on their feet had, as surely, kept the crofter and the cottar in their excruciating servitude. Now, it seemed, the crofters were to lose their teetering independence and, maybe finally, all dignity. If Hallerton's threat were real—and he had little doubt of it—they would all of them be in the hiring fair come next year's Whitsunday Term. Pringle pondered the rapacious hunger of the lairds for land and silver that so threatened the crofting existence, and going slow round his study desk, undid the hasp of his diary. Dipping his quill, he began to write:

March 24, 1879.
There has been lately in this parish of Kilbirnie a big improvement in the farming practices on those previously seen, in consequence of which there is now much evidence through the countryside of the new mode of agriculture. The oxen have been replaced in the furrow by the horse, the heavy wooden plough by an iron, smith-made implement of some grace and scientific design that has eased the draught requirement. This century has seen, generally, what can only be described as a revolution in the fields: the fattening of cattle beasts for the London market is now commonplace though the droving men who once took them south on the hoof are nowadays superseded by the steam packet that uplifts them from the northern quaysides. Land brought into prime condition and farmed well is bringing the big men of the farmtouns and the lairds letting them a fine turn-round in profit.

Alas, at the other end of the scale we see the price in human cost, and the decay of the old rural order of things, for the great farmtouns of this Improvement Age have cast the peasant folk adrift from the land, from the pendicles they kept and cultivated on their own behoof, and the big touns now are run by teams of men housed in large bothies where they are often left to shift for themselves insofar as their food, welfare and morals are concerned.

The creation of wealth for the farmer's pocket (and the laird's coffers) has become a first concern above and beyond that of a decent way of life. There is much iniquity in the sordid quarters of the unmarried men. Where once the master and the guidwife of a toun might have guided their workfolk in the ways of God there is now a laxity born of their own wellbeing and young men and young servant lasses are too often left to their own devices, with the result that there is an indiscriminate mingling of the sexes. In places where God's Writ does not run there is a slackness at times beggaring all description: fornication is a commonplace of the life when the day's work is done and the appetites are inflamed by the telling of coarse stories, the exhibition of coarse behaviour and the singing of most questionable songs that they call the bothy ballads.

The farmtoun servants think nothing of it that a kitchen maid who has been the concubine of a toun, with the horseman when opportunity afforded in his bothy or in the night-time privacy of her own kitchen bed, will on his moving to another toun fee herself in like manner to the man who takes his place with as little concern as though it were the most natural thing in the world. Mistresses of touns have even been known to countenance such looseness as a means of keeping a good horseman about the place when his six-monthly fee alone would have been but poor inducement.

Such is the breakdown of the old society of country life. In this howe there was but seventy years ago a parish of such spiritual and social homogeneity that one man could not endure without the goodwill of his neighbour. The plough was communally owned and plied as were the oxen that drew it in the old run-rig cultivation of the time, the men of the hamlet taking rig and rig about for their crops, the good soil with the bad. Kilbirnie then was a hamlet of a hundred souls, four of them dykers, three at least of them tailors and six of them souters.

What is presently seen is altogether a different picture: in the laird's refashioned landscape each farmtoun is in the lease of only one tenant, a man of some substance like as not pursuing his purposes with little thought for the folk dependent upon him, such men at times even offering a day's work or hire to those with whom they formerly held land in concert. There is bitterness and division where once there was (admittedly) common poverty and common grace. Lairds, be it said, have vied with one another to create such a changed landscape not for altruistic reasons but in order to raise their rent rolls, careless of all consequences or of human heartbreak. Some in their grand designs have ruined themselves in all probity as well as financially, a fact that need not weigh heavily on our sympathy. Most grievous of all, however, has been the plight of the crofter folk, of whom I have many, squatters in the first instance to be sure but folk

39

whose will was too proud to bend to the yoke, who found the patch on the hill preferable and biggit their dwellings there in the consciousness that it was no man's land and that none might move them from there. Alas, they could not escape the driving greed of men.

Wearily Pringle put down his quill to read the words he had written; it was unlikely that posterity ever would see them, he thought, little knowing that one day we would find them.

So how was it with you, Old Woman, in those endless grey days when the drudge of your work took you out of the lonesome warmth of your kitchen box-bed each day at five into the flichtering candlelight of another morning and returned you to it only at ten at night? I would not blame you if life then took you to the edge of despair . . . How was it then, in that early time between you, with the ploughboy Ewan Carmichael, when you gave him his meat in the kitchen: just the two of you there and him little older than yourself but a man already with his pair in the stable and his own plough in the rig? You did not speak of it often, those early days at the Mossgair when you would be ordered out from the house in the afternoons to help with the threshing in the barn, lowsing the bands of the sheaves for him . . . But there was a something, a tenderness in your voice when you spoke of it all the same so maybe it was fine you liked him, the quick smile of him as he gathered the loosened sheaf from your arms to feed into the maw of the mill, his wide bonnet pushed back on his brow, a look between you maybe as he mocked the sad forlorn Campbell, aping his limp to make you laugh when the old man's back was turned. There was mischief in the loon from far Bogandie, you had known that then, kenning already there was something between you you could not put a name to so that whiles it made the colour leap into your cheeks when he looked at you . . .

The seedtime was late: it was the end of April before the harrows took to the ploughed ley to make ready the corn's seedbed, May ere the neep-ground was sown and into June by the time the drill ploughs of the farmtouns raised the pattern of ribbing in the fields that would take the turnip seed. Earth that should have been friable loam, warmed by the sun, remained a heavy lumpy soss as intractable as ill-made brose. Hillhead was the first into his ley parks with the harrows and his Clydesdale pairs; he was always the first. It was, folk said, kenning his strong kirk bonds, as though he'd gotten the word from God and maybe he had for his judgement was sound. As the springtime came round folk took to waiting for him to make a move and would have felt they were incurring divine wrath had they usurped him. Hilly, on the other hand, was extremely modest about it all; he took no credit personally.

With his men in the parks, it would seem suddenly that the howe was full of horsemen, legginged and booted, striding purposefully ahint the grubber and the harrows. Men whose pace all winter long had never been more than a saunter lengthened their steps under the grieve's gaze, and Campbell like the lave sent his foreman and his new man, Carmichael, out to sow the parks of Mossgair. Busy the toun then, the clatter of hooves through the close and the cry of the men one to another, the strident cry of temper as they loaded seed corn from the loft and bone-meal from the implement shed. Ewan with hardly time to gobble down his noon brose before he was up and out again to see to his horse in the stable before yoking them again to the harrows. Crippled, the old Campbell could not sow his own seed as he might have done; with his limp, it would have been like a lass with a stammer singing an aria. So Charlie Skene did the job, pacing the fields with the seed hopper, a fine figure then with solemn strides. Fine it was then with the land smiling and men in tune with the land, a fine joy in your heart at the seeming order of things.

If the work of the howe dachled at all that spring it was only when the men in the parks paused for a moment to watch Miss MacFarquhar go panting round the countryside with the young Davidson loon at her side. Turning his neep-barrow at the rig-end John Lorimer cried over the dyke to the second horseman of Sheilhill, seeding the neighbouring field, 'Caroline, wouldn't ye say, Tam, is built more for comfort nor speed. What think you?'

And Tam MacCaig had given his orra lauch.

'Aye mebbe so, John. But that's a damned sight better nor

41

getting yersel cuttit tae pieces while yer takin' yer pleasure.' So they just leuch the ill-minded pair of them then and yoked back to their work.

All the same, there would be a kind of respect for Caroline in John's off-taking voice. Devil the hair cared she for what folk said of her (he liked her for that) for she felt as daft as a foal just finding its legs. She trailed the Davidson loon that was going to be a doctor away round the side of the Croft Hill, out of the sight of the village, to the sad and dreary isolation of Kynoch's Castle in its wooded cleft above the loch, a black uncanny chancy place where nicht hung like a ghoul among its guardian trees. In its long gallery, roofless now but hooded from the sky by the tall firs that brooded over it, black witches to some hellish pottage bent, she told him breathless: 'It was here they say that Kynoch was found—his throat slit open like a bleedy mou' and his bleed going pleep-pleep on the cold stone floor.'

Her breath fanned young Davidson's cheek and her wet, excited mouth was but a heartbeat from his own. That had feared the young Davidson loon. So she had taken him down to the rickle of stones of the old abbey at the end of the loch. Black and reekit they were still with the fire that the legends told of; heich and excited her voice when she told him of the terrible ill-deeds of the monks who once had lived there, of what they had done with the lasses whose bones had been found there. Near to fainting she was with the thought of it.

That spring too the folk of the howe had the chance to take a look at the new man at Mossgair, little more than a loon he seemed but for all that, folk said, he could fair handle horse. They liked the set of him fine as he stepped out behind the harrows with the bonnet pushed jauntily back on his brown curls. He had a fine open face folk said and they hallo'd him as they passed by on the road. 'Fine day,' he'd cry back, as though he had kenned them all the days of his life and been born among them.

'A fine drooth,' they would say, pleased he had spoken.

So you had wondered whiles as Whitsunday drew round would he be off, up and away like the other bothy loons of the parish to a new toun and fresh fields, for they did not stay to put down roots those restless horsemen cheils. One morning, not able to bear it, you had asked *Will ye be thinking of biding on at the Term, Ewan?* Quiet you'd said it, pouring the boiling water over his caup of brose meal and just the two of you there in the grey kitchen light of the morning. He had looked up at you, close beside him. *Gin I be speired, I will bide*, he had said, no more, but in that moment you had known there was a strange kind of compact between you. *And you?* His gaze solemn on your face. *Mebbe—gin I be speired tae bide . . .* Casual and shameless you were with the joy of it, a licht o' skirts to tease him. Well-pleased the old Campbell had been, little knowing, never able before to keep a bothy loon for more than a six-month. Och, fine it was then (so you thought it) that a man had noticed you so.

Pringle's quill tore over the paper in hurried, impatient haste to be done. The preparation of his Sabbath sermon, he silently acknowledged, gave him less and less pleasure, fewer reasons for personal satisfaction. In its arguments and persuasions lay the hollow ring of his own lack of conviction, the words but the echoes from a teem surplice. His method was simple: headings—at most cryptic paragraphs—that would guide him through an enunciation of the precepts of the faith he represented and which it was expected would be heard from him. It was not that he feared that he would lose his way in his argument; it was rather that he needed their discipline to inhibit him, for Pringle lived with the increasing fear that he would one day denounce God. His headings were maps—signposts—for a lost soul, one tormented not by a sense of sin but by a knowledge of shame and of his own inadequacy.

The hurt and loneliness of his plight had grown with the years, an inward pain that nourished itself on every single, separate doubt, on every pathetic excuse he could give for his deep disillusionment. Griefs gathered within him bringing him at times close to sickness. He had never spoken of it; not to anyone. Nor hinted at it, even to Munro, whom he trusted. But it was not fear that held him, only a strange loyalty. He put down his quill to move to the window to look out, as he so often did, at the brown fields, tidied and sown, a committal of faith by men who never questioned their destiny or their inability to alter it. Men of the soil, their creed was acceptance, sparing them all doubts.

The fields lay placid under the evening light; across the haugh, the dwellings of the Croft Hill were already dimmed by its shadows. His gaze keened over the maze of small fields where the thin corn of autumn was ready to burgeon. Strange he thought it, that love unreasoning that bound a man unquestioning to the soil, to poor ground that first broke his heart and then broke his soul; that dangled him in life like a helpless fly in a spider's web between the promise of comfortable circumstance and the abyss of poverty and want in a land where a man came to fear the laird more than he did his God. Did they feel, those broken men of the crofts in the last of their days when all hope had gone, that same bankruptcy of the spirit that now engulfed him? This countryside had grown to be part of his being. What memories were they that held him there, so deep, so abiding, so indelibly etched in him and burned into the membranes of the mind?

A last gash of red that was the dying light sank into a dark streak of cloud. It was the end of the day that yearly reshuffled country society, blowing its folk hither and thither without motive or design, pawns in a game like the chessmen that stood at times on the board between himself and Mungo. A sadness crept into him for all the casualties of progress, for the fragmentation of human kinship that came always in the worship of Mammon. If he could not condemn it—for there was no arguing against the need or inevitability—he would not condone it. Drawing the curtains on the night he lit the lamp that stood ready on his desk and undid the hasp of his daybook to lay a page of its cream vellum open to the yellow glow of its flame. His quill sped like a bird across the waiting space, draining from him the burden of his despair.

Whitsunday, 1879.
This day is the Term Day; it has come round as it always does with an inordinate haste so that it seems but yesterday that I looked out on the Martinmas scene. Where the plough was, the seed is in and the corn, God willing, will braird soon in that eternal cycle of decay and renewal that is the destiny of all things. Man and nature jostle here in this lonely

44

howe where once the wild boar grunted through the dense undergrowth but little ahead of the hunter. It would be fine to say that man is the nobler beast but I doubt gin it be so for this landmark of the farming year but engages the fancy with thoughts much to the contrary. Man now preys on man: in the hiring fair the cottar, with wife and bairns at his back, is trapped as surely by a malignant fate as the boar was by the posse. His worth in an overcrowded market place is but a fraction of what it should be, for farmer and laird now ride on his labour, careful of their own interests.

Cruel men stalk the feeing markets, men with a cold gleam in their een for the poor cottar is at their mercy. Nor is the single, bothy-housed man in much better case: his seeming freedom is a sad illusory thing, his squalid hut but the marrow of its neighbour at the neighbour toun. It is on the tide of such misery and inhumanity that the new farming has amassed its wealth these twenty or thirty years bypast and the squalor of those lives is not easy to countenance in a country where God is so publicly acknowledged. In some hearts, to be sure, He must be a stranger: how else could men treat their workfolk no better than the beasts of their byre and frequently worse than any other creature they have about their place?

Tomorrow he would see them, strangers in the pews with their kirk lines clutched in their hands: see their burnished, upturned faces on him as they listened to his Sabbath sermon: the faces of young ploughmen but newly-wived, of wives new-bairned and lasses guiltily new-bedded, faces flushed not with piety but maybe with hope. Maybe even in their thankfulness (he dared to hope it, acknowledging the sin of avarice on the kirk's account) there would be tangible tokens of their gratitude; he heard the dirl of sustentation pennies, maybe even the crisp reeshle of a note passing agreeably on to the smooth silver of James MacCaskill's collection plate . . .

Pringle scowled, rebuking himself. But he knew he could not disappoint them; that he had to keep faith with them.

That night Lander Gregg had brought the ironmaster Gurney to a house of some ostentation and grandeur in the Queen's

Road fringe of Aberdeen whose purpose in life was not immediately apparent and was still unknown to most of its neighbours. They had dined well—at the lawyer's expense—on salmon taken that very morning from the mouth of the River Don and on fine slivers of Aberdeen-Angus beef, and now walked through to an adjoining annexe where drinks and cigars awaited them. Only one or two of the comfortable chairs were taken by seemingly solitary men in a state of some unease. Gregg, however, was no stranger to such places, nor indeed was his guest of the iron industry, who had been forced from time to time from his wife's coldness to pay infrequent visits more for the comfort of human contact than any real need of the services.

Gregg helped his guest to a cigar at the central table and lit his own in a prolonged ritual that proclaimed the poor boy's preoccupation with the illicit pleasures of life, puffing a hugely enveloping cloud of smoke. Finally, well-pleased with himself and the world and all the folk in it, he led the ironmaster to a chair in a discreet corner of the room. Over dinner they had talked of commerce, thriving business, the grip of Gladstone and the probability, fervently to be wished, of Victoria's long and continuingly profitable reign.

'God bless her,' Gregg said, raising his glass. He sincerely meant it.

'Indeed,' said Gurney, easily concurring, for she was doing him no harm either. She had brought with her times when a man could make something of himself, given some discretion in his affairs and a solidarity with the respectability of the merchant classes. And Gurney was not the man to sneer at that.

They spoke for a time of other things, matters of the day and of empire in which neither was that night seriously concerned, before Gregg shuffled himself more deeply into his chair, and, musing diffidently at first, began quietly to draw out his companion.

'Ye'll mind, Mister Gurney, that we were speaking once of the investment in land—of the value that might have for instance for a man like yerself?'

'At Hallerton House, I believe that was, was it not?' Gurney's tone was reflectively casual; he swung the brandy round his glass, focusing gaze and thought on its swirling viscosity.

46

'I believe so,' Gregg's tone was equally off-handed, hiding all disappointment. He allowed himself a long satisfying pull on his cigar and then let a speculative edge gild his words. 'I'm wondering, ye know, if Hallerton himself might not indeed be thinking of giving up the estate.'

'Has he said as much, then?' Gurney feigned surprise.

'No, no . . . at least not in so many words, ye understand. It is just——'

'Then what is it makes you think so?' The ironmaster's guile was near impregnable.

'Ach, it's a feeling, Mister Gurney, no more, as his man of business . . . He is—beggin' his pardon and the trust of your silence in this—he is not the laird his auld father was by all accounts. Not a bit of it! No interest in the estate's management or in farming the land . . .' Gregg sighed expansively, conspiratorially. 'And her ladyship noo'—it was a confidential whisper for the ironmaster's ears only—'. . . she's nivver there for long enough to speak of. Always away in London. And the laird, given that circumstance, little better. If ye were to ask me, it is where the both of them would like to be. He has city interests, shipping they say, though you'll understand I am not involved in that side o' his affairs. And again'—Gregg's slight shrug of the shoulders was the very eloquence of understatement—'he has nivver been at home up here, only in the Southern society of his social kind. No, I tell you plainly, Mister Gurney, it would surprise me none to see him sell it all up!'

'You feel so?' Gurney's guile capitulated at last.

'Och——' Gregg's glance spoke volumes, confidences, assurities. 'I have little doubt about it. In fact, I'd say . . .' he leaned with some difficulty over the big arm of his chair to speak directly into the scaly cavern of his companion's ear, 'I'd say maybe the only thing that's standing between him and that is that he has not the heart for the public upheaval, for the social obloquy if you will, that such a step would bring upon him. For all I know he is but waiting for the chance to shift Hallerton off his back at the first discreet opportunity—something that would not expose him to the charge of betrayal of his heritage.' Gregg slid back into the comfort of his chair but kept his gaze on the other man's face. 'Ye'll ken what I mean, Mister Gurney?'

47

'He would be open to offers, you're saying?' The directness of the ironmaster's response surprised even Gregg.

'Oh, yes, I'm sure of it!' Lander was emphatic, unshaken.

'He'd be open to offers?' Gurney persisted.

'Ah well,' Gregg demurred only slightly, 'to negotiation anyway, Mister Gurney.'

The ironmaster smiled. 'Through your own good offices——'

'Through me, Mister Gurney.'

'And Hallerton, am I to assume, does not know of our meeting?'

Gregg for once looked sheepish. 'I neglected to mention it, Mister Gurney.'

'Just so.' The ironmaster tweaked the tip of his beard, a player as yet with faceless cards. 'You would be acting for me, Mister Gregg?'

'For both parties, Mister Gurney. Think of me as the intermediary, the go-between, seeing fair play to both parties as my profession warrants that I must.'

'That way you earn only professional fees, surely?'

'Maybe and then maybe not,' Gregg's smile was openly frank. 'I would suppose you might need a man to run your estate's affairs, as Hallerton does, somebody who knows the immediate countryside, the local dignitaries and landed gentry.'

'I would expect to make changes——'

'Not impossible, Mister Gurney.' Gregg's grin invited suggestion.

'That damned Croft Hill cleared——'

'The Croft Hill, Mister Gurney?'

'Cleared, its people evicted——'

'Cleared, Mister Gurney.' Gregg took the liberty of correcting his new client. 'If I say it can be done, can we leave it at that?'

'I've your word?'

'Rely on it!' The words between them now were sharp, chiselled, the weapons of men whose destiny it is to take a grasp on the lives of others, to manipulate society like secret puppetmasters. They had an understanding at last, one in which each had laid bare an interest and an undertaking. Gregg rose to pour himself a fresh brandy, returning to sink himself into the chair.

'I was wondering, Mister Gurney, whether you would have made any arrangements for the rest of the evening. I sometimes——' Gregg's tone held again its earlier inflexion of professional servility. He took the heavy leather-bound album from the small table between their chairs and laid it on the armrest of that of the ironfounder, flipping over its pages as he did so. They fell open at the illustration of a dusky woman spread sensuously couchant on a richly-embroidered counterpane. The photographer had done his work well; his art had softly suffused the flesh, the backward alluring gaze, the buttocks raised to his lens.

'The mulatto,' Gregg explained, suddenly a little breathless.

'That will not be necessary Mister Gregg.' The lawyer was aware now of the ironmaster's contempt. 'But you can let me know Hallerton's price in due course, if you will.'

'Of course.'

'Goodnight to you then—no, please.' Gurney's restraining hand kept Lander in his chair, leaving him with the open album on his knee. Gregg watched the retreating figure then turned back to leafing through its pages, each showing a discreetly voluptuous arrangement of the human female figure, inviting, beckoning, smiling, endlessly promising. He turned back to the mulatto with the fine buttocks and the eyes veiled with a secret excitement. She had the most magnificent haunches.

The rumour was out. It fed upon itself like a fire in the heather, compounding concern, turning, tortuously engulfing an insidious hope. The folk of the Hill were loth to believe it. It was not that they had great reason to put their faith in lairds—for were not some of them the bairns of folk who had once fled the Clearances of the West?—but that they recalled to mind the gentle paternalism of the old laird, Hallerton's father, a fine old man who had come north among them with the late spring each year from his London haunts to let them see he was well and walk about the Croft Hill and take through-hand with them the state of the work, the progress of the new-sown parks and the prices they might get for their stots. They had not prospered as he would have wished in his benign shadow but neither, in a time when heartless lairds were hoisting their estate rents to keep them increasingly in a comfort to which they had little entitlement, had they come to grievous harm. Nor had they seemed likely to: for the old laird had assured them he had siller enough to put past the rest of his days and it was freely better to go to Heaven (so being that was his destination) with a clean slate than a fat purse. In their hearts they had never doubted but that the son would be a man of his father's word. Now though, their mood was less certain. When the rain of that spring had let up for an hour or so, the croft men, where they might have hallo'd in the passing, could be seen to be gathering in knots about the hill, groups inanimate with a silent dejection. Opinion was freely given and counsel canvassed. They still could not believe it, though their suspicions were fed by the fact that Hallerton's ground steward Farquhar Douglass had taken suddenly to keeping out of their way or, when cornered in the wood setting his snares, become unexpectedly affable and in a hurry to win home.

Rumour was hunted to its source: was it not Margit Taylor had brought it home on her half-day to her old mother's house in the kirktown? And what would *she* know, they asked one of the other. Was it likely that the laird would be telling her his secrets? And why shouldn't he, some said, for did she not gey more often than not slip into his bed to give him what the mistress could not and get some pleasure for herself (so to speak) in the by-going? So their hope wore thin at last, and the heart went out of them. It was nearly with relief that they received their notices. Bland and innocent they were in their buff envelopes, like the first intimations of bastardy proceedings; they were brought round in the evening gloam by Hallerton's French chef when he had sent the last coupe of syllabub through to the dining room. M. Jacques delivered them, smiling the twist of his Gallic smile, uttering shyly when questioned his *je ne pas compris*, like a soft benediction at their doors. Sullenly, but with dignity still, the envelopes were taken from him—even by Andra MacGillivray who had said to him *Fine nicht, eh Jack!* but had gotten in reply for his pains only a pained look and *je ne pas compris*. (In his astonishment, Andra would say later, he had quite forgotten to put his boot in the

Frenchman's arse.) Under the Gothic brutality of Gregg's notepaper they were informed:

I am instructed to give you due notice that the present leasing arrangements under which you hold the tenancy of cottage, byre and the buildings together with a stipulated acreage of the Croft Hill on the Hallerton House estate will as per your agreements cease from and after the Whitsunday Term of next year; and I am further instructed to give notice that the expiry brings to an end the current rents under which you hold your land and that it is the intention of the Hallerton Estate to re-enter into further leases only at economic rent levels.

It was no less than they had expected. Between the bald lines of Gregg's words they read plainly the course of their future. It was a fate already familiar to them; they had seen it gathering an impetus through the land, that savagery of rack-renting that could drive the small man off his ground and leave it for the wealthier farmer. They knew the pattern: the incomer invited to bid for a particular croft, himself a victim of that same insidious greed, land-hunger, the sitting tenant counter-invited. It set crofter against crofter, family against family, the covetous rich in contention against the hapless poor. It inveigled all the unprincipled qualities of human nature in a melting pot in which guile and siller would decide a man's case and the old loyalties would count for nothing.

'But why, in God's name, Patrick?'
Munro in his puzzlement took the Lord's name in vain and was reproached neither by his host's look nor frown. Pringle indeed, for a moment, seemed not to have heard his words.
'Five and forty families, Mungo, maybe some two hundred and twenty souls that we both of us minister to, to be cut off from the very roots that have nourished their lives—from their native culture—with a diabolical subtlety, and all of it legal!' Pringle tilted the whisky tumbler in his hand and watched its faceted design shoot lances of light into the hand that cupped it. He handed the doctor an equal measure. 'I can tell you,

51

Mungo, I little thought to see the day when our society should come so savagely under the stroke of the Shylock's pen!'

'But why?'

'Och! Easy enough, Mungo—just the saving of siller! The croft biggins—put up by the croft folk themselves, mind you, at not the cost of a single penny piece to the estate—are beginning to go done. Honest lairdship would demand that they be put into a fit state of repair, and doubtless that would cost Hallerton siller he could profitably spend on his own pleasure in the London clubs. So what better remedy? Now he's either to cover the cost by a high rent or he's to be rid of the need to keep the croft biggins in repair.'

'Can they afford the rents he will ask for?' Munro had tethered Hector out of the wind at the back of the manse and come in as usual for his Saturday supper.

'Verra few of them, I'd say.'

'What's to become of them then?' Margaret Pringle paused in the preparation of her table.

'Pushed off the hill? Oh, they'll become day dargers, cleaners of ditches, piecework navvies at the mercy of the estate itself, always supposing they can find a habitation somewhere in the howe, which itself must be exceedingly doubtful——'

'They will keep body and soul together though?'

'Pyach!' Munro winced almost at the wrath he had unexpectedly unleashed from the old man beside him. 'Body, aye Mungo, but soul? I doot it. A man's more nor flesh. He is made up, Mungo, of hopes and dreams. Strike at a man's dreams and you strike at his frailty. Strip him of his human dignity and his een will go blank in his heid, for his soul will have gone dead!' Pringle looked at his guest under hooded brows, softening his voice. 'There are dreams on that hill, Mungo, dreams of a kind you might not credit, the kind of dreams men don't speak about, hardly admit to themselves . . . Oh, hopeless dreams, I grant you, as all dreams are. But without them where are you?'

Margaret ladled the soup, a clear cock-a-leekie, and they sat to table. 'My favourite,' Munro said, lightening their mood, and she warmed him with a smile.

'So what will they do?' Her question was for Munro.

'Go South, Margaret, maybe . . . Head for the city, some of

them anyway, to fester away their lives in rotting slums and die early deaths from tuberculosis since they will not have built up the immunity against it.'

'Some will go to the coast,' Pringle paused in mid-sup, 'to drown themselves in trying to be fishermen, an impossible thing for a man to be who has not been born beside the sea and has not known it all his days and studied its moods. And some, I wouldn't wonder, will take a ship that's going to carry them as far as possible from this place of their sad disillusionment.'

That quietened them then; they ate in silence, giving way finally to the kind of small-talk that usually punctuated their meal.

'Mistress Campbell's nae very well, I hear.'

'Not very, Patrick.' They had long taken advantage of the occasion to compare community notes. 'I doubt that she'll last the year out.' Pringle nodded, unsurprised by the quiet intimation of mortality for it was the constant of his world and he had come almost to look forward to his own end without tears. 'Just so—and how's MacCaskill's lass managing?'

'Most wonderfully well.' Munro's voice held unconcealed admiration. 'And getting little thanks for it, as you may imagine.'

'It's always been Campbell's way . . . the human contact mystifies him, that limp draws him in and to himself. And her ladyship's home I hear from the South with the fine weather coming in.'

'The other day.'

'Will she stay long?'

'Only for as long as it takes her to kick Meg Taylor out of the laird's bed.' For the second time that night the doctor's forthright words escaped rebuke, evoking neither frown nor disdain.

Their conversation died over Margaret's excellent apple pie, causing a gloom in which Munro desultorily dissected pastry from the sweet contents. Hunger for once had left him, immersing him deeply in his own thoughts. 'I suppose you'll both have thought,' he said finally, 'of the place we hold in this community. It's——'

'The middle ground?' Pringle finished the thought for him.

'We're neither martinets nor hired men——'

'True.'

'If you could fee us like ploughmen or stockmen, we would know where we stood, but where do our loyalties lie?'

'As the disinterested custodians of truth and justice, if that doesna sound too pompous?'

'Maybe.'

Pringle plucked his red, Paisleyed napkin from his collar. 'It cannot be simple for the likes of us, Mungo. Education and enlightenment brings its own obligations.'

'And the cloth, Patrick?'

'Aye, the cloth especially, Mungo.'

Pringle stopped, listening. 'Was that a knock?' Motioning his daughter to stay seated, he rose and stepped into the manse's darkened lobby, and, in a moment, Margaret and Munro caught the murmur of voices, followed by the sound of footsteps ascending the stair to Pringle's study. Pringle's own step turned back along the hall and his head for a moment appeared round the door.

'It's James MacCaskill, wi' some business. I might be some time Mungo, but tak' yer ease by the fire. Margaret will refill your glass.'

He shut the door to leave them alone, immured in each other's company, tentative friends, a man and a woman. It was the first time since Munro had come to the howe that fate had contrived it.

'Sit round to the fire,' Margaret said, rising to get the decanter.

'A small one, please,' Munro begged, settling himself into the stuffed armchair in which Pringle read Walter Scott long into the night—so late whiles that the croft folk across the haugh on an unslept night with a calving cow, would joke, *Patrick keeps late hours for a holy man.* Munro noted that Margaret did as he bid her, pouring him only half the dram that Patrick would have deemed the very plimsoll line of hospitality. 'Much as I favour whisky I have never attended a patient yet in a state that in any way impaired my diagnosis,' he said. There was an edge of pride in his voice.

'I've never heard it said otherwise,' she smiled, taking her own seat opposite him so that the flush of the fire logs gave a ruddier glow to her pale face.

'Your predecessor was less particular,' she said, surprised after all this time by her own bitterness and wondering if Munro had noticed it. 'He drank like a man with a thousand sorrows.'

'That would be Gordon Craig—I never knew him.'

'Aye.' She watched Mungo's hands cupped round his whisky tumbler, stroking, gently caressing each other as he gazed into the fire. Like lovers, she thought, in their restless, relentless shifting, their final and brutal commitment of loving, used and using, savaged and savaging, herself and Gordon on the nights he had come to her bed, her lithe body wakened by his touch till she would shamelessly beg for release; the guilt of it all only after, near morning, when she woke to the light creeping in over the parks, Gordon gone with the dark. Herself in the bed and warm with him still . . .

'He died,' Mungo said, jolting in on her thoughts.

'He drowned,' she corrected, finally facing it. She had been young then, not knowing the world.

Into the listening pools of quiet that fell between them there impinged the drone of voices from above, threatening almost in their unreality.

'I was interested, Mungo, in what you said about the three of us occupying a special place in the community.' She wondered if Mary Dougall who was his housekeeper lay down with him in the night, in the close confining dark as the world slept; in the night all cats are black.

'About our being between the two factions, so to speak?'

'Aye.'

'Which side do we stand on?'

'Aye.'

'God knows, Margaret, but, you know . . .' Munro tamped a log into the fire with the heel of his boot, 'it can be damned lonely whiles out of the crowd. Serving them but not of them.'

The drone of the voices, a sinister buzz it seemed in their foreboding, and the mesmeric sputter of the sparks from the fire-logs drew them closer, a need and a want exposed to the raw edge of the night.

'I know.' She smiled indulgently, for he had expressed a sorrow that had haunted all of her days. 'Loneliness is the hairshirt of the countryside's professional classes.'

'Maybe education does a disservice when it separates a man from his roots?'

'I sometimes think so, Mungo . . . And if you're going to be philosophical maybe you had better have another dram.' She was bantering, near kittenish; he had not known it before.

'Dammit, I think I will, thank you Margaret. And then Hector and me—or is it I, damned if I know—will run you home to the schoolhouse.'

'That would be kind of you.'

She rose to fill his glass and brought it to him, brushing a tendril of hair from her fire-flushed brow. There was a softness in her he had not been aware of till now. His voice was uncertain, diffident even: 'Have you ever thought, Margaret, that there is an intimacy of the mind, of the soul if you like, that can be as fulfilling as the——'

'Intimacy of bodies?'

'Yes.' Her bluntness neither surprised nor amazed him. 'To find a like mind in this world is like finding a rare pearl on the bed of the ocean. Or maybe a diamond in the glitter of the desert's sand.'

She nodded smiling. Her agreement needed no words.

Going in from the marbled cool of the Mossgair milkhouse you had paused by the kitchen door to feel the sun's growing heat like a kiss on your cheek, and hear through the still air the distant voices of the horsemen in the fields, the delighted bark of a dog, the sharp keening cry of the peesie-weeps as they whirled and birled and cried their raucous cries, their white and bottle-green a gash of colour against the grey of the warming sky. But the rowth of the work of the land went on heedless of their lamenting squawks as the harrows harried the stark utility of their nests, hurrying on to gather the fibres of last year's growth and fashion the tilth of another year's seedbed. You had longed for the spring, forgetting it would come, forgetting how it had been the last time and the year before that; only the old remembered. It was funny you forgot. You made a mental note to remember, knowing then in that instant, in a flash of utter and lucid clarity, how it would be to be old, to see winter come and wonder in your heart to see another spring; knowing then what it meant to the old men who came out, racked and worn and with the work of their days behind them and their days numbered, to sit in their fragile frailty at the doors of their biggings to watch with watery een the on-go of work, the dust of death already on their parchment faces.

Spring: that was the measure of their content; to sit childlike saying nothing: that was the sum of their longing. They had spanned their number of years and bedded their lottery of women (with love if they were lucky, but what mattered that now) and dreamed their quota of dreams. But the souls had gone out of them now; they were but the shells of the men they had been. What thought they on, all the day long, you would wonder whiles; what dreams had they now as they sat in the sun, silently musing? In their brittle, febrile frailty it seemed as though the wind might blow them away—*Pouff!* Already they were but the ghosts of yesterday.

Not that you'd think on it long for there was a time to be old, time yet to be wise; a time still to dwell in the kingdom of dreams . . . So you watched young Ewan from your kitchen back window (for so you once told me) at work in the fields of Mossgair, at the harrows or the hyow or catching his Clydesdale pair in the park. Neat he was in all his movements, not like the other men. You wondered at that too for it seemed to you whiles that he might be come of better folk though he had not told you. In the kitchen at evening, though Campbell himself might be there, you would see to it that it was Ewan got the bowl of best cream for his brose, the maturest crumbles from the kebbuck that he liked so much. His gaze thanked you for that. Fine it would be then, knowing his een upon you as you moved round the kitchen, not needing words to tell you what it was he was thinking; it excited you whiles just to think of the things that they told you.

You'd be minding that still going out to the evening milking, hearing the strains of his fiddle in the bothy, and afterwards as you gave the calves their milk: they came running as you rattled the pail, shy on spindly legs as yet, their silky noses rubbing impatiently against your hands. It was then, like as not, he would come on you and wait till you did your last jobs in the milkhouse before trailing you away to the hill or the moss, a strange restlessness in him. You'd go willingly with him, sharing his mood, to set a sly snare for a rabbit to cook in the ash of the bothy fire. Already you sensed the conflicts in him, heard in the music of his wild fiddle the dissonance of a disturbed soul, saw as you watched, the violence in him as he broke the necks of his trapped victims without qualm. You would turn your gaze from the last pleading in their een. But it excited you too, the cruelty that was in him, knowing in some deep and secret part of you that you too were its prisoner.

The entry in the old day-book is faded now by the years, the impact of its words diluted in a world grown old with the burden of greater wrongs. Yet it is possible, still, for the mind to be strangely moved and to imagine the tremor of the fatigued manse hand as it enunciated a sad social injustice and uttered, that early summer night, a commitment on its own behalf. For the Free Kirk's minister, as he left Mungo and his daughter alone in the kitchen to follow his late visitor up the stairs to his study, there had come a moment of painful choice.

June 10, 1879: midnicht
Have this nicht received and been entreated by one of the crofter men that I might prepare for them a petition anent their sad predicament and their grievances against the House of Hallerton in its measure that must starkly and inevitably add to the misery of their lot, and after due consideration of their pleas agreed that I would so draft for them the substance of their complaints. I do so in the full cognisance that my own cause, and that of those close to me, and my standing with the laird, cannot but be damaged by it. Still and all, it is but meet that I be forced to choose as indeed my conscience has beseeched me that I should. I regret nothing in that. Accordingly, I have this nicht, in the hours since James MacCaskill's departure, prepared as they instructed a petition that details their grievances and adds in its sum to a most damning indictment of lairdship as it is presently seen in its presumption of an inherent right to profit from the land at whatever expense. The crofter men's cause is poignantly laid bare and potently argued in the points they make, namely:—

　　1) that they seek of Major Macleod an early meeting,

along with his factor Lander Gregg, to put their case for a reduction in their present rents rather than the upwards revaluation that now faces them.

2) that the practice of revaluation of their holdings should no longer be exclusively in the hands of the estate alone but should include the view of a representative from their own ranks to speak for their interests.

3) that any consideration of the above should take into accountability the fact that farming is now bent upon a decline the full extent of which can only be guessed at but one, beyond doubt, in which grain and fatstock prices can only further decrease in the face of increasing and substantial imports of beef and cereals from abroad.

4) that, most importantly of all, any increases in their rents at the present time and in the onset of such a depression can but result in their being driven from their holdings by their inability to meet the laird's demands.

5) that, may they respectfully remind him, their holdings were riven from the Hill by their own or the sweat of their crofting forbears and at not a single penny cost to the estate; that the present state of cultivation of their ground has been achieved entirely by their own efforts and that any review of their rents must in common justice take account of this fact.

6) that the biggings and dwellings that stand thereon were in like manner raised by themselves or their predecessors stone upon stone again without one iota of cost to the laird.

7) that they humbly beg, given these incontrovertible facts, any raising of their rents to an 'economic' level would be neither fair nor just nor in keeping with the wish and declared policy of the old laird who gave the land for a crofting colony.

By the grace of God the laird's heart must surely be mellowed to grant them the simple justice they seek.

The night of their sought-for confrontation came soon enough and their anger had not subsided. If anything, the few days' delay spent awaiting Macleod's reply had fanned it higher so that their slow, soft voices were automatically raised whenever they gathered to speak of it. They met by custom rather than consent at MacCaskill's croft, where James gave each man a dram as he came in. Its warmth was welcome, for in spite of the time of year it was a cold night with a bitter nip to the wind.

'T'se like winter near, Mistress MacCaskill,' MacGillivray said, diluting a little of the room's tension; he had that affable social dexterity that could knit opposing views and keep sworn old enemies from coming to blows in the drunken bonhomie of Hogmanay, and could with admirable deftness translate a barbed insult into a point of mild disagreement. He asked graciously was Morag still liking her place and went on to say what a time of rain they had had and surely they would have won over it soon. He was the kind of man who could fill an empty room by himself.

MacGillivray was an atheist but MacCaskill liked him in spite of it for he was always the first to offer help, be it beast or sick bairn. He had fine ginger curls and was unshaven on the upper lip even tonight. His Sabbath-black suit, getting an unexpected airing for Andra kept it up mainly for funerals, had always sat better on his old father.

Rob Maglashan arrived and had his new wife well sought after and said shyly she was fine and as well as could be expected in her condition. He was followed in by Wattie Skene strangely silent and pale, and by Gavin Morrison who said his old mother had been so bad with the bile she had not been from the house in a fortnight. Murdo Maclean entered with a funereal nod to the room in general and took his dram standing against the wall, the way, folk said, that he always ate his porridge . . .

So, one by one they filed in, bonnets in hand or rolled nervously in the palm, mostly shaven and sober-suited, solemn faced at the thing that had come on them. They deferred willingly to MacCaskill, their leader without election, for he had their respect as well as kirk office to give dignity to their cause. Scarfed and bonneted, he led them finally into the night, new faces with those of old friends down the hill road, Maglashan with Morrison whose sister it was he had unseasonably bedded in her thirty-eighth year when all hope had gone, Skene with the even more morose Maclean, MacGillivray in the lead with MacCaskill till they turned on to the turnpike and coalesced into groups of four and five. Out of earshot of their families their speak was sour with the taste of betrayal.

'Come a twelve-month, we'll maybe all of us be on a steamship for Australia.'

'Not me, I'll tell ye! I'll tak' a fee aboot a farmtoun afore they force me oot o' the pairish.'

'There will likely be work in the toon,' piped a third voice, perverse in its reasonableness.

'Aye, and they'll likely hae muckle need of a lot o' crofters there, I'm thinking . . .'

All of them aware of the irony, knowing that with only their landsmen's skills they were orphans in an increasingly industrial age. In their silence the collective scrunch of their boots on the Big House's gravel was almost deafening. Within sight of Hallerton misery had numbed them.

Margit Taylor it was, inscrutable and polite, recognizing none though she had known all of them most of her days, showed them into the library, leading deferentially with a *Come this way, sirrs*. In an accomplished way she bestrode two worlds.

It was spacious and grand; Macleods, the whole long line of them it seemed, pickled flatteringly and forever in their prime in the preservative of oils, watched them enter their sanctuary from heavy gilt frames, innocent of all involvement. It was warm in the room; they were to be betrayed in comfort. And why not, MacGillivray thought: why dirk a man when you can as easily starve him to death with a writ and a clear conscience. He warmed his chilled hands over the tongues of flame that lappered over the larch logs throwing their resined scent into the room. Curtains of a deep crimson brocade, gold-ribboned and gold-tasselled, had already been drawn on the night. (*I doot that the entrance to Heaven is as grand*, Andra said surveying them.) In a corner a long table had been loaded with scones and cake and three decanters of whisky.

'You are to help yerselves, sirrs,' Margit said, a smile at last for MacCaskill whose dignity was in no way discomfited. 'The gentlemen will be with you presently.' She retreated, closing tall gilded doors behind her, imprisoning them with their thoughts. Quietly, drams in their hands, they took their seats: chairs collected without discrimination from every corner of the house and set now in rows, a cherubic pink chair from some secret boudoir cheek by jowl with a stately throne from Hallerton's dressing-room; incongruous they were, the pair of them, like a nun at a Presbyterian wedding. As they waited, MacCaskill, at the front with MacGillivray, began to feel their anger grow behind him, a sullen simmering in the blood, a bitterness that had permeated down through the generations.

The murmuring died as Hallerton entered wearing Lander Gregg by his side like a shield, a man facing a formidable moment of accountability. Taking their place beside the fire, the two men faced their restive audience. In Macleod's clipped military bearing and tailored figure the croft men saw clearly the very antithesis of their own order; never had they been more aware of the gulf that separated him from them. His voice was rooted in the fine pristine clarity of another land, an English they understood well enough but which registered none of the couthy undertones of their own Scots. Now it jarred more than ever.

'Gentlemen, I have asked you all here tonight—at your request—to explain to you the reasons for the re-setting of rents in the re-leasing of your holdings. These, let me assure you, will be no more than the economic rents of our time.'

Hallerton shifted his weight from one foot to the other, allowing his gaze to wander over them, careful to avoid the direct challenge of their eyes. 'It is a step unpalatable to you— to me!—but one that has become inevitable, as you will know from its repetition on estates all round the North. It is a matter for regret——'

'No more for you than it is for us!' The voice was from the back, its source unidentified but it rekindled the anger of the croft men. Its bitterness made Hallerton flinch.

'A matter for regret——'

'For shame,' corrected another voice more strident. He felt their hostility, the coldness of their een. Their murmuring swelled.

'In brief, gentlemen——' Dissent now drowned his faltering words, and at once Lander Gregg flitted to his side, a wraith, a sinister bland shadow that usurped the laird's role and allowed him to retire to the support of the mantel; it was what the lawyer was paid for and he did it with superlative ease. Almost before they realized it, it was he who was addressing them.

'What aboot our new agreements?' It was MacGillivray.

'They will stand for twenty-one years—as did the last—so being the usual conditions are met—and the rents paid.'

'They're owre the heid, man!'

'They are a substantial increase,' Gregg parried, 'but no more than would be asked for elsewhere, as the laird himself has told you.'

'That disnae mak' them richt!'

'Nor yet does it make them chusst.' The speaker was a tall man with piercing een as bright as a hawk's that gave him a fearsome authority. He rose to make his point, unafraid, and the crofter men recognized him as the Highlander Sam MacAllister. His words held the lisp of Gaelic still, but they rang through the room.

'Let me tell you, Mister Factor, the story as I see it—as we all of us here see it. It is an imposeeshun without regards to history, withooten heed to the past, for it beggars the man who has put his sweat into the business of winning the ground. Not a penny piece has been paid us for that, nor yet for our biggings, yet here you tell us the laird is to charge us for the very thing we created. Is that not a terrible and painfu' interpretation of lairdly obligation, think you? My folk came from the West, turned out of their holdings for the sake of sheep. Yer father, sir'—he looked directly at Macleod—'took pity on us here in the East and feued out the hill. That wiss forty years ago nearly. A fine man he was, we wiss glad of him I can tell you. Fifteen acres of the hill I took on then, at a pound in the year for the first seven year, rising then to two pounds ten shillings for the next seven and syne for the latter seven years to a level of five pounds the year. Now, I hear, you are speiring more nor double that. You are setting value—asking a price, like I say—for the verra things I have mysel' created. How muckle think you it would hae cost Hallerton estate to clear only my bit o' the hill? I'll tell ye. It would hae been cheap—taking regard to biggings, draining, fencing and trenching—at £300. And what is it now ye propose? No less than tae deprive me of the capital I hae built with the years. And this, mind ye, at a time when we are in the face of foreign compeetishyun and lang past the time when a short crap meant lang prices. What has the laird putten into the ground, I ask ye? Not a damnt thing I tell you! Nothing!'

MacAllister's raised fist punctuated his words.

'I tell you this, Mister Lawyer Man, gin ye proceed with this scheme ye will bring down disgrace on the old laird's heid.'

The room was silent; breaths held slowly expelled, tensed buttocks eased themselves.

'Is there nae appeal?' Gavin Morrison rose as MacAllister resumed his seat. 'Nae appeal against what is jist the laird's valuer's ruling——?'

Gregg, badly worried by the turn of the meeting, had heard enough. 'There is aye a lang line o' folk waiting for croft holdings, gentlemen,' he said. The reminder was a warning to them. Well he knew the power of the threat implied there, the doubts it implanted into a man's psyche. What was he to do? Flit and leave all the hard work of his years—of his life—to another? That was against the human grain, against the pull a man would feel for land he had himself broken in from the hill. The question was always: how much rent would a man stand for not to be rented out of his own improvements? Aah, it was subtler far than simple eviction with all the social protest it evoked and a surfeit of ill-will from the South. Well Gregg knew it: behind each man there that night was another, some-where out there, with his heart set on a patch of poor ground on the hill and prepared to pay to invest in a dream. It was Gregg's last card and he had not meant to play it quite so forcefully. But now the deed was done.

'There will, gentlemen,' he said, facing them, shaken but determined, 'be no revaluation. The estate has come to its decision. Your new rents will be notified shortly.' Turning quickly, he ushered Macleod from the room as the anger flared behind them. Men driven to the edge of despair rose to their feet to hurl insult after them.

'Judas!'

'Swindler!'

Oaths unheard of hung in the air but all of them now knew the choice before them: submit to the growing plague of rack-renting or quit the Croft Hill for ever.

★

The long days of that summer made a mockery of their despair for they held an unaccustomed warmth that made the farmtouns' haytime a joy. Men worked in the fields while the sun burned them a berry brown; in Miss Pringle's schoolroom its heat gathered as in an oven, stifling bairn and teacher. It swung through the arc of the sky to dip in the hours of late afternoon and send a stray beam through the screening firs and in at the window where Margaret sat at her desk, a tendril of heat that caught her like a caress between the shoulder-blades and sent a tremor of delight through her. She took her watch from her fob pocket, casting a glance at its faded gilt numerals.

'Two minutes yet,' she told herself, letting the sun's ray warm her back through the summer-thin material of her frock and dulling her mind momentarily to the scraich of pen on protesting paper, to the sound of a fly buzzing drowsily on the pane behind her.

'All right, girls.' The words fell metallically into the languor of the small schoolroom. 'All right, that will do for today. Finish your essays at home and I will read them in the morning.'

Her voice drowned in the reeshle of papers, the scrape of stools. Bodies that had been unnaturally still for too long, thumped, bumped and jostled each other in the constricting passages between the desks as they fought their way to the door, a city liberated, a civilization disintegrating. She had not the heart to rebuke them. Tolerant now, she was envious only of their youth, of their lives unlived.

'Goodnight, miss.'

'Goodnight, Alice.'

''night, miss.'

'Goodnight, Katrina.'

Then they were gone, chattering voices retreating down the dirt road to the turnpike, and finally mere echoes lingering on the membranes of her mind. She went through to the room then, behind the partition, an austere place that had but lately had a touch of comfort added here, a dab of colour there—an embroidered cushion on the hard seat that Mungo loved, a new quilted overblanket for the bed in the corner bought with a bride's blush from Scroggie the Merchant. It was a room which, while it still denied the flesh no longer sought to rebuke it. Besides the bed, it held a bookcase well-stocked, a plain table scrubbed as clean as that in a croft kitchen, four straight-backed chairs in which ease was impossible (parents were encouraged by them to cut short their gossip) and, grotesque in its opulence, the splay-footed chaise-longue that betrayed not the wayward romanticism in the soul of Miss Pringle but that of her predecessor who had willed it along with the appointment.

Unbuttoning the neck of her frock, she plucked a finely-bound anthology from the bookcase and, riffling its pages, went to sit in the pool of sunlight that splashed over the chaise-longue's fading brocade. The book had been a present from Gordon, strange she should choose it. Her eye skimmed the ragged lines, catching their savour from a single word, a random line. Some were ballads, their images earthy, crude and unmistakable. (*A book full of dung and peat reek and fertility,* he had promised her, *but fine poems all the same. They have honesty.*)

Poor Gordon, he'd had too fine a soul to deal daily with death and suffering: he had come to her like a fugitive . . . She let the book and her hands slip into her lap and closing her een, let the sun's warmth bathe their lids. Her mind turned in on the tumult of her thoughts. So, long ago, Gordon Craig had found her, over on some innocent errand (she never had known it) half-fainting in the heat of a yellow afternoon, loose-bowelled with loving.

Maybe the men that long-past harvest time had halted briefly in their bouts to see her stravaiging with the doctor; she did not know now one way or the other. She had heard them in her mind, the rough speak of them as they watched the pair of them set their stride to the steep of the Hill to take them up and away by themselves (free souls in communion) to the dreich isolation of Kynoch's Castle. Release there had been when their eager strides had carried them into the welcoming dark of the wood. There had been a freedom there amid the mossy silence of its ancient stones; a sanctuary where she could prattle her girlish joy safe from the hard eye of society, a hush that secreted from the world all the things they did there, her breath tight with knowing they could neither of them wait, her relief shameless when he had pinioned her with kisses.

There would be a peace between them afterwards, a quiet

66

tenderness, a fragile joy in which she measured his gratitude, glad it was her he had wanted. Below them in the lap of the hill as they came home in the last lilac light, the wild geese would return with piercing cries and a riffle of wings to disturb the evening quiet of the loch: benign it looked and so you might think it unless you knew it in winter with the wind moaning over its grey water. It sounded like the crying of lost souls, some legion of the forever damned so that long ago they had called it the Loch of Mourning. All the same, she knew only that she loved its brooding sadness, had shared for as long as she could mind its fearful melancholy. By it, they said, (she told Craig, a stranger still in her landscape of childhood) the clansmen had rested going home from Harlaw, bloody and ragged, back from the battlefield, the deid still dying upon it . . . You could feel it still, the lingering of ghosts there, the ghosts of those men hirpling on with swift jerky movements, their black-ringled een sunk into their cheekbones—endlessly marching those men of the claymore and suffering, a kingdom of the dead . . .

The gentle pressure of his fingers in hers would draw her back. Skirting the kirkyard in the last of the light they would strike down the hill beyond Mossgair to turn on to the turnpike the way of the schoolhouse, steps quickening in the comforting dark . . .

In the schoolhouse Margaret Pringle buttoned the neck of her frock against the unexpected caller.

So that was the summer, Old Woman, that you told me of; telling it for the first time in your life with long pauses when memory choked you and the tear ran from your eye. I loved you then, Old Woman of the ingle, in all the frailty of your years, all the warmth in you and the gift of laughter. You gathered the days of that summer like flowers in an album, petals of a special time so that now in the winter of your life, shawled with remembrance, you would recall the cadences of love: the work of the hayfield when you were ordered to tramp the ricks as they grew by the dyke and Ewan throwing forkfuls full at you and the wrath of Campbell's glower on your merriment and the secrets between you. You had not known days so still and golden; it was fine that year with the hairst coming early, the sun yellow of the grain kissed slow to the colour of faded gold. Slowly the barley heads drooped and the oats reeshled on the stalk as the days fell together into the immemorial pattern of the year. But there was a sadness in you too, the sharp memory always of the anguish of the croft men as they saw the work of their years begin to slip from them, held up for the highest bidder. Your father was among them and going home for the Sabbath afternoon you found gloom in the house.

The night of the meeting had hardly been put past before Farquhar Douglass, Hallerton's ground steward, began to be seen where his presence, before, had not been conspicuous. He had been sent round the Croft Hill to assess, to speir, as he said to his wife, *fittin' wyse they wis thinkin'*.

He found John Glennie in his small cornyard weeding foons ready to take the ricks of harvest. Farquhar was affable. 'Fit think ye o't, John? She'll be a guid crop the year after all, would ye nae say? Six, sivven quarters to the acre?'

'Fowr, gin I'm maist damnably lucky, that's mair like it!' Glennie, like his crofting neighbours, had little time for the cocky little man with his sly manner and his cavalryman's breeches.

'Losh, mair surely . . .' Douglass feigned astonishment at the other's modest hopes, then added quietly: 'Ye've put a lot of wark into this place John, that ye have . . . A lot of wark owre the years.'

'An' I micht hae saved myself the trouble!' There was no mistaking the crofter man's bitterness, nor did he any longer seek to disguise his dislike of the ground steward.

'Fat mak's ye say that, man?'

'By the time I've payed my half-year's rent tae yer laird next year I'll hae damn the penny piece left to keep wife and bairns let alone buy the next spring's seed. Ye maun ken that weel enough, surely?'

The ground steward inclined his head, excusing himself of all involvement. 'Ach, John, it's nae me that sets the rents, it's weel ye ken't. It's that plukey-faced cheil fae Aberdeen. Gregg, the lawyer lad. He has the say——'

Glennie in his anger stepped closer and for a moment

Douglass feared violence to his person as the croft man balled his fists in suppressed rage. 'It's ticht enough noo, nivver mind double the rent. I'll be oot, my wife and bairns wi' me. And whit for?' Glennie spat close to the factor's boot. 'For the likes of Macleod, a man fa's nivver daen a hand's turn on the grun but just grabbit aye the siller it has made him. I carena should he gang tae Hell for it, I tell ye!'

'But ye'll be able tae raise enough, John?'

'Nivver! Nivver!'

In the days that followed their encounter, the ground steward's wanderings took him round the neighbouring crofts in a slow odyssey that was intended to arouse no suspicion but allayed none of the crofters' fears for all that. Slowly, slyly, he analysed the position, sifting the compliant and the complaisant, those who would stand and those who would tumble; those with nowhere to go and with no hope but to pay should they have to cut their own lives to the line of starvation. His last call, since it was an outlier, was on the MacAllister place.

Sam, he of the hooked nose and the sharp hawk's een, watched the squat figure approaching on the croft road and let him near to the croft steading before he set Mirk, his spotted collie, on him. The tall crofter man watched from the door as the dog put his teeth into the ground steward's breeches and then worried at his ankles till Douglass in his very evident terror tripped himself and fell headlong, swearing. He attempted to get up and was at once discouraged from doing so by Mirk's bared teeth and panting tongue. The beast's hot breath fanned his face. Only then did MacAllister make shift to go and meet his visitor, walking down to where the ground steward lay.

'That's a damned vicious dog, Farquhar,' he said. 'I dinna ken why I keep haud o' him. Come!'

With a snap of his finger the crofter called off his dog and brought him to heel, and waited while Douglass rose shakily to his feet. Terror and rage twisted the little man's features in equal measure and a vein thickened with blood throbbed in his sun-reddened neck. He spluttered his wrath. 'By—— By God, MacAllister, ye'll pay dear for this. By God ye will——'

'Likely then, man. A'thing's dear roon here. Rents warst ava.'

'By God, ye will!'

'But nae at your hands Farquhar, I'm thinking.' Unaccountably short on the Highland guile that should have been his birthright, MacAllister was taunting him.

'The Hill's gaun tae be rid o' your kind! Weel rid of you, the whole damned kit and caboodle of ye!'

'And that's what Hallerton wants, likely.'

In his anger, the ground steward's guarded caution of the preceding days deserted him. 'Yer damned richt it is! The hale shebang! Guid riddance! And mind this, MacAllister, there's plenty o' folk that would like a placie on the Hill—and yours in particular. There was a man at me but yesterday speiring aboot it and gin ye were tae quit.'

'Bribed by Hallerton's siller nae doot.'

That had been the pattern, the insidious blackmail that Farquhar Douglass had taken round the Hill in those days of high summer, a threat difficult still to believe yet bewilderingly clear.

'He'll tak' your place tomorrow, I can tell you!' Douglass seemed ready to bluster it out, but MacAllister had seen enough of him. 'Gang hame, mannie, the way ye cam' . . . Noo! This meenit, afore I set the dog on ye again!'

With a terrified look at Mirk, panting at his master's heel, the ground steward did as he was bidden, stumbling down the track. His backward glance spoke vengeance.

'Ye'll hear mair aboot this, MacAllister, I promise ye.' Hatred rose in him like a bile.

And that night when it was decently dark Farquhar Douglass slid out from under the Kynoch firs where he had been setting some circumspect snares and, sure-footed as a cat, took over the night-shadowed fields to Hallerton House. A fleeting wraith in a copse of yews, he slipped into the House's big garden through a little-used side gate and took a path up to the mansion. He skirted round the west wing to a door, iron-hinged and heavily-panelled, a door that a man in the long-ago time might have entered a friend and left, betrayed and in chains, to a traitor's scaffold. He glanced round him in the dark, a raking look that judged every wind-fluttered leaf, before pounding the door with the heel of his fist. It opened almost at once, swinging back easily on well-oiled hinges. He had been expected. He was let in by a grey-faced maidservant, a tall figure made sinister by the black of her uniform.

'Himself is in the study,' she said without civility.

Through the labyrinth of the house's long corridors, Douglass glided like a ghost to the laird's room of business. The door was open and the ground steward barely had time to doff his bonnet in servile salute when Hallerton's voice bid him enter.

'Come in, Douglass—and shut the door, man.'

The laird was behind his desk; with him, as Douglass had expected, was Gregg. His arrival, it was obvious, was keenly awaited. Quickly the laird shuffled the papers he had been studying to the side of the desk and, leaning back in his chair, crossed his hands on his tweed waistcoat. Gregg ushered the little man to a chair.

'Now Farquhar,' he said. 'Let's have your news.'

So your golden time, Old Woman, lengthened towards the clamour of harvest. As always, as the howe waited, there was work to fill the days. Your love had grown with the corn seed of spring, like the tender fronds in the fields, in tentative shoots of awareness you extended one to the other. Strange you thought it, bewildered at times, sick whiles inside you for you had not known it before: what it was to love a man. As you moved quietly about the Mossgair kitchen at your jobs in the evening quiet, or, late and alone with your thoughts in the blue-dark in the Campbell bed, you would hear him playing still in the bothy and you would marvel whiles at the music that was in him. Often it would have a sad, dirge-like quality, a disturbing melancholy so that you would stop to hear it. What was it he mourned, you would wonder whiles, for it minded you then on laments and clansmen and things long ago. No proudness in it but something all by with now and emptied of feeling, a long sigh of sadness that folk weren't caring. Och, but fine all the same the way that he played it: you would smile to yourself and go round with a small bowl of tomorrow's broth to the bothy door and just leave it, knocking lightly. He would bring in the bowl in the morning and thank you with his een, his een on you as he ate his brose and his bite of breakfast; it made you suddenly breathless. And

71

whiles with Campbell gone to the inn and the mistress asleep in the ben-the-house room you would go round to the bothy to sit by the door as he played in the warm evening air, in the long dying-away murmur of dusk broken only by the bark of a croft dog somewhere on the Hill or the scraich of the geese coming home to the lochside through the lonely darkening sky. And putting his fiddle away, he would come to the step to sit with you; to speak shyly of his music, so different a lad from the sturdy horseman cheil that you watched stride the fields at the harrows' tail. Whiles as he spoke his hands smoothed tenderly over the bellying curves of his old fiddle so that suddenly—bewilderingly—you were jealous of it, wanting to destroy it, to smash it into a thousand smithereens, to shout at him heich: *Ye canna bed wi' a fiddle, Ewan Carmichael!* It was an unreasoning shriek of pain that tore through you. And once he spoke of his mother in far Bogandie and of their life in the island before they had come there. It was his fiddle that linked him most of all with his melancholy childhood, with old Niall of the Sums who was schoolmaster and registrar, elder and councillor all, and who had once admiringly told him, *If you had a mind to it boy, I would not say but that you might play yet in the great assembly halls of the mainland. It is possible—chusst.* Little more had the old man honestly been able to say of him for he gave little heed to his lessons, playing truant now and then to scour the cliffs for the delicacy of a gull's egg. Yet beyond the cat-and-dog battle they had fought with each other across old Niall's books, over the slated muddle of his baffling sums, he had known the old man's appreciation of his music, his nodding assessment and assent that in this, in its beauty, they were at one, that for a tune played so all could be forgiven. *A man that can play like that,* Old Niall had said once to his mother, *even were he the blackest of black-hearted rogues, might charm his way into Heaven. Maybe,* she had said, and then banteringly, knowing the old man's fondness for her, *I wonder how Nero got on? Ach— chusst so. Chusst so!* the old man had smiled, but meeting her een then, Ewan had seen her pride. She had smiled her tender-soft smile, the secret smile he had seen whiles on her face as she gazed over the minch as it lay sheet silver on a slow summer night. She would stand, not moving, not speaking, a mist in her een and her shawl drawn ticht about her so that

72

whiles he would be jealous, not knowing her thoughts only that he was shut from them, that whatever it was came between them . . .

He had hated the sea, young though he was, knowing its cruelty and its ravening fury; seeing a boat go out and not coming back, the men of the township saying little, only the women bourached black by the harbour wall—more than one that had lost her man to the sea and married to live it again. The women not liking the sea. Whiles he would wonder: did they come back from the sea those men who never came home, with weeds in their hair and their een hazed with the thing that had come on them? To look at their women in other men's beds or take a last peek in the cradle? Came they back in the dark over the shingle to slip away with the dawn, the sleep of the dead coming back to their faces like men going away to a war? Remembering, he understood her joy and her sadness, her pleasure and flurried consternation of relief at the sight of Murdo, unexpected on the brae; Murdo who came with the smell of the sea and brine about him and maybe the present of a Shanghai shawl and who stayed long after he had been put ben to his bed to lie and listen to their silences and sudden laughter; his mother quiet for days after Murdo had been . . . Black Murdo that was his mother's love, that was his father and him not knowing it yet . . .

So that hairst had come on, Old Woman. It was Campbell sent the two of you to the barn to twine straw ropes that would be needed for the rick thatch; you worked well together, Ewan feeding in the straw, yourself winding the thraw-crook, speaking little so that he would tease you at times for your silences. Charlie Skene would cry in on you to see what the pair of you were up to (you thought) with a coarse laugh as though he'd expected to find him on top of you. Together you'd watch through the barn door Miss Pringle's pupils home-going, one day unaccountably early. *Miss Pringle must hae a man to meet the nicht*, he had said lightly, and looking again at his watch: *She's let them oot early. Only the Doctor seems welcome*, you'd said. *Aye, he goes regular to the manse. Ach, he's a freen o' the minister's*, you'd said. *That'll be his story likely* . . . His careless laughter took the breath from you. *I wouldn't wonder— Dammit!* He swore. It was the first time you'd heard him. The rope flew asunder as he loosed it to squeeze the fleshy part of his thumb. *A thistle stob.* Little sympathy you'd given him, just leading him to the light at the door. *Serves ye richt, I'd say, Ewan Carmichael for makin' fun o' Miss Pringle.* It lay a black dot, embedded deep under the skin but with a tiny end of it showing. In an instant you had bent your lips to it, your teeth sharp on the flesh. *There—it's oot!* A boldness in you as you lifted your face, the barb still on your lips. So tenderly then he had picked it off, brushing the place on your lips with his own. Then quick and urgent his arm round you, his mouth on your own and his thigh thrust into the heat of you so that you melted and quickened against him and his mouth and fingers were feverish at the coarse neck of your workaday frock. *No!* It had been almost a scream as you pulled from him trembling, knowing in that moment the feeble strength of your denial, that you were different now from what you had been; sick with loving.

Pringle came down the Croft Hill with the step of a man nearly half his years. The ash staff he swung at his side was more companion than crutch and as he walked he raised it in a sweep of greeting to the croft folk working their patches at the side of the track. Theirs in all conscience was a meagre hairst but in its meaning to them maybe it was as steeped in symbolism as that of their farmtoun neighbours. He had never doubted it, for it paralleled the very pattern of life itself. He had just called on Kirsty Maglashan who had been Kirsty Morrison to bless and to handsel her bairn, a new life in the howe, and was now on his way to Mossgair where Mistress Campbell, poor body, had speired for him since she was, she said, shortly to leave it. All round him were the familiar sounds of harvest, old in the land, old in the mind but as fresh to the heart that year as they had always been, as blithe as a bouquet of gowans. Along the howe, as he stepped down to the turnpike, he could see Hilly's new reaping machine at work with Hilly himself walking proud behind it in the bout, and the Clydesdales leaning bravely into their harness. Was it not a divine, he reminded himself, who had invented the machine? Driven by pity for his flock? Away up the strath, where it opened to let down the sky, he saw there was another at work on a brae-side park, a moving dark dot on a golden square.

For the rest of the farmtouns, though, the patterns of hairst were those that had held there since early in the century and the sweep of his gaze took in no fewer than ten teams, each of five men, scything their way through the grain. Behind them, gathering the sheaves and making the bands, were their women partners, bareheaded some of them as they swooped and stooped, working in the blaze of the sun. This was the time when he liked the howe most, for he had never lost his love of the parks and their seasons. There was hardly a day—not even in the dead thraw of winter—when his tall broad figure was not seen on the road, hallo-ing tink or cadger man, laird or ploughman.

Stepping down the croft track, he minded well the early folk of the Hill, the first scattering of the few, squatters at will on the face of the brae before the old laird had decided to allow it to be colonized. They had come from God knows where, glad of a place to bigg their poor dwellings—some of them, like MacCaskill's old father, from the West; all of them men with that most fragile of dreams: the creation of a kingdom they could call their own, that would prosper under their own industry. Year by year he had watched them taking in a fresh bit of their hill ground, copying the new crop rotations of the farmtouns that lay below them in a mad mockery of self-sufficiency for their neeps were rarely worth the growing on that poor land and their corn was a pitiable travesty of their dreamed-for bounty, both a tribute only to the remarkable hopes and persistence of men. Theirs had been a long betrayal of sweat and hope. Sad in his heart he had watched the dreams die in them, a little more with each passing year. For that was the way of it with the crofting men. Their fragile dream faded and their een dulled and their once-blithe steps grew weary. It was not hard to excuse their failure of spirit, even their diminishing faith (for so he supposed it) for His mercy on them seemed at times singularly slight. Death emptied the cot with an appalling frequency; fevers and the scourge of diphtheria took the young and the brave early into the kirkyard. Maybe it was in watching their despair that his own belief had waned . . . he did not know now. Yet it seemed to him that

75

there were times when God did not deal fairly with those who sought Him. Worse still was the plight of their womenfolk: their investment was not in dreams but in the men who had bedded them and their reward had been to watch time and circumstance crush them. They had not had the privilege of choosing their own destiny; the love of a man it was that had brought them to the Croft Hill and into the long days of its slavery. Bonnie they had been some of them in the first of their days, blithe and fair to the eye; too soon they had grown hard in the bone and string-wiry in the flesh, tanned to leather in the skin with their constant exposure of work in the fields, making dutiful shift in the wan-weary hours of the night to give their gudeman his pleasure whenever he had need of it. Maybe it was the nearest they came, some of them, to the gift of loving, that moment in the snibbed dark of the box-bed, holding him while he laboured at them, the last thing in failure that made him a man. Their despair in time had congealed into a haze of numbed existence in which one day followed another without hope or meaning. He forgave them their bitterness.

He hallo-ed Martha MacCaskill, working her heuk at the rig-end, working with fine rhythmic movements, her fingers deftly gathering the corn stalks as they fell before her flashing blade. She straightened as Pringle drew level.

'Yer gathering it in, Martha,' he said. 'It's that time again.'

'The seasons nivver fail us, Mister Pringle. They aye come round.'

'A middling crop, would ye say?' His eye knew better.

'Puir for the year, Mister Pringle . . . There's but little grows weel on this rauchle o' stanes.' She looked blear-eyed out and beyond him into some corner of secret remembrance, musing almost to herself. Guiltily she glanced back at him.

'I would hae tae gang and marry a crofter man! My auld mither, I can tell ye, had me weel warned what tae expect . . . and she wis richt. She used tae say it wis naething but travail till ye gid tae the grave an' I widna gainsay her.'

'Life itsel, Martha, has its ain strange harvests whiles.'

Was he chiding her, she wondered.

'Och, it is true richt enough: the life has its independence o' a kind. Till ye come tae tak' the measure o' it—and then ye see fine, there's nae independence at a'.'

76

Her hazed een looked down the patchwork fields that fell from the small croft steadings, down the flank of the hillside to the bigger farmtouns of the howe where a more bountiful hairst was being reaped, where the gangs of men and women crowded the parks under the burning sun. Her eyes swung back to the minister's face.

'D'ye ken this, Mister Pringle . . . There are times when I think Jeemes deserves better nor this—this puir hand-tae-mooth existence that we lead—for he's a guid man in his way.' She nodded down to the howe. 'See half the dykes doon there? What he didna bigg himsel his father biggit afore him. Both of them selled their labour owre cheap when they micht have held laird and fairmer tae ranson, and look at's noo . . . We're finely balanced, us folk o' the crofts, atween existence and eternity. What comes in wi' this year's hairst will gang oot for oor next year's seed. The sower, I'm thinking Mister Pringle, disnae aye get his just reward.'

Pringle was silent. There was no anger in her voice: just a sigh, if you understood and could hear it.

Beyond her, seated at the door of the croft house, Pringle saw Grandfather MacCaskill, the man who first had claimed the croft's acres. Wrapped now in the frailty of years, his pale een blinded by the sunlight, his parchment face smiled often but he spoke little, his staff tapping accompaniment to the febrile *Tchech, tchech* that regularly escaped his lips. It might have been an expression of joy or disapproval, you could not have said, or the wry amusement that came from some secret inner commentary he heard in his mind. His face wreathed as Pringle came up to him: a familiar figure whose connection with his own life he could no longer understand. In his few lucid moments the world had become an embarrassment to him: each day he retreated a little further from its hurts.

In the hairst parks of Mossgair, Old Woman, you had followed that end of summer at the tail of Ewan's scythe while Clara Skene gathered and bound to her man Chae. Sweet it was the sound of the scythe—*swish, swish*—a somnolent rhythm that matched Ewan's mesmeric movements—*step, step*—and your own with every sweep. He kept close to Chae's heels, getting a curse for his pains.

77

'Haud back, ye bugger!' Chae shouted to him, over his shoulder without pause. 'Ye'll hae the legs aff me!'

And Ewan had laughed, not caring, that low lauch that made your heart-strings tighten and leap; you liked it fine that he could match Chae in the scythe now as well as in the plough. So the four of you had taken that same bit lauch, sitting down to your forenoon piecetime by the side of a stook: oatcakes and cheese and the honeyed ale that Mistress Campbell had made for hairst before taking to her sickbed.

'Morag,' Chae had said, 'ye will hae tae see if ye can dae something tae slow him down a bit. He's owre——'

'Wheesht, Chae,' Clara had said sharp to him. 'Fitten a like thing tae say tae the lass!'

'Ach!' Chae for once had looked sheepish and said no more. Fine you had kenned what he meant and Ewan too from the look that he gave you. You liked Chae for all that, for there was no hurt or harm in him, not like some.

The crop that year was a heavy one on the loamy Mossgair acres and the work was hard; your face and arms tingling under the sun and as the heat rose on the day Chae and Ewan would tirr to just the breeks and boots and you saw then, smooth-skinned and already near as muscled as Chae, the fine ripple of his shoulders as the scythe swung.

'Come, lasses, doon tae the petticoats, eh?' The droll lauch of Chae made the rest of you grin till Clara scolded him. 'Aye, ye big sumph, ye'd like that fine, widn't ye?' and turning to you: 'He has naething else in his mind I think whiles!' That made you blush.

But the days going by in a blink, the oats at last cut and stookit and the weather so fine that year that you were into the leading almost before the scythes were put away. You had biggit your first hairst cart then, trampling the sheaves down into the well of it, the sheaves that Ewan forked up to you, building them, as the pile grew under your feet, round the rim of the harvest frames. You had not known such days of work before, the night never coming soon enough. You'd had a distance between you the two of you since that day in the barn dark, but a tenderness too for all that in the quick step or two he would take from the table to the kitchen fire to set a heavy pot off the crook for you, or maybe in the way he would take your Sunday Bible from your fingers to find the place for you before sliding it back into your still, gloved hands as you sat together in the Campbell pew. So close you took the heat from his thigh. You liked that, his nearness to you. You did not say, Old Woman, how it was between you then; we did not speak of the agony and anguish in you then nor of the bewilderment of loving, for it had been a secret thing between you. I cannot know how it was, only how it might have been.

The day simmered down to the pulse of the night. Hot it was still, the last-shafting sunlight lengthening into the glimmer of dusk, laying shadows long ben the howe but plashing still over the crown of the Croft Hill. Peace reigned owre the new-shorn parks and where the ricks rose daily, one beside the other, in the Mossgair cornyard. The cool shadows between them it was that had drawn you there in the late-evening quiet to be out of the house, away for a moment from the fetid odour of sickness that gathered uncannily, undisturbed, in its airless corners and hung like a curtain in the ben end where Mistress Campbell now lay, silent and smiling, brave soul that she was.

It hurt you to see her.

But more now to your life than the clammer of pans and the milking of kye and the meating of men. Men needed more than brose in their bellies, more just than the work of their days. You'd as lief lie down and die now gin that's all there was—you'd be a saint not to think of what more they would want, not to think on the day you would sleep in some man's bed and sifter his nights with laughter and love from the tyaave of his days, for there was a time you kenned for every mortal thing, a time and a season for ilka whim you had a mind to, for every heartbreak you were heir to. Now was the time to laugh your fill for you'd be old soon enough and burdened with despair and broken dreams. It was a time (the dusk hid the blush of shame that rose to your cheek) to dance like a dervish to the tunes of love, to play the fool with a man, to be cuddled and fondled and feel his hands on your dowp. You were young with the rest, blithe and bonnier than most: John Lorimer, still, would watch you go past his road-end, coarse tink: you would ken what it was *he* was thinking. You would not be unwilling with a man that you liked, a man of your own; your blood would lowp to his touch for you'd need more than a spinster's bed with its prim starched sheets and its waukriff nichts stretching into the dawn; you wantit to wake to each day tousled with love. It would be fine that a man wantit you so; you'd not blame him for that . . .

On the warm breath of the evening Ewan's playing carried to you, a strange dwam of compulsion on you then as you turned out from the cloistered dusk of the cornyard back to the steading and slow, slow up the stone stairs to the bothy, the door they forbade you, your father and Campbell. But you pushed it gently, all the same, the blood quickening your heartbeats; it swung back on Ewan, rapt in his music. *You're practising*, you said, the words a bridge between you. He started and turned, still playing. *Aye.* In his voice there was still the Highland softness of his boyhood; it was a caress to your heart. The melody faltered. *Dinna stop!* you had cried. His stillness had made you breathless and uncertain so you wondered: why had you come? So he played and you listened, some strange enchantment it was that possessed you . . . Unnoticed the mirk gathered far ben the howe and spread slow up the Croft Hill in a mounting gloaming tide. Now it was dark in the loft, only Ewan's profile as he bent over his fiddle under the skylight pane and the blurr of his fingers as they flurried and danced on the strings, the music uncanny in the things that it told you. You thought you never would tire of it. Wild it was too in some way that excited you. And Ewan black-brooding owre it: it hung round and about him, a tapestry of forgotten things woven in the patterns he played; a tenderness too, that quality of yearning (you had heard him before) as sharp as the cry of a keening gull.

You encouraged him: *Come owre that one again, Ewan, for I liked it fine.* So, in the blue dark of the summer night the golden cadences were wrung from the fiddle's strands to dance on the fiddler's bow, for Ewan Carmichael had the pure soul of a poet; the music flowed from the heart of him, all of it part of him. Held in it were all the strains of a Gaelic lament and maybe all the words of the world's love songs dwelt in its melody. Maybe too—for it was something you could not put a name to—there was all the weariness of Scotland, distilled and eddied in the attar of singly mellifluous notes that sprang from the wells of his being into the springs of your own. You warmed to the music, to its depth and its longing, its tender responses . . . The tempo quickened: from sweet strathspey to panting, ranting reel, the music ebbed and birled, buoyant, joyous, quicker, wilder till the whole loft bothy was filled and alive with the sensuous, thigh-stroking throb of it . . . till you wanted, achingly, to lie with him there in the comforting dark . . . to take into you all the anger and hurt that was in him . . .

The music stopped, as though maybe you had spoken the thought, the loft a cage with just the two of you in it. Time congealed the moment. You tensed to his movement, his shadow beside you, not seeing his mouth but finding it with your own, glad of the night so that only his hands would know you. *Is Campbell——?* His voice harsh, your own near inaudible. *He went to the inn.* There was no one to hear you, no one to hear what you did but no sense of reasoning now in you as you slid with him to the floor feeling the urgency of his hands as he uncovered you, the shrug of his body as he unbuckled his moleskins and finally found you . . .

Long after, sea-wrack on a gentle incoming tide, you heard Campbell come home, the ring of his steel-heeled boot on the farmtoun's cobbles and the speak of him heich and muddled with drink, going thud into the stable door before he could open it and now, below you, newsing still to the beasts as though they were creatures of his kind. Sometimes, Ewan said softly, he grat there like a bairn.

In that time before dawn, the day as yet was but a hint of pewter behind the distant hills, the thunderous knock tore Sam MacAllister out of the turmoil of sleep and drew him, reluctant, to the comprehending edge of consciousness and finally, resentful, from the warmth of his bed to the door. He slipped its bolt, unsuspecting—and was immediately sent sprawling as it was flung back in his face.

'What the hell——?'

Blinded by the sudden glare of lantern light in his een, he struggled to rise, the anger growing in him, and was at once pinioned firmly to the floor by a boot wedged on his upper arm.

'Lie still, man, gin ye ken what's good for ye,' a voice

advised, and travelling his gaze up the leg that held him to the figure looming over him, MacAllister looked into the face of his tormentor, a heavy, hard-featured man muffled in a reefer. Behind him, from the fringe of the lantern's light, other faces looked on, plainly enjoying his predicament. They were all of them strangers, faces unknown to him.

'Yer makin' a mistake, I'm thinking,' the crofter man protested.

'Is yer name MacAllister?' The questioner was the man whose boot kept him tightly captive.

'I'm nae the Queen of Sheba.'

'HelpmaGod, we have a humorist!' The big man feigned astonishment. MacAllister for his pains had the sharp nails of the boot jabbed more viciously into his muscle. The length of his arm was numbed.

'I was asking gin you were MacAllister—gin I want comedy I'll gang to the music hall.' The voice had a city slur that placed it, in the crofter man's mind, from somewhere down in the south. 'And onywye, I didna come here at this hour tae bandy repartee wi' the likes o' you,' it warned.

'I'm MacAllister,' the crofter man admitted dourly.

'You do yerself a kindness, Mister MacAllister.' The boot eased its pressure but remained firmly on the crofter's arm.

'Ye're a wee bit inclined tae dispute the need for higher renting of the Hill holdings, I'm hearing.' The big man turned to his companions. 'Did any of yous hear that too . . .?'

'Aye, we heard it.' They chorused sinister agreement.

'Aye, and so I do dispute it! It's a damnable injustice!'

'A what, Mister MacAllister? A what did ye say?' and again Sam MacAllister winced under the pain of bootnails savagely re-applied to the tender padding of muscle and the now-lacerated flesh. The big man's voice insinuated astonishment, a pretended shock. 'You maun be careful with yer words, Mister MacAllister. Careful——'

'It's nae mair than the truth and Hallerton kens it. It's——' Deftly inflicted pain cut the crofter man's breath and further protest, but the voice was almost reasonable as it continued: 'All the same, Mister MacAllister, it would be fine if you could see your way to changing your opinions about that. My principals are much aggrieved, Mister MacAllister——'

'Ye mean Hallerton?'

The big man shrugged, his patience endless, as with an intractable bairn. 'We will not speak names, Mister MacAllister. Ye understand?' The heavy-featured face bent concernedly over the prostrated crofter. 'There is neither of us would be the better for it now, would we?'

It was an appeal to reasonableness. 'Let us, in the bygoing, Mister MacAllister, just say that our benefactor is a shy man——'

The remark brought snickers of suppressed laughter from the faces grouped behind him. 'Is that not so, gentlemen?' He appealed to them again, his face breaking in an odd, crooked grin.

'Aye.'

'To be sure.'

'Verra shy . . . oh, verra shy indeed.'

The quick chorus made clear, if MacAllister had doubted it, the big man's unquestioned leadership. He turned back to his hapless victim. 'He would take it as a special kindness to himself, Mister MacAllister, gin ye were just to pay up—or, of coorse, quit yer place if that is what ye have a mind to. The one or the tither—whichever is convenient to ye. But nae fomentation, nae upstirring, Mister MacAllister, among the crofting community. He would not like that. Not at all, Mister MacAllister.'

'An' ye can tell Hallerton——'

'I said nae names, Mister MacAllister, nae names.' Through the numbness that was the leaden lump of his arm MacAllister was aware of the new excruciating stoon of pain that travelled out to the very ends of his splayed fingers making them twitch and leap there, disembodied and beyond his physical control. 'He is a reasonable man, Mister MacAllister. His concern I may tell ye, is only that a handful of folk, misguided like yersel, should not stand in the way of farming progress. Or make trouble of a really upsetting kind. No more nor that.'

'Tell ye yer maister . . .' The crofter's anger rose above the heightened threshold of agony. 'Tell him, gin that's what he said, that he's a damned liar, nae less. His concern is with the siller in his pooch.'

The big man chuckled menacingly. 'It could indeed be as ye

say, Mister MacAllister, but . . .' Again the boot jabbed cruelly, forcing a cry from the crofter's lips. 'I did advise ye that we would avoid that kind o' remark, did I no' ?'

'I'll be damned first!'

MacAllister, in his semmit and drawers, was becoming by the moment more aware of his vulnerability and the heedless character of the men who had burst in on him. Now without moving his boot, the big man knelt beside him.

'A promise of yer respectful silence. That is what I need from you, Mister MacAllister. What my principals need. Do I get it, no?' A rough hand shook the crofter man's shoulder for one irritated moment. 'Aye or no, Mister MacAllister? Aye or no?'

The crofter man's silence seemed only to sadden him.

'That's nae verra co-operative of ye, Mister MacAllister,' he sighed and was again immediately supported by a barrage of feigned regrets. The big man rose and nodded, finally removing his boot from the crofter's arm. It was the signal the watching faces had been waiting for. Suddenly, before he could summon movement into his limbs, MacAllister found himself hoisted from the floor and hurled bodily against the wall: spread-eagled against its crumbling lime-wash and pinioned in the vice-like grip of four pairs of hands. His head cracked back on the rough stone of the wall, blurring his mind and vision, making him only fuzzily aware of what was happening. His senses reeled, but slowly, close up to his face now, the features of the man in the reefer came into focus, curiously impersonal. A hand seized the front of his flannel vest as though forcibly to shake the answer from him. He felt the waist button slip loose and then, in the same moment, his long drawers yanked savagely down to hang round his knees, exposing the dark, knotted hair of his nakedness.

'A promise, Mister MacAllister, of yer respectful silence on the matter of which we hae spoken. Nae fomenting of disenchantment or the like. What say ye, man?'

The voice now was low, soft, persuasive, almost pleading; the low up-thrust blow that drove hard into the crofter man's groin smashed sleep-swollen scrotum with a savage, knuckled vengeance, cutting off breath, making him leap like a man strung on wire; making his haggard face in the lantern light a

84

staring mask of pain. Again the balled fist, hard, upward, burying knuckled bone in the spongy open vulnerability of the crotch of Samuel MacAllister, crofter man, so that his whole body jangled and danced and recoiled to its uttermost nerve-ends with the shock of it; so that his limbs lost their coherence one with another, making them spring and twitch grotesquely as though at the hands of some drunken puppetmaster; making his bowels move.

Again . . . and again. Quick. Pounding into the soft, pudding flesh, compounding damage, the scream of pain cut from MacAllister's lips before it could be emitted by the counter-pain; its cry suffocated in the frantic contraction and suction of tubes, bronchialed by seasons of mists and damp beds, as they heaved to suck back the breath so sharply expelled from them. MacAllister gagged in his throat, somewhere on the fringe of consciousness.

'He will spew all over yer boots.' The big man, warned by one of his companions, shifted deftly, stepping back as the crofter man's stomach, unable to bear its body's pain, threw its meagre contents down the front of his vest.

'God, but I hate tae see a man make a fool of himsel by not being able to keep his meat doon in a wee moment of excitement,' the big man said. He had lost heart in the work. He nodded. 'Let him go,' and watched MacAllister's legs make a valiant effort before they buckled under him and let him slide near-senseless to the floor. He bent down to the crofter man's ear, seizing his vest to drag MacAllister's head from the floor. 'Nae tricks,' he whispered, 'mind noo. Nae tricks, fae ye!'

Outside it had started to rain, the drizzle of a raw unshaven morning as the first streak of day lifted itself on to the shoulders of the hills. With a shiver, the man in the reefer drew a flask from the inside of his jacket and giving himself the first swig, offered it round his companions. Crouched against the rain they set off across the silent parks round the shoulder of the Croft Hill, cursing the clods that broke under their unaccustomed feet.

Suppered and sated and with the on-go of hairst behind them— in that pause of the year in which the touns took their breath— the two men in Mossgair's kitchen sat on into the gloaming,

one at either side of the long scrubbed table, their faces lit by
the glow from the peats as Morag readied Mistress Campbell's
evening bowl of gruel. Campbell was sober, not seeking the
inn for once, the speak of him, after the curses of harvest,
conciliatory now and Ewan well enough pleased to let him
have his say. Taking the bowl through to her mistress, Morag
listened as their voices carried quietly through to her in the
ben-end as she waited, Campbell's the firmer guttural tone of
the region, Ewan's softer, lilting. She knew what they would
be discussing. MacAllister had been found in the late forenoon
by Henry Coull the Post, concussed and in a semi-conscious
condition, not able, rightly, to say what had happened to him.

'Wha in hell would have done sic a thing?' Campbell said;
though no friend to the crofters, he was genuinely shocked. He
did no more than express the general loathing of the howe for
an act of such violent outrage.

'MacAllister threeshed?' folk said, incredulous, one to
another. 'Surely *that* canna be!' It was not that they had any
great notion of MacAllister, only that such an unprovoked
thing was inconceivable in their backwater community.

'This morning, sometime in the early hours,' Munro told
Pringle. 'I have never seen a man's body bearing the marks of
such savagery.'

'Kens he wha did it?'

'He says he never saw them before—. They just came in on
him.'

'Somebody kens!'

'If they do, they may feel it a bit safer to forget.'

'Aye.' Pringle pondered that, nodding his acquiescence. 'So
they would . . . And where is he noo?'

'Martha MacCaskill has taken him in.' Aye, that would
be typical of MacCaskill, Patrick thought. They had carried
MacAllister in a blanket, crying his pain almost with every
step, to the elder's croft house. There, in the ben-end bed,
Martha MacCaskill had administered to him till Munro arrived.
There he would stay, MacCaskill had said dourly, till he was
good and well and wanting to leave.

'He had a bit of a confrontation with Douglass, a week or so
back, I'm told.'

'Ach, so I heard——' Pringle stroked his beard reflectively.

'But no. No, Mungo!' The minister shook his head self-reproachfully. 'There canna conceivably be a connection.'

Munro shrugged. 'A mere opinion, Patrick.'

'No—— I canna think it.'

So Munro had left him, late in the afternoon, seated in his study armchair, outraged but impotent in his wrath, unable even to countenance such ill opinion of any of his flock. He took down his Bible, for once, for consolation (for guidance, he wondered to himself?) rather than for the preparation of his sermon, and plucking through its gospels came to the Old Testament pages where Abraham and Moses and Isaiah had their being. It was his favourite part of the Book: he loved its bold imagery, its simple, crystal absolutes, its studied vengeance, its clear affirmation of life: Lot's resolute firstborn going finally to her father fevered and drugged in wine, stirring his manhood, deft strokes known in her blood and her own growing excitement . . . the old flesh quickening, erectile. Impaling herself, gasping as she gathered the unexpected ecstasy and . . . exquisitely, unquenchably spending. . . . Where, Pringle wondered, had the world gathered so much doubt? Become grey with uncertainties? The couplings of our existence so frail and febrile, so careful of life?

His supper untouched in the kitchen below, Pringle sat on into the gloaming, till night filled the room and reclaimed its shadows. His whisky glass trembled a little in his fingers; from frailty of years? Perhaps, but maybe too from the suppressed hurt he felt at the stupidity and greed of men. . . . So he sat on in the night-still house as it sifted its shadows, its peace filled with yesterday's voices, the palm of one hand round the worn leather binding of his old family Bible, his father's before him, a link with what he had been, the palm of the other clasped round the tumbler of whisky. It did not seem to him incongruous that it should be so for were they not, such things, the tokens men lived by: the Book and the Water of Life, the restraint and the release turn and turn about, the joy and the sorrowing, the one at times almost indistinguishable from the other, the divide so delicate it took but a word or a stray thought to shake it.

He rose to the window finally, to draw the curtains on the last dregs of the day, and momentarily stayed his hand as his desultory eye picked out the dark speck moving in the last lilac light, a point of interest on an otherwise still countryside that enlarged itself as he watched to form the silhouette of a shawled girl and distilled finally into the unmistakable identity of Meg Macleary turning up the minister's brae. She paused as he waited, glancing uneasily about her, then came on hurriedly to the manse door. Her hammering was urgent, as though she feared something in the night behind her. Pringle, already half-way down the stair, opened the door in an instant.

'Meg!' His greeting, for all that, held some surprise.

'Mister Pringle.'

'The hour is late, lass.'

'It is, Mister Pringle—it suits the errand!'

'Why so, Meg?'

'Let me in, Mister Pringle, and I will tell you. I wouldnae want to be seen tae be hanging about on yer doorstep, nae offence tae ye.' Without waiting permission she slid quietly past him and into the manse's lobby. 'There's folk as widnae like tae see me here the nicht.'

'Just so,' Pringle said, some recovering his humour. 'On my side likely, Meg, as well as your own.' He closed the door on the night. 'My elders micht want an explanation, eh?'

In the darkened hallway he felt rather than saw her conster-nation. 'Aye—— I nivver thocht, Mister Pringle, so help me. Maybe——'

Pringle's chuckle surprised her. 'Come through,' he said firmly, silencing doubt and leading the way into the manse's living-room where some embers still lingered in the hearth. 'We will let them think what they like, Meg. Sit ye down.' Lighting the lamp, he waved her to a chair by the fire. 'Will ye have a dram?'

'Aye, thank ye, gin it please ye, I will. If it's agreeable tae ye that is, Mister Pringle, for there's some as says it's unseemly in a woman.'

'I too have heard it said,' Pringle acknowledged dryly, 'that the good Lord adjudges his sinners on the strength of their liking for the whisky bottle.'

'Aye, weel . . .' Meg Macleary's gaze rested reflectively on the dull glow of the peats, 'gin it be so, Mister Pringle, I'm thinking it will mebbe not matter tae me one way or the tither.'

'Maybe, Meg. And then maybe no.'

'I will roast in Hell, minister—it's yerself that kens it.'

Pringle turned up the wick of the paraffin lamp he had left burning low on the table, and now, as he did so, his visitor pushed the shawl back on to her shoulders and he saw the dark, crow-gleam of her hair, the delicate oval of her face and the deep brown een that had made her a lure for men. Old though he was, he could understand the passions such a face might yet awaken.

'There are worse sins, lass.'

'Than being a whoor, Mister Pringle?'

'Than being a comforter of men,' Pringle said. 'We hae that in common, you and me. They come to us at the two extremes of existence, Meg. We stand, the both of us, slightly to the side of life, gin you see what I mean——'

'I've nivver herried anither wumman's bed, Mister Pringle,' and then contritely, almost with innocence, 'Well, just the once, sohelpmeGod, I couldnae help it—it was something beyond me and maybe beyond him too—I nivver speired at him.'

'There are the money-changers of this world, the self-righteous, Meg. The hypocrites and the avaricious——' Pringle seemed not to have heard her.

'The what?'

Pringle shrugged. 'No matter.' He gave her a half-tumblerful of whisky and watched her gulp down its comfort. 'You're afraid, child!' Her hands trembled. 'What fears you?'

'Aye, I'm feart! Feart near for my life!' She eyed him directly, watching his face. 'They say that Sam MacAllister's been terrible mishandled, awful malagaroosed?'

'The tongues ye heard are not liars—I would to God they were!'

'And would ye call the man that set on poor Sam a sinner, Mister Pringle? Maybe waur nor me?'

Pringle drew breath carefully, seriously, nodding slowly. His words were deliberate. 'I believe I would, Meg . . . Yes, I believe I would, that is gin it were a calculated malicious attack with the sole intention of grievously harming the man.'

'A waur sinner nor me, Mister Pringle?'

Again, the minister gave her words the most earnest consideration. 'I might well judge him so, Meg—I do believe so, though I canna answer for God, ye understand.'

She took another gulp of the whisky, staunching her courage, debating something within herself.

'I ken the man,' she said flatly.

'But surely there were several of them?'

'The ane that ordered it, arranged it, like—and paid for it!'

'Yer sure?'

'As sure's death.' Pringle accepted the oath.

'You were with him?'

'Just after . . . He came tae me.'

Pringle rose from his own fireside chair to draw the curtains. Now he could understand her fear. 'You are wondering,' he said slowly, reading her thoughts with a clarity that made her jump in her chair, 'whether you should tell me the name of this man, Meg?' His voice, it seemed to her, had distanced him from her.

'Aye.'

Pringle slumped thoughtfully back into his chair. 'I would think you have tae consider your reasons for telling it.'

'The man's a criminal, Mister Pringle, isn't he noo?'

'In the law's een certainly. But—and I'm sorry it needs sayin'—ye micht well have private reasons, lass.'

'D'ye think I've nae conseedered that? Askit mysel' that?'

Pringle's tone was conciliatory. 'I'm sure you have, Meg. Forgive me.'

'I'm sorry for the croft men, Mister Pringle. For what's happenin' tae them. There was nivver one o' them that laid a heavy hand on me, or ill-used me . . . them that's come tae see me whiles, that is, their wives heavy-bairned mebbe . . . Ye ken hoo it is wi' men, Mister Pringle?'

Pringle nodded; he knew how it was with men. Did folk, he wondered, suppose otherwise? There was silence now between them, broken by the sputter of the larch logs the minister had thrown on to the fire.

'It was Farquhar Douglass.' Her voice was a whisper. 'Hallerton's ground steward——'

90

'Douglass? Yer sure of it? He told you?' Pringle's voice could not disguise his disbelief.

The black-haired quean nodded vigorously. 'He'd had a skite owre much tae drink, him and the rest of them likely. He wis gigglin' like a lassie near, like he'd taen leave o' his senses. He feart me . . . He is a vicious man, Mister Pringle.'

'He laid hands on you?'

'Ach, and nae for the first time. He is an evil man. He gave me a guinea and warned me that should it come to it I was to say he had been wi' me a' the time . . . Said he had only to give the nod and he could have me thrown out of my hut. I can tell ye, he feart me!'

Pringle's silence alarmed her, increasing her agitation.

'I did richt, Mister Pringle? Comin' tae see ye I mean?' Anxiety quickened the question.

'Aye, Meg, you did richt.'

'It's eased my conscience some to speak of it, I can tell ye. I couldnae sleep, onywye. I thocht someone else should ken, in case——'

But Pringle again seemed not to have heard her; he rose, his dismissal kindly enough for all that. 'Go home now, child. God gang wi' ye.' She rose eager to leave.

'You'll be safe?'

'In the dark ye mean, Mister Pringle?' Her tone held amusement. 'In the dark? Oh, aye, Mister Pringle, the nicht is a friend tae the likes o' me.'

He screwed down the flame of the lamp all the same, so that its glow through the manse's thin curtains should not betray her departure, and with a quiet 'Goodnicht' let her out to the night. In a moment she had blended with its shadows; below him the village slept, drugged by dreams.

With a hesitant hand Pringle hazarded a knight from the safety of his chessmen's ranks into the open arena of the board, savouring as he did so, the feel of its old polished wood.

'Is there nae something satisfying—holy, almost—about the feel of wood, Mungo?'

The doctor smiled good-humouredly. 'It's an association of your ecclesiastical mind, Patrick, Christ being a carpenter.'

'Ach, maybe so.' Pringle was in no mood to pursue the

argument for it was the first time in some weeks that he and Munro had had the board between them and though the game lacked its usual single-minded challenge, he was quietly enjoying it. He had, so to speak (he smiled to himself at the muddle of the metaphor), a card up his sleeve.

The minister's study below the eaves was stuffy still with the unexpected heat of the late-autumn day, and with a ploughman's lack of ceremony Pringle drew out the gaudy neckerchief that served him for a handkerchief and wiped the sweat on his brow.

'Ironical, isn't it,' Munro said, 'that if we'd had a few summers like this in past years the croft men would maybe have been able to give Hallerton the increase in rents he is asking for.'

Pringle nodded. 'That would not have made it just, but to be sure, the sun seems a cruel benison on their troubles.'

'You think me an irreligious man, Patrick.'

The doctor's statement took the older man by surprise, drawing his hawk-like gaze from the board. 'No, Mungo,' he said quietly. 'I have never thought that, how could I?' His features softened in a grimace of dour amusement. 'Lacking perhaps in the outward appurtenances of piety, but unChristian, no. . . . Man, I have watched you from this very window on a winter's nicht set away down the howe up to your fork in snowdrifts to look to a sick bairn! No, Mungo, gin ye were to be called unChristian I would be bound to say that God was a poor judge of men.'

'Does he care, think you, Patrick? God, I mean?'

'What mean you?' Pringle's tone now held an edge of rebuke.

'Well, take the croft men—years and years with poverty and want for a friend, good-livin' folk in the main, doing their best. And now: I see only the triumph of the machinations of men. Where is your grand design? The reward for honesty and effort? Man's taking responsibility for his own destiny?'

'It's the new lairds that are tae blame.'

'To be sure, Patrick. They are men who see the land a bit differently, who know nothing of that old bond between men and the soil and would little care one way or the other if they did. They will tear man out of his true context and spread him like an angry contagion over the face of the earth, like a wandering bullock, a rootless, feckless creature not sure of where he is or where he should be going. Then—and here's the important bit, Patrick—he'll be no threat to them then. We'll have a land fit for gentry.'

Pringle slid a bishop to the protection of a lonely pawn. The impulsiveness of the action halted Munro. 'You are over-zealous of your flock, Patrick,' he smiled. 'I doubt if that pawn was worth the saving!'

'Ah,' the minister parried deftly. 'But wouldn't he be a poor minister who weighed humankind in so calculating a scale? Which reminds me, I had a visitor the-streen.'

'Oh? An emissary from Hallerton House, perchance?'

'Deed no, far from it, Mungo. Meg Macleary, no less.'

'Meg!' Munro's curiosity was sharply whetted. 'What in heaven's name brought *her* to the manse?' The doctor's astonish-ment was undisguised.

'In Heaven's name as you say, Mungo.' Pringle paused to give point to what he would say. 'She told me the name of the man behind poor MacAllister's thrashing.'

'You believed her?' Mungo's brows lifted in doubt.

'Why not?'

'But Patrick, she's a——'

'Whoor?'

'Aye, if you will then!'

'And so they say was Mary Magdalene . . . Yer saying I should not believe her?'

'I'm saying,' Munro said quickly, almost heatedly, 'that Meggie in her time has had some violent admirers. I know, I've had to treat her. She could be paying off an old score.'

Pringle nodded, acknowledging the possibility. 'True, she is at the mercy of men, Mungo, without keeper or kirk, but I ken she was telling me the truth. It is the luxury of God's poorest creatures that they can afford an unbiased honesty. And besides, she was frightened, badly frightened.'

Munro nodded thoughtfully, quietly perceiving the other's dilemma. 'So now, you have a decision to make? Whether to let the culprit await God's judgement or face punishment here on earth?'

'Alas, there is but the one way to be sure of justice.'

'True.' Munro hid his astonishment. Pringle sighed, his een

quizzical with amusement. 'After all,' he said, 'God himself is a great sitter-on-the-fence, as any student of theology like yourself must know, Mungo. Margaret, in her student days, was forever chiding me with the fact that judged alongside some of his martyrs the Almighty disnae emerge as a man of action.'

Pringle in fine fettle then: it was as though suddenly some burden had been lifted from him or some break, some gleam of light, had broken in the darkness of the squall. Through his agency vengeance might still be the Lord's.

So that was the nights drawing in to the fa' o' the year; that sadness you'd known took hold on you again. The stubble raked and the horsemen of Mossgair and Littleshin and Lochhead and all the other grey touns of the howe making ready their ploughs for the start of the new farming year and the plight of your folk (and all the ithers forbye) on your mind: what would they do? For all that, though, you had something now to kindle your days: to tumble you out of the big kitchen bed of Mossgair in the morning and send you back to it dwamlike and still with each night. You lay by your lone for Mistress Campbell's pain kept her waukriff at nicht, but as evening came on Ewan came in from the parks to linger over his supper brose till Campbell himself had gone through; secrets between you now that bound you quiet and close, strange you thought it the way they held you at times in that sweet poise of doubt and daft bewilderment so that with your day's chores done and the evening milking behind you, you'd be drawn to the bothy not able to help it . . . till long after in the lonely dark, halffainting, you would thrust him away and run out to the nightstill close, the night quiet and only the sound of your heartbeats in it. Running into the house owre the weed-happit stones of the Mossgair yard, you'd look ben the howe to the last lights of Kilbirnie blinking out, cats' een on a cushion of black, yet hardly aware of them, kenning only the sweet sob and turmoil of your mind. Behind you, you'd hear the door of the loft slap back on its latch.

In the kitchen quiet, the peats burned out to an ash, you sat in their dead warmth in the comforting enclosing dark till reason came back and your heart stopped thudding into your breast—Campbell not home yet, lying drunk in some ditch like as not, the drink a new thing to him as yet. But syne, on the listen, you would hear him come home, maybe swearing and singing, stoitering aboot, going clyte to the wall, out from the barn and in to the byre to sleep with the beasts, spouting out of his stupor: poor man, you wondered whiles what it was that hurt him so. Ewan too would hear him. *What says he?* Once you had speired at him and Ewan had said sadly *Wha kens?* for it was no language he could understand only a blethering of words, some tortuous litany of indelible despair.

But dreams too in your heid, Old Woman, as you lived out those days; gathering about you, tentatively drawn, so that when you saw the notice in the *People's Journal* you had spread the paper on the table before him after he had suppered. *Read that*, you had said and then watched his eye travel down the ink-blur of the type. He read slowly, literate just; fumbling the words:

MUSICIANS WANTED: Marshall Pierce's renowned Scottish orchestra, based Edinburgh, needs talented musicians to fill several vacancies for the new season. The orchestra is one well-known for the quality of its repertoire and only exceptional applicants will be invited to audition in the capital. As a preliminary, Marshall Pierce is himself travelling through the North-east Lowlands to select those considered suitable for audition. He will be visiting the following venues in the coming weeks . . .

Ewan's eye skidded over the listed villages and dates to halt finally on Kilbirnie. *Friday fortnicht, Morag. He's here at the inn* he said. *Ye'll gang?* you had speired. *What think you?* His een held you, caressed you. *Ye should* you had said, your joy suddenly muted. And so it was settled, and a queer pride gripped you. A sadness, too, you could not put a name to.

The fluttering candle flame, at the mercy of every draught that could find a chink of admittance into MacCaskill's barn, threw its eerie yellow light on the tight circle of faces, the faces of haunted men, dark with anger. Chae Bonner's slow droll voice, speaking from the shadowed edge of its illumination, heightened the aura of unreality.

'It would be richt, Jeemes, gin I were speiring, tae assume that this trial has substance neither under God nor the Queen?'

MacCaskill's reply was quiet but unresentful. 'It micht be fairer, Chae, to say that it has no validity under the Queen nor the Procurator-Fiscal. Withoot labouring the point owre muckle, I would say that all men are under God and under trial and because of it, let me remind ye all, for what is decided here this nicht we will all of us be accountable. But . . .' the tall crofter man met his challenger's gaze squarely, 'yer concern, Chae, does ye credit.'

MacCaskill scanned their faces, their een intent on him.

'It is something we should all of us be clear aboot; this gathering has nae standing under the law. And it isnae a trial. . . . We are meeting this nicht to pass sentence for an injury done tae one of our own. Sam MacAllister lies in the ben-end of my hoose here, in pain still from the savage attack made on him a week since. It may be that in what we are tae do we are protecting others of the Hill from the intimidation of a like attack.'

'Ye believe that, Jeemes?' a voice asked.

'I do.' MacCaskill, as was his way, was unequivocal.

There was silence then; pipes were lit and puffed, men nodded their acceptance to themselves of what they would do, turning finally one to another to affirm their belief. There were fewer of them this time than had followed the elder-crofter to Hallerton House but a few weeks earlier: fifteen, twenty at most, and not all of them crofter men, for the news of Sam MacAllister's thrashing had angered the horsemen of neighbouring farmtouns who knew him, Ewan Carmichael and Chae Skene among them. There was reason enough for the diminished number: the last month or two had eroded some of the croft men's resolution, blunted their anger. Determination had been loosened by despair; men who knew their families would come to the edge of starvation doubted the wisdom of extreme attitudes, and only the few now fought against the feeling of futility that had begun to overwhelm them—MacCaskill because it was in his nature to hold to a cause however lost, Bonner maybe because his dour, defying nature impelled him to it, the others (who could say?) for similar reasons. The horsemen's presence, the tall crofter man knew, was out of respect for MacAllister the man. They had all of them come late owre the gloaming parks.

'What matters it, one way or the tither? We're surely nae concerned here with justice but wi' simple retribution——'

'A Biblical vengeance.' The voice, bafflingly, remained unidentified.

'—— wi' simple retribution, on the man who mischieved Sam.' The speaker now was a tall red-haired man, Lachie Leggat, who had an outlier place round the flank of the Hill.

'On the word of a whoor,' Chae Bonner reminded them, his droll voice unsettling them.

'As sworn to a minister, Chae,' Lachie retorted.

'The word of a whoor,' Bonner said, with the same slow insistence, his mind unwilling to go past it.

'Meg is no more than we've made her,' Leggat said quietly, his anger for once controlled. 'I canna for the life of me see whitten hell her whooring has tae dae wi' her word.'

'I'm satisfied she telt the truth,' MacCaskill said.

'Meg's nae a liar, whatever else she is,' Leggat said, and finally drew a murmur of consensus.

'I'm wondering all the same, gin it be richt tae be trying a man in's absence,' Bonner insisted, unwilling to be silenced, and immediately lighting Leggat's fury.

'Goddammit, Chae—he's nae here for trial! We've said as muckle! What we're looking at is his sentence. Aifter a', he's damn-well confessit his guilt!'

'Verra weel.' Bonner quit, unable to resist a last salvo. 'But it's drumheid justice.'

'An' sae mebbe it should be in these times.' The voice was from the shadows but its view gathered to it a growl of common consent.

'Gentlemen——' MacCaskill brought them again under his chairmanship. Turning to the dissenter, he nodded with understanding. 'If yer nae happy, Chae, ye can leave noo, taking an oath on yer silence. There will be nae ill-will amang us——'

'I'll stay,' Bonner said, snubbing the offer, surly in defeat or maybe because his loyalty had been called into question. 'I'm as muckle in this as onybody.'

'Sae be it, then.'

MacCaskill, quiet-voiced, met the ring of een above the

97

candle's flame. 'Now we have tae decide what's to be done about it . . . If anything's tae be done?'

'It's but meet that Douglass be punished.' It was another voice from beyond the candle's glow; it held neither anger nor sorrow, only an unshakable conviction. 'Tae allow it—sic a thing—to pass unheeded would be tae invite its repetition ilka time a man dissented from the lairdly view. Next, it could be any of us——'

'He should be thrashed like a beast,' Leggat said. 'The way that puir MacAllister was, and nae mercy. I'd give him nae mair conseederation nor a cantankerous stirk. Nae mair, nae less.'

Assent rippled in the barn quiet then, no denial came.

'So we're a' agreed?'

'Aye, Jeemes.'

'As ye say——'

'Hear, hear!'

But the moment of their frenzy passed, subsiding again into a silence of expectancy. It would be an eye for an eye, and why not? What was there wrong with that, for hadn't it always been that way among them and didn't the Bible tell them so?

'So, we maun appoint a man—nay, men rather—tae carry through the sentence, to be as Lachie Leggat has expressed it.' This time it was Andra MacGillivray who coalesced the feeling.

MacCaskill nodded. 'Aye. But nae in ony public kind of way for to do so would be to expose the men tae blackmail, maybe many years fae noo. But there's ae sure way, gentlemen . . . We'll draw the straes.' MacCaskill stooped to pick a bundle of short oat straws from the floor. 'I have them here . . . ready. As mony as matches oor number. In ilka ane there's an oat . . . But in twa of them there's the ear of a black oat. The men that draws them tae meet in the auld gallery and confront Douglass in Kynoch's Wood as he's at his snares three nichts from now. Agreed?' His gaze swept the serried faces, gauging their resolution. Not an eye wavered from his own.

The crofter man shuffled the straws in his hand and then fanned them in a semi-circle on the crude kist before him: short, strong straws that had been sealed at the ends with clay, giving nothing away.

'See!' MacCaskill shuffled them together again into one pile

98

with a sweep of the fingers. 'They are a' identical. In size and length.'

'Chance and the Devil decides,' said a voice.

'We could mebbe hae thrown the dice for it, Jeemes.' The speaker's light-heartedness betrayed only his nervousness, now that it had come to it.

'Identical,' MacCaskill stressed, his dark een searching them for objection but finding none. Deftly his hand again threw the straws into their half-circle. 'The twa that draw the black oats will deal wi' Douglass as we hae agreed. Justice will be in their hands, as will the severity of the sentence.'

'Kill the little bastard, I say.'

'Garrot him wi' ane o' his ain snare-wires.'

MacCaskill's silencing hand stilled tongues loosened by the heightened atmosphere, by the palpable tension of nerves shaken by the weeks of strain. 'If yer agreeable then, we will draw on it. Pick ye each man a strae as ye leave,' he said, himself taking one and putting it into his waistcoat pocket. 'The anes with the black oats hae Douglass's sentence in their hands, three nichts from noo.'

So, slowly at first, some with reluctance, hands stretched from the shadows into the circle of candlelight to hesitate for a moment over the semi-circle of straws before grasping one. Quietly the men filtered out to the night.

Miss Pringle, awake in the early grey light of the morning, had risen to the schoolhouse window where a frolicsome wind tossed and riffled the lace of the curtains and now blew welcomingly on her face, on her neck, flirting delicately with her hair, loose still on her shoulders. Awake in the dim before-day light, the loch as yet but a streak of leaden grey against the brooding black blur of the Hill.

She breathed deep; with it, the wind brought the odour of earth new-freshened by a smirr of rain. Like a drug it revived her . . . so that gradually sanity returned, flowing through her, deadening and dispelling the dream, the nightmare that had woken her: the dream in which nightly she appeared trem-blingly at the bar of her own conscience to plead before the figure of her father (he was judge and prosecutor both) and a jury composed variously of Scroggie the Merchant, sleekitly self-righteous; the inn-keeper Miller, severe and stucco-straight; Mistress Miller, too, ringed and sanctioned for her man's pleasure; James MacCaskill, soberly-suited, dour-faced and determined not to understand; Meg Widow Taylor, mouth piously pursed in disapproval, never kenning about Margit . . . and others, a numberless host, whose faces blurred before her, stark in their condemnation.

Margaret Pringle, spinster of this parish, you are here arraigned on the charge that you did severally and many times commit the gross and unforgivable act of fornication with Gordon Craig, former doctor of this parish, to the scandal and disgrace of the community, the violation of the memory of your dear departed mother and the eternal shame and disgrace of your father. How plead you: guilty or not guilty?

'Not guilty!' In her dream her voice rang shrilly, its echo answering from the darkened, high-vaulted roof of the building in which she alone occupied the one dazzling pool of light.

You deny it then? That you submitted your person to the kisses and embraces of men——

'No, I deny nothing, but——'

—— notwithstanding that you knew this to be sinful. That the said acts took place in the schoolhouse where the young people of the parish were daily entrusted to your care and came under your instruction——

'I don't deny it, but——'

—— that you not only submitted but invited these gross attentions?

'Not gross! Not evil! It was——'

Here in her dream her voice would break on tears of remembrance.

Did you or did you not encourage and allow this man to gratify his lust upon your person. Lie with him wantonly, to the dereliction of your soul?

'If you will have it so, yes!' Here in her dream her head would come up, her een blaze defiance of the shadowy figures around her. 'I did not proscribe the limits of love. Scruple for decorum's sake!'

Answer the question: Yes or no.

'Yes!'

So be it, and turning away, the figure of dark judgement would instruct: *Men and women, jurors of all that is just, I charge you to consider your verdict on this sinful woman.*

Guilty, m'Lord. It was instantaneous and unvarying.

Thank you. A faithful verdict.

And turning back now to face her: *Margaret Pringle you have been found guilty of shameless fornication to the peril of your soul. You will roast in Hell.*

So it was still, after all these years.

'Dinna torture yourself so,' Craig had said. 'The hell is of your own making.' But the black-browed image of her father had shouted her shame down the long corridors of her mind, branding her with names that made her skin burn.

'The hell is in yourself!' Craig's voice had been soft, persuasive in her ear, his lithe fingers already unbuttoning her, 'a gallery of alcoves filled with dread—your own dread, your own imaginings!'

'I will roast in Hell,' she had said, suddenly sure of it.

'Pyach!'

Worsened by drink he would be, like as not, coming in from the inn and the speak of him heich so that she had been feared that folk going by on the turnpike road would hear him and know then of this terrible life of lovers they led.

'Your own imaginings——'

'No! No! No!'

The hell had been real enough then, awake as well as asleep— a tangible world of evil, of women naked in the throes of bearing the Devil's children, of lovers locked forever in stale embraces, and murders lying bloody on a bed. Better to him far to have held his tongue for he had been but a lone voice crying in her wilderness of tears. She had known then that their love was a doomed thing. And so it had been. She had hidden the pain of it all, knowing the world would not understand . . . But that had been the ballad of their days, the ballad and the ending, her days hurrying out at the end of the world . . .

Now she was calm and fully awake. The growing light began to give texture, contour and dimension to the morning landscape, defining the outline of the loch in the lap of the hill. As she watched, four figures—croft men, from the set of them—moved up from its edge, a pathetic bundle between them. Death is without grace, she thought, knowing already in her heart that the loch had widowed a croft wife.

★

Ewan going down to the lochside, going down and liking the night and the dark about him, wondering what black things were in him. Going down to the loch in the stillness, dark things in the night around him, the stillness so silent it thundered at him. Fear and exultation gripped him as he thought of the monster they said slept in the loch's dark waters.

'Tyach! A fig for their legends,' he told himself and unlocked fear, all the same, in some secret chamber of his being.

A rustle of grass behind him, a frolic of some stray torment- ing wind awake in the night made him gasp so that he turned, quick, half-expecting—— What had he expected? The ghost of Kynoch who took a dander now and then owre the parks, in the night (so folk said), his head lolloping down on his back and him terribly embarrassed by that, not wanting to meet folk?

Or was it but some phantom clansman, stirring there in the quiet lost hours, his hands hackit off at the elbow and the blood dripping still from their bloody stumps; a shade trailing a tattered plaid endlessly on through a night-land filled with his moaning, finding no place to lay down a dead cause. Weighed down (Ewan wondered) with the sorrow of what had become of his country?

Or had it been only, after all, but the soft reeshle of a surplice, the wail of some old Covenanter's spirit as he roamed his ghost over the hills protesting still at the injustice of men, his hands hanging giblets at their arm-ends, his mind sick with the madness of the killing there had been and the suffering endured; all the holy lust unleashed in that time when fine preachers had been hunted like beasts owre the land. Maybe, still, the pain of it all had not died away, for often enough he would think on all those men who had given their blood to this earth; their blood and their sweat and their bones, to manure it. They had committed their souls to it, their seed and their savings, and in the cycle of the appointed seasons had reaped from it but grudgingly. For the land had given only sufficient to whet their appetites, never enough to realize their dreams.

It was the dead glaze in John Glennie's een that haunted him still.

Now, he judged, it was time to climb the hill to Kynoch's

Castle. Glad he would be to be on the move, though he knew it was not the night air made him shiver. Fear, apprehension (whatever it was) quickened his stride. Soon the black and lowering hulk of Kynoch's keep loomed over him, sinister in the silence of all the dark deeds laid to its history. He edged in through the main crumbling portal past shadows so solid he put his hand out to touch them, feeling the reek of its evil. A bird, disturbed on its roost, squawked its alarm shrilly and went past his head so close in a shrieking flurry of fury that he felt the edge of its wing brush his face. The fright made his blood leap. To brace himself he put a hand out to the wall and felt horror crawl on the back of his neck, and the first impulse of panic as it plunged into wet slime, a slime he normally would have known instantly as dew-sodden moss. He steadied himself, waiting for cool reason to return, then found the broken stone stair leading up to the castle's long gallery. His back braced against the wall, he edged upwards a step at a time, knowing that a careless slip could pitch him into the sunken courtyard below. The flat flagstones of the gallery, when he gained them, felt reassuring under his feet. He took a half-dozen steps along it to safety, then stopped abruptly when he realized that the iron scrape of his heeled boots rang and echoed through the chamber.

'Yer a noisy sodger, Carmichael—you'd stand damn the little chance of getting through the enemy lines, raising a din like that!'

Ewan spun in his tracks.

'Lachie?' His heart raced.

'Aye.' The voice identified itself.

But still he could not see Leggat, though he realized now that he must have walked close past him.

'Where are you?'

'Here man!'

Ewan saw a shadow move beside the head of the stairs and materialize into the outline of Leggat as it approached him. 'This place fair scares me,' he confessed.

'Aye,' Leggat admitted. 'It does cast a wee bit of a chill on the blood, right enough. Bring a lass here about this time of nicht and I'd say her only concern would be to let you get yer jobbie done quick as you like so she could get the hell hame again. Eh?' Leggat chuckled. For all that he said, he seemed to have little fear of the place, or of anything that might lurk there. Below them some creature of the night scurried across the causey stones of the courtyard. They listened for a moment.

'A rat, most likely,' Leggat said, then, serious now: 'Have you the stomach for this night's work, lad?'

'I drew the other black oat,' Ewan said, thinking it answer enough. But the other man's matter-of-factness disturbed him. 'We're nae gaun tae——'

'To kill him? No.' Ewan felt the weight of Leggat's hand, a pledge on his shoulder. 'No, we canna kill him,' he said quietly, 'but we'll maybe tak' him to look owre the brink of eternity. We owe that to Sam MacAllister, and mair nor ivver noo tae John Glennie's memory.'

'What're you thinking on?'

'That the essence of punishment is first that its receiver should fully understand the justice of it.'

'What mean you?' Ewan was puzzled. The Lachie Leggat who spoke to him now was a different man from the one who would stand most of the night in Miller's inn telling his coarse stories.

'Just this: that Douglass is an old sodger as I'm an old sodger, and that if Chae Bonner the ither nicht thocht oor crofter's court a drumheid hearing then it might be but seemly that we render unto the sly Douglass a drumheid punishment. So he'll understand it, ye follow?'

'I wouldnae quarrel with that. It seems nae mair nor fair.'

'Fine then! Since we canna lay our hands on the wheel of a gun-carriage there's the grille owre the old well doon there in the courtyard . . . That'll hae tae serve.'

'We'll bring him here then?'

'Ach no, man. Tak' yer ease.' Leggat chuckled. 'We will wait. He will come to us.'

'You seem damnably sure of it,' Ewan said, aggrieved now that he had been so little consulted about the arrangement. Leggat had slid down to sit on the gallery floor, his back against the wall; Ewan did the same.

'As sure's the snares he has set roon the back of this very wall. The earthworks roon this place are a warren of rabbit runs. Four of his snares are fu' already,' Leggat said. 'I've checked them myself. Jist afore it came doon dark.'

'Ye've been busy, Lachie!'

'I have, man, I have.' It was not Lachie Leggat's way to be behindhand with a show of false modesty.

'Mebbe he's already cleared his snares?' Ewan said, the thought suddenly striking him.

'I think it hardly likely,' Lachie's voice was cool as you please.

'You seem damned sure about that, too, gin I may say so,' Ewan said, feeling resentment again rising in him.

'Ach, and so I am, man. This nicht Douglass has had ither songs to sing . . . He's with the black-haired lass. I trailed him there from Miller's bar.'

'Meggie?'

'Wha ither? She will throw him oot when she's sookit the sap oot of him, and him likely dead drunk forbye. Douglass had a half-bottle with him.'

'It'll be licht soon,' Ewan said. Looking up, he could already distinguish the outline of the shaggy Kynoch firs above his head.

'Give it an hour or so . . . It will be dark enough.'

'And after?' The words thickened in Ewan's throat.

'We will cut him free and leave him. An hour after that the cords we tie him wi' and the thick rope—I gave it just a wee touch of pitch on the painful end—will be burning away under the peats that heat ma porridge. And you, Ewan Carmichael,' Leggat's hand clamped his knee, 'you will be sleeping like a lamb in the loft at Mossgair. Nobody the wiser!'

'But Douglass! He'll ken—— He'll see!'

'Naething! He will see naething. We will slap a blindfold on him afore he kens we're ahint him.'

'He'll ken yer word. And mine.'

'In his befuddled state? I hardly think it likely. But even so, what of it? If later he has some glimmer of a recollection, what of it? There will be Meggie to say they had the nicht thegither, that they were drunk as tinks, that her memory of that night is imprecise . . . But oh-ho, all the same, he left her three shillings.'

'So that's the way of it?' Ewan said slowly.

'That is the way of it, Ewan lad! And think you noo that her ladyship up at Hallerton House would be pleased with the news? Her ground steward taking up not even decent-like with one of the housemaids but with the strath's common strumpet?'

Ewan laughed, still uneasy. 'Lachie, you're the cunning one, richt enough,' he said.

'We are maist of us, after all, trapped by our own weaknesses,' Leggat said lightly, and added, his voice hardening for the first time, 'and besides, in case yer forgetting, John Glennie was a guid neighbour. He leaves a helpless widow, and fatherless bairns.'

'Aye.' Ewan was contrite. 'I was forgetting.'

Ewan felt the older man's hand clamped comfortingly on his shoulder. 'Ach, Ewan, it would be a fine world indeed'—he was his soft-voiced self again—'gin we could all of us keep our hands clean. Eh?'

He paused, releasing his hold, drawing his breath in slowly, 'Wheesht noo!' Above his whisper on the night air, Ewan heard the sound of a faltering step and growing clearer and nearer, the lurch of a tune on lips no longer in control of it. In the dark of the gallery where Kynoch, cornered by the fates, had gladly slit his throat, Lachie Leggat nudged his young companion's elbow and passed him the blindfold . . .

'He will live?'

'No question.' Mungo rose to throw a fresh peat on the fire. 'But he will have a profound desire, I'm thinking, to sleep for some months on his belly.'

'It's savagery, Mungo, all the same. They were saying in Scroggie's this morning that the skin was hanging off his back like tatters of ribbon.'

'Maybe.' Mungo was oddly non-committal. 'Myself, I've little liking for the man. There's few of the croft folk with a good word to say about him.'

'But you treated him?'

'As though he'd been Hallerton himself. After all, he's likely no more than the laird's tool—or more likely Lander Gregg's from what they say.'

'He will be bedded for some weeks, likely?'

'Indeed—as Sam MacAllister's likely to be.'

'It was brutal all the same,' Margaret insisted.

Munro doubted she knew of her father's part in it, and forbore to enlighten her. 'It was thorough, I'll say that.'

'Has he said who it was attacked him?'

'Says he never saw . . . that they blindfolded him when they set on him as he was checking his snares.'

'What manner of men must they be?'

Munro was silent for a moment. 'Ordinary men, Margaret. Just ordinary men, driven to the limit. And beyond it. Like Glennie.'

'I suppose so,' Margaret Pringle conceded, sad beside him now, sad for the broken dreams of men, and for her sons unborn as he slid the hampering blankets from them, shy of her nakedness still before him . . .

So Mungo, after all, had stepped in for a nightcap of hot cocoa and stayed to become a lover. Strange Margaret thought it now, lying there beside him in the bed's shadows beyond the circle of fading firelight; had they met somewhere in the commonality of their despair, somewhere in the haunting memory of all her lonely sad summers? A thing of the mind near, it had been, a kind of contentment, a usurpation of will as he took her, melting slowly away all the dread of her days. . . . She had been woman enough. Fine it had been, all his tenderness surprising her and rousing her, rekindling forgotten fires till she had moved nakedly to him and with him. So long it had been . . .

'You've had women?' she had asked him, not wanting to hear.

'Very few . . . and you?'

'There was a man—long ago.'

It had been enough, the past defined, the rest unspoken between them.

'A doctor's gig excites no comment on the nicht road,' he had said, a compact between them.

So it had been; already their speak was filled with the peace of old lovers.

'I saw you go up the Croft Hill the day,' she said.

'Mistress Morrison.'

'Maybe it is a mercy.'

'Maybe,' Mungo said, death still, for all his experience, a

defeat to him. 'Maybe . . . She was eighty. She said she was not sorry to be going—she'd been born within sight of the Croft Hill, had been bairn and lass, bride and widow on it, and forbye, she said, she had been the old laird's tenant and he was long away. . . . She was too old to set sail again.'

It was quiet and still in the room; in the warm dark of the bed Mungo's breathing rose and fell rhythmically against the glow of her cheek. Outside, a fir cone lost its grip on the branch and crashed on to the schoolhouse roof, disturbing the silence beyond the curtained panes.

'There's a wind getting up,' Mungo said. 'Winter'll soon be with us.'

'What about Hector?' she asked suddenly, for thought of the world outside had brought the beast guiltily to mind.

'He is comfortable, drawn well into the trees,' Mungo said soothingly. 'He has his nose in a bag of good oats and a warm blanket over his flanks—more than you have yourself!' His hand on her haunch was a delight to her. 'He's a dutiful beast,' Mungo chuckled. 'And what he can stand for medicine he must surely endure for love.'

'I'm indebted to him,' Margaret said lightly, and felt Mungo's fingers run down the long curve of her naked back, soothing and caressing, awakening desire . . .

'I have the appetites of a whore,' she said suddenly, knowing her body would shame her.

'Wheesht, my dear . . .'

His voice was a whisper; he quieted her with kisses.

It was the speak of the howe, Old Woman, for that and many a day after (for so you told me), the tones of shock muted by the dislike that all of them felt for the ground steward who had been so quietly, insidiously, insinuatingly blackmailing them, the smile of affability on the face while the bunched fist struck at the balls. Not sorry they were, for there was a justice in what had been done, but fretful for this festering sore that had erupted at the heart of their community. They wondered one to another who was it could have done it, the women looking strange at their men and the men of the Hill saying little about it, telling nothing of that night in your father's barn when the straws were drawn but each maybe looking a bit speculatively at his neighbour, not knowing what violence was in him. You had not known about Ewan, never suspecting; he would not tell you. It would be long years after you would learn of it from Lachie. Lachie generous with praise for him, though he had not liked it. *A fine loon he was, Morag,* he would tell you and the tears, all that time after, would well into your een. Silly you could not help it, that ache you carried inside you; that ache and that longing that no other could still in you. *Why, why?* you had speired whiles when the pain of it gripped you; you speired it of God but no answer came.

So the men of the strath took John Glennie slow down to the lochside on a day when the sun hung still like a golden ball in a cloudless sky. 'No break in the weather,' they said one to another, differences forgotten. They had come up the Croft Hill in their sober suits, tight-breekit, the skin on their sun-reddened necks hankit into unaccustomed collars; they were the suits they wore for christenings and weddings and Sacrament Sundays, the three other occasions that gave depth and meaning to their lives; they were the only suits they possessed—they had lain all morning, brushed and ready, on the closet beds of the croft biggings.

'We are needing rain, now the hairst is in,' they said.

'The parks are parched for the want of a shoo'er.' They spoke of the fields with love, their speak low, giving death its due dignity. They had stood quiet round the door of the Glennie croft, taking off their cloth bonnets as the coffin appeared, to be edged out through the door and on to the shoulders of MacCaskill and MacGillivray, Murdo Maclean and a Glennie cousin who had travelled up from Kinlochleven to be with his kin at the last. They set off then, Pringle behind them and at the head of a slow caterpillar of men, mourning now in their mien . . .

They came slow down the Hill, looking across to the outlying places away behind the Pringle manse, where the lower hills rolled away to the north, taking through-hand the heavy harvest bypast, men bound in a long compact with the soil.

Whiles a man would go forward from the ruck of the mourners to put a shoulder under the coffin and give one or other of the bearers a rest. Only Andra MacGillivray brushed their offers aside with an impatient wave of his hand.

He set the pace. He was calm, unhurried. He spoke low to MacCaskill. 'John's gotten a braw turnoot.'

'Aye,' James said.

'I've seen lairds go to their Valhalla with fewer folk for company.'

'Aye,' MacCaskill replied. 'And soon they will maybe hae fewer to follow their corteges—none but a rich farmer or two and a handful of gentry.'

They fell quiet then. Down the hill now, they struck across its gentler slope to the lochside, their step easier, their burden more equally shared with the men behind them.

'He should hae had a piper, Jeemes,' MacGillivray said, his tone tinged with regret that he had only just thought of it . . . 'To have played him down the hill and into the kirkyard——'

'Mebbe then.' MacCaskill was non-committal.

'The Floo'ers o' the Forest maybe,' MacGillivray said.

'It's a fine tune,' the elder allowed. 'Aye it is.' He remembered his soldier's years.

'There's nae man that doesnae merit a lament, Jeemes, when life itsel' forecloses.'

Fiona MacGillivray watched them go out of the sunlight into the afternoon dark under the yew trees; she had watched them slow-stepping down the croft hillside, her man at their head his stride unfaltering, his face, heavy-tanned and soberly set, and felt a pang of pride go through her for this man that was hers. Soon now he would be home, heavy with the sorrow of a man who loves life yet sees its days siftering slow and slow through his fingers. She had known it before this sadness came on him: he would sit staring into the glow of the peats, drink silently the tea she would bring him, cupping his hands round the bowl as if warming them from the chill of the grave. Till by and by, rising from the fire, he would go through to hang his best jacket in the press with his Sunday bonnets, and cry through to her *Come ben, my lass.* And so she would go to him then, through to the closet bed; quick and trembling and savage he would be, it excited her still that he needed her so. It was something to thank God for: a man who could make you a woman. It was cold and dank in the grave; she wanted to go to it warm with loving.

From the schoolroom window, the scraich of slate pencils behind her drilling into her thoughts, Miss Pringle watched the final black-suited figure disappear behind the yews, and felt the sadness claim her. Her heart went out to Margit Glennie, new to her widowhood, for little though she had known John Glennie, Margaret knew he had been no different from the rest of the crofter men. He had been a man with a dream; it had been this; that the croft acres would be his kingdom; that by skill and thrift and sweat he would win crops from his tiny parks, that he might in time lease two or three more acres, that by and by his industry might be such that the laird would give consideration to letting him have the lease of a bigger place . . .

So, *Pouff*!

It was gone in a blink, that fragile dream, like winter sunlight, like thistledown on an autumn wind. She looked up the Hill to the patchwork of bare parks. Drab and grey, they were, reflecting her own melancholy. What they were burying now in the kirkyard was not the cold, lifeless body of young Glennie. It was the broken dreams of men. A kist of sorrows.

That evening an elegant Hallerton table was graced by Gurney and Gregg and James Grant (brought in, so to speak, to make weight, for the mistress herself, in truth, had little time for his simpering gentility). As a privilege, perhaps as a foretaste of lairdship, Gurney had been allowed out with a gun that afternoon in the estate's pheasant wood without harming the expectations of the man to whom it was regularly let. Only Hallerton himself was in poor spirits; some malaise of the soul gripped him, turning sour the anticipation of Gurney's silver.

'I hear they buried that poor young crofter today,' the laird said, pushing away his compote of pears untouched and reaching for the last dregs of his claret glass.

'So somebody was telling me,' Gregg said, tackling the dessert with hedonistic relish.

'I was hearing word of some rebellion against the new leases.' Gurney showed signs of unease.

'Nonsense! Rumour!' Gregg said, not only with his mouth full but with an ill-mannered wave of the spoon as well, at the same time outstaring Grant whose een accused him as a bare-faced liar. 'Nonsense, Mister Gurney.' Gregg turned with a show of frankness upon the ironmaster. 'True, there's no gainsaying that one or two of the crofters would sooner stay where they are at the kindly rents they have now. That's natural enough, surely? But they'll see reason, never you fear. They'll see reason . . .'

'All the same,' Gurney persisted, 'I would like to think that every consideration that *can* be shown, *is* being shown to these folk.'

'It will be, it will be,' Gregg's spoon promised his assurance.

'And there's that business about your ground steward, Haller-ton,' Gurney said.

'I was for reporting it,' Hallerton said. 'But Gregg would not hear of it.'

'Well now——' Gregg wiped his wet lips and settled back in his chair, 'You're surely not thinking there is some connection?'

'I see no other reason, Lander.' Hallerton was curt; he was drinking less and, uncomfortably for Gregg, taking some interest in his affairs.

'Well . . .' Gregg smiled down the table at the mistress, '. . . and begging your pardon laird, Farquhar was a man inclined to be over-familiar with the ladies. I think what has happened is clear enough. A croft wife perhaps . . .' he raised his eyebrows, letting his gaze travel round them. 'Need we say more?' He smiled again down the table, his frank and open smile.

'These things happen, Mister Gregg. Love has its casualties, always has had!' The mistress of Hallerton was gracious, understanding, an ally he could count on. 'They do, Mister Grant, in a far-from-perfect world, don't they?'

Grant settled gallantly, hardly squirming, on his cleft stick.

'It is so,' he admitted, compliant.

'We had a housemaid once—you remember, James?—with whom he formed some sort of liaison. A croft girl. I sent her from the house at once, of course. She told me some trumpery about an indiscretion. Said Douglass had threatened to tell her father unless . . .' The lady of Hallerton shrugged eloquently and arched her brows, indicating that it was unnecessary to continue. 'I should say Mister Gregg is undoubtedly right.'

'One must pay for one's sins, Mister Grant,' Gregg smiled. 'Face meet retribution. It is yourself that knows it, surely?'

'And the crofter's death?' Gurney questioned, stirring his vague unhappiness.

'A young man,' Hallerton said. 'Well thought of, I hear.'

'His widow is taking it wonderfully, I hear,' Grant said, and drew a look of scorn from the mistress. God, but she loathed weak men! They wanted their success but not the worry of a muddied conscience. They wanted the gambler's prize but without the gambler's risk. Except Gregg; she would like to see him playing a London table.

'All the same, James, one cannot but feel some responsibility,' Hallerton said, idling with his claret as though it were suddenly a poisonous potion.

'And I can't help but feel a slight share in that responsibility,' Gurney added quickly, penitent before Grant, who did not disappoint them; he was quick with absolution, with God's forgiveness.

'You need feel no guilt, I'm sure,' he said, so pat and facile it was plain that God himself had not been consulted.

'In fact,' Gregg said reasonably, 'you could say that Glennie might have done the same whatever problem it was confronted him.'

'Indeed, indeed,' Grant assured him hastily, never seeing the hoop, let alone realizing he had been cleverly induced to jump headlong through it.

Gregg looking down the length of the table was rewarded by the mistress's tight smile of amusement; here indeed was an Antony who knew that to get to the top you had to put your boot hard and firm on another man's throat.

'All the same, Mister Gregg,' she said, 'it would be as well that Mister Gurney should know that there *are* just one or two unruly elements on the Croft Hill, prepared neither to heed his right to enjoy his land nor the legal title he might one day have to it.'

Gurney glanced up in alarm, from the mistress's face to Gregg's. The lawyer shrugged (*the betraying bitch*): 'A handful, Mister Gurney. There are, to be sure, always a few trouble-makers.'

'I—— I'd rather it were all discreetly handled.' Gurney was

anxious. Down in the South he had customers with a social conscience.

'It will be all legal,' Gregg assured him. 'All legal-like, Mister Gurney.' Only the mistress noted the hasty qualification; in such times the gentry had a need of such men.

Beyond the tall dining-room windows night had fallen, leaving only the dark phalanx of the policies' pines against the sky. Pringle, up in his eyrie, had watched the late-autumn day go out in a winding sheet of gold, marvelling at the beauty of the universe, the innate splendour that bathed always in the cosmic sweep of things. He had seen the mail coach, late in from Aberdeen, draw in to the kirktown below him and observed the stranger descend from it. The man's name was Marshall Pierce. Nothing was known to him, neither to the good nor the bad, and he was more than civil to Miller. Stepping across from the coach to the inn he speired *You'll have a room?* and was told instantly by Miller *I have more nor that—I have a whole house full of them.* That pleased Pierce at once. He laughed delightedly; they were cronies under the skin, men of the world for whom a penny turned easily and a promise sat lightly on the conscience; hearty, quiet blasphemers who moved in a ambience of easeful whisky and for whom a solitary evening was the thief of life. Nobody had kenned then, Old Woman, how his coming would alter your destiny.

In Miller's bar-room later that evening, in the flichtering light of the swinging paraffin lamps haloed by thick tobacco reek and peering like distant worlds from their misty galaxies, Andra MacGillivray fell in with Ewan Carmichael who, unlike Campbell, was not a regular patron. Carmichael's een, he saw, were watering.

'Miller's brew owre strong for ye, laddie?' Andra speired heartily.

'It's nae that,' Ewan protested. 'It's yon damnt lamps. They're damned-nearly poisonous!'

'So an' they are,' said Andra, for the air was acrid with their smell. 'Miller couldnae trim a wick tae save his life, let alone think of giving the lamp glasses a bit whisk wi' his duster now and then.' Andra lifted his whisky from the counter. 'I'll put this whaur it'll dae me the more good,' he explained, and tossed it down at a draught. He waited for it to siphon down to the region where it would spread a little warmth through him, then sighed: 'Aah! The solace of mankind, Ewan man, the blunter of all barbs of remorse. The world has a damned lot to thank the Gael for, Ewan! A damned lot!'

'It has shown him little kindness though.' Ewan's tone was quietly light and conversational.

'By God, it has not!' MacGillivray exploded, buffoonery forgotten, his voice serious. 'Nae mair it has us . . . Come this time next year, Miller will be lucky gin he be turning a penny, nivver mind twa.'

They were quiet for a moment, letting the hum of conversation from the shadowed corners of the room flow round them. 'Crofting despair is fair bringing him a fine profit the meantime though—even if it's nae doing anybody else much good!' Andra said.

Ewan nodded. Since the plight they faced had fully dawned on them the men of the crofts had taken more to the inn, driven some of them by the sorrowing faces of their womenfolk to find common cause with the other men of the strath in its whisky-engendered warmth. There at least they found talk, commiseration, a unity in their common betrayal.

'But where else I wonder would a man go when life has kicked him in the ballocks?' Andra mused, more to himself than to Ewan.

They were interrupted by a step on the stair as Marshall Pierce, who had suppered in his room (putting his hand the while on the maidservant's rump as though testing its ripeness), wandered down for a dram to dispel the bone-tiredness of his journey.

'Miller has a guest staying,' Andra said quietly. 'One of the gentry, would you say by the look of him? Or maybe a corn seedsman, would you say?' (Andra had bought more bad seed corn in Miller's bar-room than he liked to remember.)

'That'll be Pierce,' Ewan whispered quiet as they waited, expecting the stranger to take his drink through to the inn's ben-end where the tobacco reek was diluted and the howe's genteel drinkers sipped circumspectly in the cozening comfort of weary wicker chairs. Instead, though, Pierce moved along the length of the bar towards them, pushing his whisky before him.

'Fine evening,' he said. He was maybe a youngish forty, with crisp, greying curls, clean-shaven and Gladstone-collared. There was in his bearing that stamp of superior effrontery of a man who has traded for a lifetime in lean kine and speyed horses. It was a quality MacGillivray instantly recognized but could not put a name to.

'Fine evening,' Andra responded reluctantly.

'It was spring-like the day.'

'It was.'

'Summery almost,' Pierce persisted, as though he were pushing the crofter to the limits of credulity.

'Almost,' Andra said.

'The name's Marshall Pierce.' The stranger nodded to Ewan, then at the violin case that leaned against the front of the bar. 'You'll be Carmichael.'

He gave a nod with familiar ease down the bar to Miller, polishing glasses.

'Three drams, Jamie.' He turned back to Ewan. 'Miller has set aside a room for us, but we will just have our drams first, eh?'

So it was that Pierce listened and Ewan played, the bow livened by the dram or two he had taken, the melodies leaping from the strings one after the other without pause in a mélange of mood and feeling, of merriment and sorrow. A mesmerized Pierce sat silent and entranced as old Niall of the island once had done, for there was no question of it: Carmichael could play. But more than that there was the music of an old Scotland in him, some well or reservoir that brimmed with the strains of ancient melody, of far-off forgotten things. It was as though all the sadness of his native history sieved through him; no doubt of it, Carmichael brought something more to the fiddle than simply the tunes in his head. Pierce listened, nodding, tapping a foot as the strains of some little-known tune took his fancy, silently letting himself go with the music, kenning now that he was listening to an extraordinary talent that might fill halls of assembly. He listened for an hour, not touching the dram he had brought in with him, the maidservant forgotten.

Finally he held up his hand to stem the tide that seemed it might go on forever . . .

'Enough, laddie! I need tae hear no more. You'll come down to Edinburgh for audition, of course, but I will tell you now, man: you have a rare gift. It would be churlish of me not to tell you so—an' it would be a criminal waste were you to spend the rest of your days wi' yer hand on the plough stilts and not on the fiddler's bow.'

For so he had told you the morning after, coming in for his brose, a quiet in him. All night you had wondered, waukriff in the kitchen bed till the dawn came, wanting to go to him in the loft but scared all the same of what it was he would tell you, not knowing then in your heart what you wanted for him, for yourself, half-feared of what news the morning would bring. *I'm for Edinburgh aboot the end o' the year,* he'd said, stirring his brose as you poured the hot water over the oatmeal in his caup. Kindly he said it as though knowing your thoughts, for that was the way of him, no bragging or boasting like some might have done. But pleased all the same. *Ach,* you had said, *didnae I just tell you so! I always kenned it.* Yourselves alone in the dreary dawn of the kitchen morning, his arm had gone round you in comfort, for you hated his fiddle then, all his magical mastery of it. It was a strange thing that gripped you then, that chilled the heart-cry in you. *But he as much as said it was but a formality. Ach,* you had said, *and so it will be.* Some day he would be famous with ruffles of silk spewing out at his collar and soft on his sun-blistered neck sun-blistered no longer but smooth from the caress of fine linen—maybe a name, as they'd said, in the assembly halls atween Inverness and Dundee, a man who could make the heart-strings dance, the equal of provosts and bailies and their womenfolk dressed in silk finery with their breists primpit up in the neck of their goons and pink in the licht of the room; and women among them with gold in their smiles and nicht in their dark sunken een, their lips mauve-painted like vulvas of torment. Already, Old Woman, you heard their brash and cymbaline merriment and the tinkle of their brittle laughter breaking into the dawn. *Ach, yes,* you had said. *And so it will be!* Sad that your heart told you so.

★

Gaunt and granite-square—it could not have been more austere gin John Knox himself had biggit it, folk said—the Free Kirk manse looked out across the thatched roofs of the little kirktown and in at the front doors of the privies that littered its backyards like a row of sentry boxes. 'If Pringle had been truly a Christian,' folk said, 'he'd have biggit it to look decently the other way.'

Still and all, fine privies they were all the same and well enough used now for it had but lately become unfashionable for a man to step out of doors to answer the call of nature simply, against his own gable end, except that is on a byordinar cold nicht or when he wanted to avoid the muddy clort of the garden path. Over the years, over the long haul of his ministry, Patrick had come to know as much about the physical flights of his flock as about their spiritual pilgrimages. And faith, if he had been at all an orra-minded cheil he could have gotten rare sport for weeks at a time just spying the way they came out to their thrones, all of them Moderators juking into a four-ale bar. Whiles Matha Moir would step out in his dotage and unattended to sit with the door thrown wide to the world, his breeks at his feet and his mind on some far oblivion as he endlessly evacuated his bowels, and Meg Widow Taylor would come out in the morning nightcapped still and fall asleep at her chore to re-emerge only at noon when the sun was high. But if the rest of the village knew it, it wasn't from Pringle's telling.

Beyond them now, as the minister watched, the smoke rose briskly from the kirktown's chimneys, and beyond that on the Hill the first gatherings of folk congregated at the Glennie croft. The sight awoke pity in Pringle's heart making him for a moment deeply conscious of the injustice that brought a man's life-dream to such a sad and humiliating end. Margit was to go to her sister's in down-country Kinneff (so she had told him) where, God willing, her bairns might grow up in a landscape where men still had a care one for the other. 'The weather at least is with her, God be thankit for that,' he murmured, for it was a rare evening for the start of November, though the breeze had a bit bite to it.

Margit would be the first to hold her roup; hers would be the start of many, for that much was sure now as folk began to take stock of their lives and started their drift from the Hill;

men were leaving their dreams behind, finally beaten, for that summer had been the fulcrum of their lives, a time that had tipped them beyond all hope.

Pringle watched Campbell go up the Hill, Gladstone-collared and sober-suited, his Sabbath best brushed down and the halt of his step marking him out conspicuously against the quiet parks; himself a casualty of life from the day he was born. Maybe we all were, Pringle thought to himself; it was only that in some the scars did not show. What was it, he wondered, that drew the tenant of Mossgair to a crofter's roup: some bond of brotherhood, a recognition that life had flawed them both? Behind him trailed Ewan and Morag together in that casual proximity that betokens ease with each other. Away to the left of his vision, round the shoulder of the Hill, two figures appeared to be identifiable in time as Lachie Leggat, proud as a peacock, with his housekeeper on his arm magnificently pregnant. They closed the two of them without apparent embarrassment upon the rest of the croft folk and, as Pringle watched, merged into them. A tiny flicker of admiration stabbed at the minister's heart, a wry reluctant pang of recognition that bold men like Lachie made their own destinies.

Now, too, he saw Grogan Faulkner's gig taking up the hill, the auctioneer, well set-up, a brown suit set off with a blue polka-dotted tie in execrable taste, his een (Patrick knew) already twinkling jovially, shrewdly surveying the crowd, a Mark Antony come wanting the lugs of his countrymen. Grogan Faulkner had a terrible coarse tongue and a reputation to match it and cultivated both assiduously in the cause of trade.

Pringle watched him now, picking his way through the piled clutter of possessions set out for inspection in front of the Glennie dwelling, stooping here and there to examine a brace of scythes, the teeth of a hay rake, his quick tongue the while giving utterance to a lewd riposte where it was expected, a fulsome greeting where it might one day bring back a guinea. A crofter's son himself, he had risen on the strength of his wit and an eye for a good beast; whatever his vulgarity, however outrageous his sallies, he would (Pringle knew) sting them this night for every penny for Margit's sake.

The first-comers had bourached themselves at the byre end

of the small croft steading, snatching what shelter they could from the keen air. They were mostly croft men and farmers from the smaller touns of the howe. Their womenfolk, tugging their shawls about their heads and shoulders, stood apart in a group by themselves, the speak of them quiet as they waited for the auction to begin. Yet Grogan, they knew, would be in no great hurry ('Anticipation is half the pleasure of purchase,' he would say); he liked time to size up his audience, to prepare himself like the great actor he was for his performance. And still they came (he was giving them time), folk from farther out, folk who had not kenned John Glennie from the next man; poor stock, it was a pity he'd drooned himself, they had come to see the fun.

Margit, watching with Fiona from the MacGillivrays' back window (she'd no stomach, she said, for another death so soon), saw Faulkner make a rostrum of her kitchen table, three pairs of hands hoisting him laughingly on to it.

'That's grand, lads, as the lassie said tae the sodgers.' The words were lost in the snicker of laughter. Grogan Faulkner had them now in the palm of his hand, hanging on his every word.

He smiled benignly down on them, well-enough pleased by their response, measuring their mood, running his een owre the tight-packed circle of faces and re-gauging their interest before bringing his gaze to rest on Lachie's housekeeper at the front.

He winked and she blushed. 'Just bide ye where you are, lass—the cradle's among the first lots.'

More laughter rippled the crowd, but Grogan, ignoring it this time, hunkered down to his clerk. 'The piss-pot, Davie. First, if you please.'

The clerk produced it with a conjurer's flourish, and inspected it studiously. Knowing what was expected of him, he had already had it in his hand. ('HelpmeGod,' folk would say whiles, 'yon twa are better nor anything you would see at the seaside pavilion in Aberdeen supposing you paid for it.')

Grogan gave him his moment.

'Nae leaks in it, Dauvit?' he said loudly, so that they all could hear. 'Ye'll hae tried it oot?'

'N-o-o, no,' said the clerk mock-serious, the pot cradled in his hands as he studied it from all angles and finally raised it above his head so that the folk at the back of the crowd could see it as Grogan now began his commentary, the accomplished patter of the showman.

'This, ladies and gentlemen—for the benefit of those of you whose education is not all it might hae been—is a chuntie, a chamber-pot . . . A very useful requisite I can tell you on a cauld nicht. I was fourteen afore ever I saw one . . . We were all sent out to the dykeside when I was a laddie . . .' Thus did he woo them, ranging himself with them. No shame or side with Grogan, they said, liking him for it. But business was business.

'Noo then, whit am I bid for this choice bit of china? Woodside, will you start the bidding . . . Thank you, well done, I'll sell your stirks for a fortune at next week's cattle mart. Sixpence, sixpence? No . . .? Thrippence . . .' His grimace registered mock disbelief.

'Fivepence, surely, Woodie?'

'Thrippence.'

'Come tae fourpence, Woodie. Fourpence, fourpence——'

'Fourpence then, dammit . . .' Neil Ferguson of Woodside nodded his long droll face in capitulation.

'Thank you, Woodside. Fourpence I'm bid for this wonderful chamber-pot. Fourpence . . . fourpenccha'penny . . . fivepence . . . fivepence I'm bid . . . Do I hear any advance on . . .? Just look at the bonnie flowers on it . . . Fivepence, fivepence . . . And there's more use than one for it . . . Sixpence I'm bid . . . My grannie used to grow flowers in one after it was no use for anything else. She'd the best geraniums in the Howe of Torphins . . . Fa will gie me sevenpence . . .'

It was his earthy vulgarity most of them had come to hear and he knew it. He'd see to it they were not disappointed.

'And fa'll give me sevenpence. Sevenpence, I'm bid. Do I hear any advance on sevenpence? Hillie, this is just the thing for you—you'll get your death of cauld if ye keep gaun oot tae the lythe of the byre these chill nights!' Unerringly, he drew a laugh at the elder's expense.

'Eightpence . . . Thank you, Kilwhinny, it's worth every penny. Eightpence, I'm bid—— Ninepence . . .'

Baikieknowe bidding for a chuntie he has no manner of use for just because he cannot bide the sight of Kilwhinny. Play your cards right Grogan and you could sell it for a thousand pounds—with Baikie and Kilwhinny both in the right humour that is.

'Ninepence. Baikieknowe has an eye for a bargain. It's stainless forbye!'

'Tenpence.'

'Thank you, Kilwh——'

'A shilling.'

'Fourteenpence.'

'Sixteenpence.'

'Seventeenpence. Do I hear any advance?'

But Baikieknowe had finished now, his discretion overcoming his antagonism.

'Seventeenpence. It's going, going . . . Gone to Kilwhinny. The cradle now, Davie.'

Grogan glanced laughingly down to see that Lachie's housekeeper was still beside him . . .

So that was the roup, the first of the many: he sang for them, the snatches of a lullaby, did a jig of delight for them, cursed them, indicted them, pleaded and begged with them. Margit Glennie's old dresser that had been her mother's dresser found a new home and all John's old implements, bought with dear siller by men who never rightly knew what return tomorrow would bring them; knew, even less, if they really would long have need of them. Hillhead bought two ricks of John's hairst oats, a surprising good crop it had been and the price had been keen on the expectancy of five quarters to the acre, and Baikieknowe bought the crofter man's hay rick and a second-year's one to go with it. A young cottar from Hillden bought Margit's tub and tressle, the fire bellows and the churn and the dung of the midden got ten shillings from the new tenant of Blaemyre.

It had taken John Glennie long years to gather what little he had of the world's gear; it took in all but an hour and a half to disperse it. Tomorrow, or the day after it, there would be a little bit of John Glennie in nearly every parish in the district, in places he himself had never set foot in. His hayrake would go on with the things of haytime, his trusty scythe would take the gold of harvest long after he had mouldered in the grave. It was the thought of it that finally brought the tears into Margit

122

Glennie's eyes. That and the emptiness that life now held for her. Tomorrow they would tell her: 'Grogan was good, Margit, by faith he was! He turned a fair penny for ye. It will take care of yerself and the bairns this next year or twa till ye see what is to be done.' And the lightening chuckle: 'Ach, Grogan wid sell his auld mither gin he got the richt price for her.'

So, she thought, maybe he would: what mattered it now, a little whoring amid the rest of the filth of the world.

Breakfast at Mossgair was a dull, uneasy affair, as indeed were now many of the meals of the day, with Campbell sitting morose, drawn into himself as though contemplating some deep and private grief. He said grace from the force of long and enduring habit, a litany of dubious thanks, mouthing the words without feeling, without thought for their meaning (whiles, you would have said, in mockery of them). Afterwards he ate untidily, the drips from the spoon fouling his beard, which he wiped when necessity demanded with the back of his hand, and his hand in its turn on the leg of his moleskin trousers. He had sunk in a steady decline, these past few months, rousing himself only now and then to rail at Ewan or Morag for some minor, imagined slight—or to glance knowingly, his een pouched in the loose skin of his face, as Morag poured Ewan a second bowl of tea.

Now he lifted his head from his breakfast bowl of brose and looked at each of them in turn. 'Well, you will both have enjoyed yourselves the-streen, likely,' he said, a sneer of condemnation in his tone. 'Margit's sale went well, thought you?'

'Verra well,' Ewan said.

'Grogan struts his stage well,' Campbell said, 'and yon performance will likely be but the first of many. Your father now,' he said, turning to Morag, 'he will be thinking on it, too, I suppose? Not many now that will be able to afford the Croft Hill, I'm thinking.'

'If he is, then I've heard nothing on it, Mister Campbell,' Morag said shortly. Her father's plans, in truth, were a mystery to her but what stung her was the insinuation, too true, of her family's poverty.

'Ach,' Campbell added, an afterthought that caught the fancy of his mind, bringing a spark of life into his dulled een, 'maybe it will not be a bad thing to have to go from the Hill——'

'Why so?' Instant anger lit Ewan's een.

'Well,' Campbell waved an expansive hand, 'the country's changing you might say. We are seeing the end of something. Seein' the start o' a new kind o' countryside.'

'Aye, and maybe with it the end of an auld tyranny,' Ewan retorted, incensed that a man like Campbell should be so ready with his bland easy pronouncements. 'Whatever else, men will become freed of an obligation to lick the laird's bootcaps.' In Campbell he saw the personification of the servility they would shed. Looking across the table with all the arrogance that youth allowed him, Ewan saw before him a hollow man, like so many more he had known. Suddenly he hated Campbell for showing him what became of a man when his courage failed, when life foreclosed on him. He wanted to sting him, punish him, kick the older man in the crotch of his pride.

'I was speaking to Hillhead the-streen,' he said, the speak of him calculating and easy now.

'That so? What said he to you?' Campbell's curiosity was quietly aroused.

'That he'd heard more nor once that I was a fair hand at the fiddle-playing. That so-being it went well with me in Edinburgh, I should take my chance with the fiddle.'

'Said he that now!' Campbell surveyed the younger man; he had derided his fiddle-playing, finding it an amusement for fools and an idle frivolity about a farmtoun.

'He was saying I could do a lot worse.'

'Imagine that now!' The mockery in Campbell's tone was a resurrection of his former will as he strove to discredit and humiliate another human spirit. 'And in time, like enough,' he added with studied reasonableness, 'you will be playing at the fashionable balls for the gentry—maybe even at the Palace of Holyroodhouse itself, gin the auld queen want a tune.'

'Maybe I will then!' Ewan's anger flared again, this time against himself, that he had so underestimated the old Campbell: he was an expert still at the quick thrust, the wounding psychic dart.

'Maybe I *will* . . .'

Ewan flung down his spoon and rose to the window. In the

early morning light the parks of the Croft Hill lay bleak and grey. His gaze, falling from their drabness, lit on the weed-ridden garden of the Campbell place immediately beyond the window-panes, on the crumpled dykes, the sad squalor that betrayed Campbell, bore witness to his mismanagement, the years of neglect. Drawn again, his een travelled across the loneliness of the howe at this early hour and rose once more to the Croft Hill, this time to pick out the outlines of the implements, the piles of the human trivialia that cluttered, as yet uncollected, round the Glennie croft, the transient memorial to another man's defeat.

'Better that, anyway,' he spat, 'than rotting like a damned turnip in this God-forsaken howe, in this rot-riddled house.'

Blind, biting anger possessed him, drove him on, regurgitating the hate and loathing he had always felt for the man who had so little cared for their distant kinship that he had treated him no better than a hired hand.

'You'll heir the Mossgair one day,' Campbell said quietly, suddenly conciliatory, sensing the younger man's despair. It was an attempt at restitution, too late.

'D'ye think I *care* about Mossgair!' Pointing savagely out to the Hill, Ewan swung round on Campbell. 'D'ye think I want to end up like Glennie—like the rest!' He swung back to the window, to the desolate parks. 'I'd sooner go to Hell first!'

So at last the hate they had hidden so long burst between them: the disgust of one, the terrible envy of the other. Campbell, too, had risen to his feet.

'Quiet! You insolent tink!' It was the roar of an ailing beast, baited beyond forbearance. 'D'ye dare speak to me in that fashion, and in my own house? After all I've done . . .'

He limped threateningly to where Ewan stood. 'By God, I will show you yet who's the maister of Mossgair.' He was sweating not only with rage but from all the defeats life had dealt him. 'What ken you about respect? Yer mither little better nor a market-day whoor that lay doon with any fisher lad that put his hand to her? You that nivver kenned yer father——?'

Ewan spun from the window, the black anger blazing in him.

'Ewan! No!' The shrill, unexpected shriek of Morag's voice cut through the red mist of his fury, transfixing his balled fist.

'No!'

Slowly Ewan let his hand slip to his side, while the anger simmered between them, cooling slowly again and at last to the level of mutual loathing. But the harm had been done; the tenuous thread of kinship that had so slenderly tied them, had perished in the heat of that moment. Next time, the old Campbell knew, it might be the long curving tine of a hayfork, sinking bloodily, fatally, into the softness of his belly.

'I was hearing the-streen on the Hill that more folk are to give up their holdings—Ogilvy and MacEwan for twa and maybe Maclennan as well.' You had risen, Old Woman, the winsome quean you once were, to the bothy's skylight to stand quiet and still looking out and away to the dark blue mound silhouetted in the pale moonlight. The cool air fanned gently on your cheeks and brushed soothingly over your shoulders.

'It is true, like enough.' Ewan said from the bed. 'And hardly a murmur among them. Their will is broken.'

'Not my father's!' Your reminder was sharp.

'No, to be sure,' Ewan allowed. 'It is not in his nature. But what can he do? He canna stay—he has nae siller.'

So he had risen then from the shadowed dark to be beside you, his arms going round you, his hands smoothing the thin stuff of your shift on the soft swell of your belly.

'What's to become of him?' Your voice was anxious. 'After MacAllister, I fear some harm to him.'

He chided you gently. 'Yer father! He's naebody's fool, nor yet a martyr unless I be muckle mistaken . . . But, sure's hell, Lander Gregg can have no love for him. Nor for MacGillivray nor the rest of them—the few of them—that think with him.'

'Gregg, ye say? What about Hallerton?'

'Hallerton drunk would little care. He is back to his old ways and Margit having to take the breeks off him and bed him since the mistress herself will not.'

'They say he has Gurney's silver already salted away with his London bankers.'

'Like as not . . . Maybe he will soon be able to show his face again in London society.'

'So it's Gregg has the say?'

'Hallerton's but his puppet, Margit says. She says Gregg is a big man with the mistress.'

'I have seen him,' you said. 'There is an evil aboot him.'

'He's a cauld fish, right enough,' Ewan admitted, surprised by your womanly percipience. 'They say . . .' His voice was soft in your ear. 'They say he offered Sarah, the Millers' maid, a sovereign and she refused him——'

'Ach, that's an ill thing to say, Ewan Carmichael!' So you had rebuked him, but without conviction. 'Even gin it were true.'

'—— that he couldnae buy with silver what the odd travelling seedsman gets with his supper gin Sarah takes a liking to him.'

'Wheesht! Ye have a coarse tongue, Carmichael,' you had scolded, laughing as his hold tightened round you. 'And a coarse mind to go with it, forbye!'

In the dark of the Mossgair loft there was freedom to speak to him so. Fine in the dark and his arms round you, his words an enchantment to you. His whispered sweet-singing words in your ear. 'I will buy you finery—silk hose and buckled sheen.'

So men had promised before you supposed and women believed them. But you trembled all the same, your body a fine and silken thing offering itself to his caresses, ashamed in that moment that his touch could stir you so; turning to him in the loft shadows, wanting now to reach into the blackness of him, to touch the strange dark core of his being . . .

So that was the year sliding away to its end, as that magical summer of your young womanhood had done, with night coming ever-earlier blue-hazed owre the late-autumn fields still already with the expectancy of winter. Hard frost in the early days of December stilled the ploughs in their furrows, the ground bone-hard so that not a plough-sock could be got into it. Days of storm lashed the Hill and the howe, turning finally to rain; little work could folk do round their touns then but stand hunched, filling their pipes and peeking out from the byre or the barn door, men bewildered by unaccustomed idleness, their winter work already behindhand. They watched with sore hearts as the puddles grew in the farmtoun closes and the mud got deeper with every passing day, all of them now but nature's prisoners.

That last Sunday of the year you had walked to the kirk with Campbell, strange by your lone and Ewan not with you, you'd think of him near with every step for soon now he would be home to tell it all to you, his long hurl on the train and what Edinburgh was like and what said they to him. Ach, but you knew he had been fine, done well, a sickness inside you that you should lose him so, as always you had known it . . . You waited half-feared, half-proud for him, Campbell stepping silent beside you, his own thoughts claiming him. It had been a fine bright day that end-of-year Sabbath, the fresh frost lifting as the day wore on, so suddenly mild for that time of year, till well on in the afternoon the wind rose and a drizzle turned to blattering rain on the Mossgair window pane. Come milking time that evening it had given way to a gale that hurled itself at you as you fought against it on your way to the byre, blowing out the lantern candle with its blast so you'd had to return to the house to light it again, the wind so strong now you'd hardly been able to shut the door against it. Back through the close you had shielded the lantern with your apron while the roof-tiles ripped from the steading roofs crashed into the close around you. It took the breath from you till you won to the byre door and threw your weight against it . . . A strange tension in the byre as you entered, the beasts standing nervous in their stalls, their een rolling round to you in the lantern glow, their necks tugging at their tethering chains. Little milk got you from them that night try as you might, as the gale vented its gathering fury on the gable corners and howled in the rafters like to lift the roof off. *Och, whatten a nicht of wind*! you would tell me, minding it still these long years after as we spoke by the fire and I watched your een haze with remembrance and the sadness gather in you. In the haughlands of Kilbirnie that night, The Great Storm spared human life—just—but wreaked a terrible havoc: roofs were lifted bodily into the air as barn doors burst open under the onslaught; steading slates, prised loose, sheeted through the night like a deadly hail, trees no longer able to stand against the blast tottered and fell, crashing in on byre and barn and stable; stones, at the very height of the fury, were torn off dykes and sent skittering as though from some murderous catapult and fences, ripped from their moorings, sailed over the parks and were scattered through the countryside like ribbons of bunting. Ricks, the pride of that year's hard hairst, lifted from their foons to take flight like airy galleons owre the parks before disintegrating and being swallowed in the darkness.

In the byre that night, Old Woman, for so you once told me, a terrible fear and foreboding gripped you that you could not put a name to, so deep the hold it took on you, a terror that near loosened the bowels of you as you sat there on the milk stool with the pail atween your knees and turned you near spew-sick with the dread of it. And down in the South it was no better and maybe worse. So folk would remember . . .

In the corner of a compartment in the third carriage of the train that left Burntisland early on that Sabbath evening the young man in the brown tweed suit who sat clutching his violin case listened without fear to the buffeting of the wind on the glass beside him. He had brown curls and blue een that smiled with secrets—or maybe at the curious young daughters of the compartment's only other adult occupant, a young woman with a strained face and features etched sharply by the day's tiredness. She too listened to the tearing sound of the wind as it rattled along the side of the carriage, the four of them contained—isolated, it seemed—in the dimly-lit swaying capsule that rocked and shuddered with the shock of every blast. The young man closed his eyes, retreating again into his reverie and his success of the day before, his triumph as tune followed tune, a joy to the heart (for they had come like magic to his bow), the one melody unfolding upon the next as though he might have played forever. All his inborn skill had been on show, consummate, effortless, as though his life had waited for that moment. As though some spirit possessed him. Marshall Pierce had been pleased, pleased beyond words . . .

Stations came and went behind the bleared blur of the North British Railway's window: he noted their names—strange places to his mind, a vocabulary not known to him—but without the true traveller's relish. Each was a stopping place on the long journey home . . . Cold now seeped through every crevice and cranny of the carriage so that presently he was forced to turn up the collar of his jacket and to shrug deeper into it, setting the violin case on the seat beside him in order to plunge his hands into his pockets, looking more like the ploughman he was. The two little girls smiled shyly to him . . .

Out of the cutting on the south, Fife end of the line, the little train swayed on to the bridge, on to the silvery, delicate tracery of its spiderwork . . . Almost at once the storm took hold of it, shook it, alarmingly, like an angry dog; doors rattled, wheels screeched, their flanges driven hard against the rails. In a further moment they were truly into the teeth of the ravening storm. The young man in the corner seat jolted wide awake and in that moment came the shriek of anguished metal as the rails were torn assunder and the slender iron tracery of the bridge crumbled . . . For a moment the moon broke through heavy cloud, then darkness engulfed them. In that moment, as he grasped for his fiddle case and clutched it to him, Ewan Carmichael felt the train begin its slow and terrifying plunge, an instant-long eternity of dread . . . In a moment the dark turmoil of the water had swallowed them . . .

That terrible night the wind spared nothing in that northern landscape, not a farmtoun, cottage or croft bigging but felt the fury of the gale. Yet all that was as nothing against the desolation it would leave in Morag MacCaskill's young heart, for she never would win over it. That night, Old Woman, they robbed you of dreams, of your future, for in his heart, for all the dark wilderness of him, he loved you, that lad with the brown curls. In the hinderend it was life itself not his fiddle that betrayed you.

So that was Ewan never coming home. Three days it was before they came to you, the police up from Alford in the station gig; Postie Coull had sent word to the Postmaster there. A fine man the sergeant: he sat you at the table of the Mossgair kitchen and speired in his fatherly way what kind of suit had he been wearing and describe him if you would: fine you remembered the last you had seen of him, looking back with a wave from the roadend. There was a tear in your eye, Old Woman, as you told me for we spoke of it often, quiet by the fire, that despair of the soul, sad and overwhelming, as a life is taken from you. It was a tear for that long-ago time and for the lad who'd been yours; fine dreams they had been in the loft's summer dusk. You had not known the world could be so cruel, the thought of him coming home from the parks and in for his supper like a tearing pain in your belly. And now no news of him, nothing to say he had been on that train, nothing to say he hadn't . . . But you had known from the first, long before the sergeant came back to Mossgair sad with his burden of surmise: *A young man in a brown suit was seen—carrying a fiddle. It has to be assumed* . . . Poor Ewan, the victim of such an indefinite death; so sure of himself in this life, so vague in his leaving it. You had never forgotten the agony of loss. *You loved him?* I asked you, needlessly but wanting to know, and watched, Old Woman, as you tugged the shawl more protectively round you. *Like nothing before it—nor since.* And my heart wept for you, for the lass you had been, for the fragile kingdom of dreams. They never would find him to lay by the lochside; sad you were without a grave to go to.

In that strange indeterminate time, while you moved through the days in a dwam, the pattern of your kitchen work a daze that you drifted through unknowingly, the year slipped away. From the mantelshelf of the Mossgair kitchen the clock, gilded and ornate, stole your young life from you, ticking thunderously into the evening silence as Hogmanay passed unheeded. Lost in that endless dwam of days you waited—as the howe waited. Strange, folk thought it, that one of their own should have been on that fateful train so far from home on such an unlikely errand. *He was a fine loon,* folk said, the one to the other. *Noo wasn't he just! And a fine plooman,* folk said. *And a braw fiddler. Aye,* they said, shaking their heads, *a braw fiddler.* The music of him stilled forever under the muddied flood of the winter river. Not to hear him more: you could not thole it, did not believe it. Campbell, too, deeply grieving—it surprised you that—coming ben to sit by the fire, saying little at first, but syne, as though he kenned how it had been between you, *Gang hame, lass, gin ye've a mind to. I'll manage fine* . . . *I'll see that the mistress gets her gruel, nivver fear.* You had not known such kindness in him. *No, but thank ye,* you'd said. *News micht come* . . . It was a slender hope that you held to, unwilling to let go; little either of you believed it. *I'll bide*, you'd said, *the mistress is nae sae weel*.

So the old year turned its back on the new, embalming its events—this first sad sorrow of your life—in the annals of remembered time, a garden of the mind where the heart keened over the faded petals of past and glorious summers. For the croft men it was like waiting in an interval carved out of time, a pause on the bridge between now and eternity. Round the Hogmanay fires they had gathered as always, to draw the tattered remains of their dream around them, calling on God's strength and whiles, when the mood of melancholy overwhelmed them, for the more immediate succour of whisky, hardly one among them who knew what the year would hold. Bereft of hope, they looked into their souls, looked back into the far distance of their lives, counting the steps and the staggers, computing and regretting the misfortunes that had clung, unshakable; all the slights of destiny, real and imagined. But all of them that night had avoided Mossgair.

Somewhere in the time that followed in some deep still pool of your being, Old Woman, you buried the grief that was yours and the pain of loving, getting strength with each day; only you knew what you'd lost, not able to tell them. The laughter died in you then, the laughter of your young life. Never again would it rise in you, thoughtless and free.

As the year turned winter set in in earnest. Blattering hail, that had fringed the fields and feathered the little kirktown's rooftops, turned to a white curtain falling slow on the world. Long the winter lay on the land. From the Croft Hill and the crusted expanse of the haughland a million pinpricks of light danced in the frosty sunshine, stinging your een with their harsh iridescence, the air so clean and strong going into your lungs it took your breath away. But fine all the same, it tingled your skin. And the howe kenned well enough: young Ewan Carmichael would not be coming home.

So winter slid toward spring. Immured in its grey, time-stretching days—for now the snow had gone—the folk of the crofts resumed the old set pattern of their lives, dragging feet to inn, kirk and market still as though they no longer could help it. But gradually all hope of reprieve on their rents and the re-negotiation of new leases, of some gesture of kindness from the laird of Hallerton, faded in the croft men's minds and worry drained the gaunt lined faces of their women.

By the Mossgair fireside Campbell sat out the days, a prisoner of his own thoughts, going out to wile a dry peat or two from the stack as the need or the fancy took him. Mostly though he sat brooding, in some private despair (you supposed) that haunted him, waiting for the night and the solace of Miller's drams. For little thanks Chae Skene ran his toun for him— unable to break his long loyalty to the parks—for Campbell seemed unwilling to. Mossgair's acres had never been the all-consuming interest, a fever in the blood, that they had been to his father or great-grandfather. For that first Campbell the earth and the smell of the fields had been something wound into the fibre of his being: the heady smell of clover in the summer evening fields, the odorous richness of dung and the warm breath of beasts in the winter byres. These things had been the touchstones of his life, the things that had steadied him in his hours of need; he could not have envisaged life without them and the howe, little though it respected him, had never grudged him that farming recognition. It disdained the great-grandson, cripple though he was, for his lack in a heredi-tary skill.

Only Farquhar Douglass, stepping ben from Hallerton, would break his lethargy, crying in to warm himself at Mossgair's kitchen fire: for hours thegither the two of them would hunch over it with Douglass giving out his heich hyena lauch now and then, coarse tink that he was with his stories and the buttons of his spaver nearly always undone and the speak of him hardly Christian-like. You wondered at Campbell taking up with his like for they were not cronies under the skin. But Campbell glad of him all the same.

She was a cold spring that year, with a scouring wind settling in from the sea forty miles away and keeping Pringle in his thickest knitted hose and muffled to the ears in his ancient clerical cloak well through the month of April. And even Andra MacGillivray, who stripped himself to the waist like a savage at the first hint of warmth did not get out of his moleskin waistcoat till the hindmost days of March. *The parks need the sun*, folk said. *Faith, they do*, they said. *And it's nae like tae come.*

But come it did through a morning of low mist, breaking the last shard of watery cloud, a shaft of tepid warmth that lifted the shawl that had wreathed the top of Croft Hill so that the pap of the hill stood stark again in its splendour. You stood for a moment by your kitchen window, aware of it, of the Hill and its folk and the way they were part of you, a part of your life. Fine it was then with the sun lying languid and warm owre the parks so that the vapour rose from them in wispy drifting clouds; soon again it would be a time of green and living things, the earth burgeoning blithely in tender fronds of liquid green and in buds that nippled, swelled and burst finally in gouts of gay bobbing colour. Stooping achingly over the trestled washtub by the window you saw Andra MacGillivray come out to the sun, scratch his armpits and throw his waistcoat over his shoulders—Andra, like your father, as yet unbowed; he would cottar, gin it come to it, about some farmtoun, he said, rather nor be vassal to some robber laird; Andra—his cow dry and down to the Mossgair for a flagon of milk—that had comforted you quietly and knowingly (how could he have known?): *I'm so sorry lass. Sae damnably sorry—he was a fine loon, we will all of us miss him.* Andra that had put his broad arm round your shoulder for a moment while the tears racked you, his lips, you kenned fine, sealed forever in silence for not even to Fiona would he speak of it. That nicht for the first time you had gone round in the dying of the light to the bothy loft, able at last to push its door gently ajar . . . the loft that was full of him still, full of his music, and saw again that time that had been. It seemed as you listened that you heard last summer's laughter, the light quick lilt of his voice as he told you of the island of his childhood and its stories, embellishing their absurdity for your pleasure.

For you, Old Woman, it had become a haven of enchantment; it was filled with echoes of that slow soft summer that had womaned you; his melodies stirred still, like his voice, in the velvet dark of its corners. It was as though all the warmth of your life had been gathered there and so in a way it had been; it was here you had come in the blue-dark of down-coming dusk to escape that endless drudge of work that filled your days and

134

darkened your life for as far as you could see . . . So long it had been; you had hoped that it never would end. Once (so he'd told you) a fine man had come up to the island from London (that was somewhere in England) on his important travels, a fat sumph of a cheil he had been with a bit stripling of a Scots laddie fawning about him like some love-smitten quean. He'd come to the isle, fat and pechy, high and mighty he had been with its folk thinking himself a person of some note. But cheap dirt he had been all the same: he had slept at the township's old manse bigging in a fine embroidered nicht-sark his feet stinking and black as the earthen floor but still and all fine sheets were put on to the bed, all scented with rosewater. But little he had thought of the isle's folk and said so, leaving *that* to posterity, a libel on fine folk who never had sought sight of him and were damned pleased to see the back of him. That once, too, he had told of his mother and Murdo that came with the smell of the sea about him; it would be strong in the house for days after he had been. Strange the ways of love, you thought then; and the private sorrowing of women.

Douglass waited in the wood across the turnpike from the Hallerton gates for the moon to slide behind a cloud then flitted like a phantom into the wooded policies of the big house. Then, only a poacher's eye would have picked him out from the twisted and gnarled trunks of the big Hallerton beeches, so silent and wraith-like was his progress. With the instinctive timing of the night-prowler he matched his movements to the pattern of the shifting shadows and even as he sidled up to the shadowed side door for admittance, his knock coincided with a bluster of wind that shook the tall trees and blattered on the old house's window panes. Only a conspirator's ear, finely attuned for it, could have heard it. His entry was swift, deft, affected by the same grey eminence of the old and melancholy maid who flitted through her days in the cold flagged corridors of the old house.

In the study the ground steward found a Hallerton ill-humoured and still unwell from the debauch of the night before. The laird had found himself becoming increasingly displeased with the events of the past few weeks and besides had just endured dinner with an affable Lander Gregg and her brightly chattering ladyship. His stomach had taken ill with both.

'You're late, Douglass,' he snapped as Farquhar eased himself into the study. The ground steward, he thought, was the only man he knew who could come through a door without seeming to open it and in his present state of nausea it was not a quality he greatly admired. Douglass, he told himself, was damnably like a bad conscience: forever creeping up on you.

'I—— I'm sorry, sir.' Douglass's apprehension did little to appease the laird.

'What news have ye for's, Farquhar?' Lander Gregg, on the other hand, was more than polite; he did not send a man on an uncomfortable errand then treat him like a pariah. 'Have we some resistance on the Hill to oor rent proposals think you?'

'Some disaffection, I'd suppose?' Hallerton added, not wanting to be left out of his own business.

'They're nane weel pleased, sir,' Douglas said cautiously, scared of the laird's tongue.

'And maist are likely tae go?' Lander asked.

'The feck o' them, aye.' The ground steward hesitated, uncertainly.

'But one or two maybe not so willing, eh, Farquhar?'

The ground steward nodded, grateful to his prompter. 'So I'm hearing.'

'Like——'

'One or two.'

Gregg reached to the desk-top for a long sheet of paper, the names abstracted a little earlier from the estate's rent book. 'Fine then, let's just check noo who's to go and who's tae bide—and who's maybe going tae be a problem.' The lawyer's finger began to trace its way down the list.

'Archibald?'

Douglas nodded. 'He's gaun.'

'Denholm?'

'Aye.'

'Duncan?'

'He'll bide on but he's protesting sair at the rise in rent.'

'Let him—Gavin?'

'He's selling oot.'

'Isaac?'

'He'll bide. There's siller there.'

'Wi' a name like that I wouldnae wonder, Farquhar!' Gregg laughed at his own joke, to hell with Hallerton and his fine sensibilities.

'Jamieson?'

'He'll gang tae be sure—I saw him but yesterday.'

'Lobban?'

'Him tae.'

'MacArdle?'

'Oot.'

'MacBean?'

'Gaun.'

Gregg ticked the names off the list, pleased with what he was hearing. 'Gurney'll be pleased, think you?' His aside was for the laird.

'I don't doubt it.' Hallerton's voice had an utter weariness in it.

'MacCaskill, the Free Kirk elder?'

Douglass's silence drew Gregg's eye speculatively from his list to the ground steward's face. 'What about MacCaskill?'

'I'm thinkin' Jeemes micht want tae sit where he is——'

'And so he can gin he pays the viable rent.' Gregg's tone was reasonable.

'He will maybe not be willin' tae do that.'

'I see . . .' Gregg pondered that before returning to his task. 'MacGillivray?'

'Aboot the same.'

'You know for sure.'

'It's the speak of the Hill onywye.'

'That they'll sit on in their dwellings?'

'Aye, and—nae disrespect—damn ye!'

'Just so.' Gregg took a deep breath, his good humour had evaporated.

'Murdo?'

'He'll bide—and pay.'

'MacLaughlin?'

'Staying on.'

Gregg looked up suddenly, glancing at the laird's slouched

figure in his chair. 'It sounds like the roll-call for some fine Highland regiment of the line, eh?'

'What other is it but that?' Hallerton snapped, the old soldier suddenly sparking, betraying anger or maybe a fear of his own conscience. 'Pick any name you like Gregg, and you'd have to trace back only a generation and no more to find a man who had fought in the campaigns.'

'Sir, you're getting sentimental, gin I may say so.'

'Proud names, Gregg!'

'Ach, I'd say——'

'Proud names,' Hallerton insisted, sick with the nausea in his stomach. 'They have a ring of history about them. Fine soldiers they were most of them.'

'Ach, and fine fornicators too the most of them.' *Damn the man, the heart had gone out of him, the will and the fire: he needed siller, what he lacked was the will to put in the dirk.*

'Some I hear are to emigrate? Is that so Douglass?' The laird turned to his ground steward.

'There's some word of that, sir—in a few cases.'

So they went on, the lawyer ticking methodically, Hallerton huddled deeper in his unease. In his mind he saw now that they were calling a roll of the dead from some past and arduous campaign. For them at least there might have been a kind of glory . . .

'You're burying a nation,' he said suddenly.

'Nonsense, laird.' Gregg scoffed gently. 'What we are doing is letting them take out a mortgage on a new life.' His smile was patronizing, unsullied by guilt.

So then there had been a rowth of work in the parks, the days of seedtime fine and clear and close to the heart of you that time when the folk of the farmtouns took again to the fields in that urgency of nature you had known since the days of your childhood, your father slim and lithe and quick then and whiles, unelder-like, putting a hand on your mother, fools the pair of them thegither as though they could not stay away one from the other. You minded that now in the quiet of your own hurt, the way it had been before the land had soured him. A fine macaroni he had been, you knew that now, his soldier's bearing making him seem proud and aloof, only you'd kenned he wasn't . . .

In that time, the men of the howe stepped boldly behind the harrows wreathed in the swirl of its dust, paced the spring-brown parks with hoppers slung, a hymn to nature and to man's place in it. Hillhead with his south-hung fields was the first (for wasn't he always?), turning the winter's grey furrows to friable tilth, the moold of the seedbed, his new broadcaster out for the first time and himself walking behind it entranced like a bairn with a new playick. That was in the howe. On the Hill the work was strangely muted; for the croft men putting seed into the ground it was a ritual without its ancient commit-ment and without hope for all but the few who knew they would be there to reap its meagre harvest. Few it now seemed would have the siller to stay; few the spirit to go. Theirs was a fine-balanced destiny. Yet MacCaskill strode his small parks as he had always done, the time of sowing a thing in the blood, something between him and the land, unable to help it, for to him as to others it would have been a betrayal of man himself and maybe of God. In your father still there was something deep and unplumbed you could not put a name to. Your mother was his acolyte in that strange compact he yearly kept, an old sacrament with the soil, filling the seed hopper on his shoulder with the calfies' pail, the golden grain scooped from the seedbags set sentinel-like and waiting silently down the side of the field. From his seat at the door of the old croft dwelling Grandfather MacCaskill watched watery-eyed, swad-dled against the sharp nip of the April wind, a ritual that had once given meaning to his days, the task that had justified his life. Interest stirred in the benign and vacant gaze, some loose engagement of the soul for an immemorial task he remembered; the folk now were strangers to him.

In their neighbouring shifts, MacGillivray and Maglashan and Morrison mirrored the age-old cameo of springtime, keep-ing each their own yearly date with destiny. Morrison was for out of it, for all that: he would roup out at the Whitsunday Term he said and look for a horseman's fee and a cottar house for his wife and bairns; Maglashan was in the same mind, less willing, for to him it was a sad return the way he had come: it would not, he said, be like working his own ground, not like watching his own seed grow or winning his own small hairst. But again, he thought, since he had a house bespoken on the edge of the village he some hoped for a bit of mason work with some ditching maybe and taking a hairst in season. Only MacGillivray and a few more were, like MacCaskill, as yet undecided.

From his study under the eaves, Pringle watched the work of that seedtime in a heartweariness his abiding joy in nature could not assuage; it was like the ache of love, deep and deep within you, buried away from one spring to the next. Down the years he had watched Hilly, confrere and confidant, step proudly about his fields; he watched him now, grizzled and frailer, trailing on at the back of his new bright-painted seed-chest on wheels as though he had but that minute invented it. Memory rolled away the years as he minded his first widower's spring in the howe. So long it seemed now, yet the hurt never-ending. After the drab causeys and grey biggings of Dundee it had seemed like a deliverance; there had he supposed been peace of a kind. As always, memories took him to the volume that down the years had kisted all his hopes and all his thoughts. He unhooked its gilt hasp, remembering the love that had been taken from him. Maybe he thought, some day he would destroy it, for it exposed him as neither life itself nor his ministry had ever done; here in its pages was the man they called Pringle, unembellished and unashamed, all his hopes and his sorrows and his dreams, and, embalmed for all to see, the crises in his faith. Today, though, he was but the recorder of his troubled parish.

April 27, 1880:
Watched this day the on-ding of seedtime in the parks of the howe: man and beast and machine astir in that old compact that man keeps yearly with nature and with God. All my days I have never ceased to marvel at it and been moved by it, this season of faith and of hope reborn in the hearts of men. Little would I have thought it that one day it might for many be divested of all meaning by the cupidity of men, the division of one against the other. Yet now it is so. Out on the Croft Hill this day I spoke with men who are sowing crops they will not reap—or who have left unsown shifts

that they or their folk once carved out of the hill to clothe every summer with crop. Come Whitsunday the hill will have been cleared of the half of its people. God knows where they will go for they are not easy, confident or compromising folk. They will drift, some of them at least, to the city: what is to become of them there one can but speculate for they have not the guile to withstand its lures and temptations; they will exist in a servitude of work that will sap their sturdy independence. Some will go to the farmtoun bothy and the status of hired help, selling their precarious freedom for a caupful of brose morning, noon and night. What rankles more than the seeming injustice of life itself is the cause of their plight: the high, rack-renting of our times. Throughout the land, men now see their hard, patient work mocked by callous lairds whose consideration is now, overwhelmingly, pecuniary. Their pioneering spirit is to be taxed.

It is a mean and vicious betrayal that does not speak well for lairdship nor for the charity that should invest men's souls. In all conscience, there is need for their rents to remain little or the same as they have been, for the years have gripped the crofter men most pressingly: oats that in the scarce times paid 30 shillings the quarter have slid steadily these past number of years to the mark of a sovereign or even less; the price of a stot for the Christmas market now down to or little better nor £25 at a time when it is proposed to lift the rents, sometimes by as much as 150 per cent.

Not all the croft men will quit, that's for sure. Some have fallen prey to that most diabolical device, the spurious bid invented by the factor or ground steward, most likely, for there is none can gauge the truth of it. In the face of it a man is put in the position of whether to pay to get the benefit of his own hard toil, the investment of his sweat over the years, or to leave it—on the principle of pride and the determination not to be blackmailed—to another to maybe reap the reward of all his work. And even then, the truth of it is not as simple as that: the croft carved out of the moor or the steep of the braeface, if it be anything at all, is more than a tribute to the persistence of men against nature, more than a viable or unviable agricultural unit, for it is a hame as much as a holding. It always has been; it has been the place where the nomadic folk of the old landscape chose to put down roots and become part of a community.

Now it seems that must change: in our society the crofter man has become something of an undesirable, a contagion on the country's hillsides, a dangerous alien, for his lifestyle (gin that be a word) exists somewhat beyond the ambit of estate government and the tyranny of the farmtoun's disciplined days. There is a move among the estates, not stated but tacitly understood among the lairds themselves, that the crofter man must be discouraged for the liability he might become and which he imposes in the upkeep and erection of biggings; for the administrative responsibilities that accumulate from his presence. Yet these very crofter men, along with the tenants of the small farms, are the very men who from the end of last century and through the present one, have between them, it is estimated, reclaimed about one-third of the country's agricultural land. Such men set up their own biggings—with their own hands—at the cost of not one penny piece to the laird: now they are to be ousted (for the outcome in reality is no less) to fatten the laird's purse and make way for the big farmer who covets their additional acres that march with his own. The laird's monopoly is ironclad. There is no appeal against the plan's iniquity nor the heartlessness of the dismissal of a well-doing folk. God pity them since the laird will not.

That spring in the stoor of seedtime the mistress of Mossgair died quietly without murmur or rancour or malice on her lips and with an almost painless ease in the ben-end of the house between her dinner bowl of weak broth and what would have been a small helping of kail brose, something she had speired for specially but not stayed to enjoy. It was a gentle release for an undemanding woman from a demanding life that she had never liked and a man whom she had never truly loved. She had given Morag little trouble for her whispers about the running of the house had long ceased as she gave it over unconditionally to the croft lass's rule. She had seen nothing strange in that: we came, we endured, we passed away, letting others take our place. When she had gone her sister, a Mistress Thomson, from Kildrummy came down in her widowed weeds to the Mossgair, a tall, tall woman she was as grey as a tombstone with dark piercing een. She glowered a long while at Campbell slumped by the fire, syne washed and dressed her sister and sent to Alford for John Soutar the joiner who came sober-like and sombre-suited and wrote his calculations with fastidious care into a black, dog-eared notebook with gilt-edging that held the record of the community's grief and syne speired at Mistress Thomson, so gaunt beside him: 'Will that be steel handles and a steel plate?'

And Mistress Thomson had glowered back at him and said crisply: 'That will be brass handles and a brass plate if you please and thank you. You will give my sister a respectable funeral, my mannie, and dinna think otherwise.'

And John, real vexed-like had said: 'Just so, just so,' and taken home flabbergasted with that flea in his ear and Mistress Thomson's breath still hot on the back of his Gladstone collar gey sorely affrontit at being spoken to like that.

So they had taken old Mistress Campbell down by, between spleeters of showers of late sleet on a dark afternoon, under the yew trees to be happit away by the lochside with that first dark-glowering Campbell and the young lass he once brought home and bedded relentlessly in his new farmtoun, and not far from the lair where the young John Glennie, but newly ensconced, slept with his ain, waiting to put his hand round Margit again, all loving done. Folk came from far ben the howe and from the Hill to give Campbell's wife their respect for she had been a fine body in life, not like her man, and mony a fee'd loon down the years in Miller's bar had spoken well of her. The heavy drops of sleet blattered on Pringle's Bible and folk bourached thegither to take sly shelter one from another; or maybe, you thought, in that moment to draw comfort of each other. Campbell and his sister-in-law stood together for that final leave-taking, silent, not speaking (she would never forgive him) and the next day Mistress Thomson had ordered Charlie Skene from the sowing of the yavil crop to gar him yoke the shelt in the gig to take her to Alford to speak with John Burness the mason about a suitable stone. And folk for once were near sorry for Campbell for she was a jad of a woman richt enough: she had harried her own poor man into the grave they said and she was now all set to break

Campbell. And faith, it was an ugly big brute of a stone that she ordered, with Cupid-like creatures perched on its corners, unseemly-like things to have in a kirkyard. But still and all, it would be a fine and conspicuous memorial and Mistress Thomson took home to Kildrummy weel-pleased with herself that her sister had been decently buried and would now, beyond doubt, be fittingly remembered.

Among the guests to dinner at Hallerton that night was Andrew MacVie, the county's Procurator-Fiscal, who was periodically invited to remind him of the side his bread was buttered on. With the mistress's return from the South the chandeliers of the big dining-room had been polished (a penance on Margit for whatever services she might have rendered in her mistress's absence) to a jewel-cluster brilliance, and the soup tureens burnished to a brightness that threw back at the diners the grotesquery of their own distorted images. Apart from MacVie there was John Gurney, seemingly in no hurry to settle his purchase, Lander Gregg, resplendently shirted, James Grant, hardly able in the circumstances to call God his equal, Pringle, surprised to be asked, with his daughter Margaret, Campbell of Glen Gloy, Hallerton's brother-in-law, and Munro, to bring up the number. It was, by the howe's standards, a glittering assembly this yearly dinner-party the mistress gave, on her return from the civilizing *ambiance* of London society, to mark her re-immersal in the cruder elements of life in the North, and in which, when he was sober and the business could no longer be avoided, she allowed herself disdainfully to be clumsily prostrated on pink sheets while the laird claimed his rightful inheritance—something he did now (and she thanked God ceaselessly for it) with a diminishing frequency. James, poor man, had never warmed her ovaries enough to put her at the slightest risk of capitulating to passion. She had taken sex into marriage, Munro would say whiles, like a condition of employment.

Though James himself was the company's head, it was she, from the table's other end, who reigned over them. A well-padded woman of fifty or so, with that puffy pink complexion of the aristocracy that betokens a trencherman's indulgence, the years had nonetheless been kind to her. Her breasts, lightly

144

browned by an early month in the Bournemouth sun, were primped into the corsage of a blue velvet gown, diamanté-trimmed so that it spangled the light with their every soft rise and fall. But that he knew her well, Mungo thought, a man might be cheated into thinking her a rose still worth the plucking.

They began with salmon, brought almost within the hour by a ghillie, new-dead from the river.

'Ye-You will have fou-found the cap-ital sti-sti-stimulating, likely?' MacVie asked. He was an unctuously polite man with an unsightly wart on the side of his nose that marred his life more than the stutter and gave many an unlucky poacher the impression that he had fallen singularly foul of some spitefully lop-sided justice.

'Extremely, Mister MacVie. Extremely!' Her ladyship was emphatic. She'd had the foresight to seat him with his wart on the blind side so as not to be worried by it. 'I always love London, don't you?' Her tone was that of the English noble-woman: high, flutey, cultured.

'They are telling me that the Queen . . .' Even in his casual conversation MacVie was given to attributing his statements so as not to be pinned down in the felony of some innocent half-truth, though for a figure of justice, his informants had a sinister anonymity. 'They were telling me the Qu-Queen . . . that the Queen is not much about in the city yet.' His serious countenance bent anxiously in the mistress's direction.

'She is little seen, certainly, Mister MacVie.'

'Mourning still, they say, for the Consort,' MacVie insisted 'After all this time.'

'Indeed,' the mistress added. James, she thought, would not be worth it.

'There would be some anxiety . . .' MacVie said carefully.

'There is some disillusion, to say the least,' the mistress said bluntly. 'Some say that she is not earning the salary the country is paying her.'

'That cannot be!' the Procurator-Fiscal said; it would pass for an expression of surprise, but equally it would do for a denial if ever it came to it.

'Indeed, but I assure you it is the case!'

'She is over fifty, of course,' MacVie said, peering under his eyebrows.

'You are ungallant, Procurator,' Gregg said quickly, and felt the mistress's smile fall upon him like a benison. 'A woman in her prime—mature, no longer skittish maybe, but—— You'd agree, Pringle?'

'Maturity indeed confers its own inequable comforts,' Patrick said.

'You are too grudging, Mister Pringle.' The mistress had no liking for the Free Kirk minister; he had strong black hairs on the backs of his hands—hands that would have been more seemly steering a plough than gripping a pulpit; they excited her. 'Grudging, Mister Pringle,' she taunted. 'Like your kirk.'

'It would be unfair—as I'm sure your ladyship knows—to judge the worth of the edifice by the ineptitude of its humble servant,' Pringle parried over his last mouthful of salmon, a past-master worthy of the duel they long had fought.

'You were closing the lid on life at fifty,' she accused him.

'I beg to deny it!' Pringle was gracious, unruffled.

'At least,' she said, more conciliatory, 'You are squeezing it dry of all excitement. And doesn't that amount to much the same thing?'

'On the contrary,' Gregg said—to Patrick's surprise at finding himself aligned with such an ally—'I inferred from what Pringle was saying that he meant maturity had its own enchantments.'

'It does allow a certain detachment of view, wouldn't you say?' Glen Gloy, with brotherly concern, bridged the awkwardness of the moment. Besides, he had a high esteem for Pringle.

'The Queen wi-wi-will——'

'They are terrible times in business,' Gurney said quickly, tired of the tiresome Queen as well as the stammering MacVie, still unwilling to be prised loose from his Royal fixation.

'It is the speak of the capital,' the mistress said. 'Is there likely to be a slump in the country's fortunes, Mister Gurney?'

The ironmaster shrugged bleakly. 'Not a slump maybe but a down-turn certainly in trade, I'd say.'

MacVie, conversationally snubbed, looked hurt, the sentence he had put so painstakingly together stuck in his throat.

The main dish was Crêpes de Porc Alsaciennes; these were

gently rolled and crusted with cheese that had been delicately browned. With them Jacques had provided a particularly fine claret and the two made a marriage that set Gregg's palate aflame with a gastronomic lust, silencing in him all further attempt at polite conversation. Fascinated, teasing her own food with a dilatory fork, the mistress of Hallerton watched his undisguised gluttony entranced, as she always was, by such gross capitulation to appetites. (The working classes, she supposed, took all their pleasures as simply and unashamedly.)

All the same, it was MacVie, gallant in defeat, who was the first to acknowledge the excellence of the dish. 'Pray t-tell me,' he begged, 'what i-is it? I don't believe it has been my pleasure to make its acquaintance on a di-di-dinner menu before.'

'Pork pancakes, in the manner of Alsace, Procurator. I doubt that the fair province will produce any more gourmet masterpieces under the Prussian heel.'

'Pray God, both it and Lorraine will soon fall back into French hands,' Grant said, lugubriously linking European tragedy with the rescue of a recipe.

'France is unthinkable without them,' Gurney offered; he was stronger on current affairs than on the culinary arts, and besides had a stomach so dried out by years of business worry that it would accept only the mildest of beef brees without protest.

'France, I doubt, has little choice but to accept her ill-fortune,' Glen Gloy said.

'She has no army left to speak of,' Pringle said.

'And she is poorly served for generals,' Hallerton added. 'And has been, surely, these fifty years past?'

Munro watched with inner amusement the mistress's obvious disapproval as Gregg abandoned cutlery in disarray all over his plate and slumped back replete, his een glazed as though from some rapturous act of carnal enjoyment.

'I put my faith in generals,' she said savagely. 'They keep the rabble in check!' Her gaze banished Gregg from polite society.

'That's a savage cure for democracy,' Gregg said lightly; he had resurfaced and wondered idly at the back of his claret-misted mind whether a guinea would make Miller's maidservant amenable.

'The world is changing!' Mildly, and a little embarrassed,

Glen Gloy rebuked his sister; he was, he had been telling Pringle, an old man unravelling the last strands of his life; he wanted to be able to wander to the last among his tenants without fear of their censure, to be sure always of a welcome and a seat on the stranger's stool. 'I canna see that the gentry, of whatever nation, can stand in the path of progress without being flattened under the press of the people. What's more, I doubt gin they have the right to.'

'You were always a one for the Communard's creed,' the mistress said sullenly, ill-pleased at being contradicted. 'And a traitor to your class,' she added tartly.

Glen Gloy reddened furiously, stung by her remarks. The others, relegated suddenly to the role of mere bystanders, waited, their expressions heightened by interest—with the exception of Hallerton, who looked strained, and Grant who registered alarm, for he had never before seen the mistress in this mood. Munro alone recognized the behaviour of a woman clamped suddenly tight as a fiddle strand with desire, without a man to bow the string . . .

But the tirade never came.

They were all of them saved by a sorbet, glacially cool, and the entrance of Margit, whose skilled hands made the soiled plates vanish by uncanny magic in front of their very een and set in their place the confection Jacques' genius had concocted. It would tease the tongue yet sit lightly on a tired stomach. They supped it in silence, without the compliments Jacques might reasonably have expected, and when they had finished, the mistress of Hallerton took her leave of them with a headache. By then, darkness had begun to slant silently over the parks as the day settled down to the hush of the night and the light, a liquid lilac mist, at last blurred the outline of the Croft Hill and its kingdoms of the small hill parks.

Later, with her whispered and furtive connivance in the schoolhouse dark, Mungo Munro took Miss Pringle, trembling, like a Naples whore against the wall with a fine and dizzying violence that drew protest and ecstasy from every sinew of her being.

'Why?' he asked buttoning, bewildered as she smoothed her

frock over her hips and tidied tendrils of hair again into their bunned imprisonment.

'Heaven knows,' she said; she felt neither shame nor disgust, only a freeing of the spirit, a satisfying honesty, some pagan acceptance of dark and elemental things that worked in the soul. Kneeling, she lit a candle from the fire-peats and he saw in the glow that her face was serene and that she had not bothered to rebutton her bodice.

In the firelight the skin of her neck, the mound of a breast uncaged, took on the rosy glow of the peats, making Munro aware in that moment of the unsurgical warmth of flesh. He had not known her like this before. Sensing his thoughts, she smiled up at him.

'Maybe I wanted to be soiled a little. Soiled by life, Mungo.' She rose to fit the candle into its tin holder on the table and came back to sit easily on to his knee in the big chair by the fire. 'Can ye understand that, Mungo?'

'Aye, but——'

'You thocht the penury of my spinster's bed all these years had turned my head, its prim sheets raddled my brain?'

'No, no——' It was Munro's turn to smile. 'No,' he said softly, his hand, in its caress, riding high on her thigh. A peat wormed and caverned by a slow devouring flame crumbled at last, its final explosion of heat striking them for an instant.

'I found Margaret Pringle the night,' she said quickly, looking into the fire. 'In that brittle and fusionless company. The real Margaret Pringle, I mean, Mungo. Her father's daughter. The one that got buried long eons ago in a welter of learning and social manners at college, the one that tried to run with the fox and hunt with the hounds—that bestraddled two cultures, had a foot in two camps yet belonged to neither. A poor dispossessed person, Mungo, in a constant state of betrayal of herself.'

Margaret Pringle sighed, absolving the world. 'She was a poor bitch, Mungo. You, of all people, must have known it.'

'No, in God's name——'

'Don't say it, Mungo!' She laid a finger tenderly across his lips, silencing him. 'She was a whore, a lady of easy intellectual virtue able to lie down with both the laird and his servant. She existed in a limbo of her own, just another wanderer in the desert that is the middle classes, Mungo. Too inferior to sip champagne, too much of an upstart to settle for honest porter.'

'I don't understand you, Margaret!'

'No, Mungo?' She seemed disappointed. 'I'm sorry. I don't suppose you do. I'd thought maybe you of all people would.' A pool of quiet fell between them, in which the known facets of their relationship fractured and coalesced, and new elements were distilled.

'I walked up the Croft Hill today,' she said. 'The first time for years I suppose, and looked at the little fields and the folk, kind still in their faces. And I knew I'd betrayed them. I owed them better.'

'What do you mean?'

'For years, Mungo, I have misled and mis-educated their bairns, sent them out into the world so innocent and ill-prepared to meet it and with such a lack of real understanding of its machinations as to be almost criminally culpable. I have stood in that schoolroom through there for the past twenty years pretending to them that theirs is a fine inheritance, that there is justice and godliness in the world, that right must prosper. Poor vratches! I have sent them into a battlefield of existence with the belief that they could be perpetual virgins. Surely, Mungo, that must disgust you as much as it offends me?'

'You're over-wrought, Margaret,' he said, finding the excuse for himself as much as for her.

'No, Mungo.' She was sad but emphatic. 'I was nivver mair relaxed.'

You could not open your legs to a man, she had found, without opening your mind as well; there was no thought now she would not share with him, no confession in the dark labyrinth of the night that offended her.

In her release, she found easier expression in the dialect of the district, the speak of her childhood, discarding the formality of stilted English, a speech she had acknowledged always to herself to be without warmth, the language of lawyers and careful men with words that made passion a mockery.

Outside a night wind had risen to sing lightly on the schoolroom's tin roof. Still, in the listening quiet, they heard it; its quavering melancholy moan stirred from some forgotten corner of her being an answering chord, a sadness at the passing of things, and with it a quiet fear. Silence, fraught and tense, fell between them; into it, out of the night came the lonely cry of a corncrake, disturbing, unanswered. Gently Mungo's hand freed her other breast from the constriction of the open bodice of her frock and took it carefully, like a kitten from a basket, into the glow of the firelight. He watched the nipple harden under his gaze, and with slow movements allowed it to bruise his hooded palm.

'The soul has its contracts,' he said, his voice soft, reassuring, and saw the tears well into her een and spill unmolested on to her cheeks . . .

So that was the courtship of Margaret Pringle. Queer she thought it, long after and Mungo gone. Strange how the wheel of destiny turned, how the world birled on its inexorable axis, how beings wove a tapestry across the bare earth, binding and loosening their involvement, their obligation one to another, clasping and sundering (she smiled to herself at the fitness, the rightness, of the phrase, hallowed with age); strange how the tangled threads unravelled to reveal the ultimate design (or was that but Calvinistic excuse for the pretty dance life led us?). Strange to think now on that time long since, of that bright afternoon, that room barred with sharp sunlight so that its images were etched forever in her mind; knowing and being known, exultant. Knowing then her need for more than a spinster's bed and dead nights stretching into the dawn. Her brow now against the cool of the window pane, Margaret Pringle saw that the wind had scoured the sky clear of cloud to bare a night clustered bright with stars.

You moved through that spring, Old Woman, in a mist of secret sorrow, one day drifting into the next as you lay waukriff and sad in your dreich kitchen bed long into the night watching the flichter of firelight blink out in the hearth, the sadness gripping you like a weight in your belly. By day the joy of the seed parks were but a reminder to you of all you had lost, for now Chae Skene strode by his lone in the fields. You minded how it had been. The house quiet then, in the night hours: you would hear Campbell come home and stoiter up through the close the way of the byre to sleep with the beasts, the news of him heich and most of it stite but maybe truth coming out with the lave. Then his speak dying down as the stupor claimed him: whatever it was, the drink deidened the pain. You felt then for the man he might have been, moved by his plight, sharing in that time the dunt life had dealt him. You wondered then in the box-bed dark, in the quiet house, what thing, what trick of life it was had brought you there that late November nicht—something strange and uncanny for you had almost sensed it then, coming past the parks in the slow creep of dusk, a foreboding within you. You minded that now, lying there by your lone in the bed where the first Campbell and his bonnie bride had once lain after the tyaave of the day, silent and quick in that stoon of pleasure before sleep claimed them. . . . The day's hours moved you from the scouring of the morning firegrate through the scrubbing of stone-cold floors, the trestling of the washday tub and the toil of the plump churn to the readying of meals and the late milking of evening . . . a dwam of days it was, for you told me so. And something else you knew as the months passed and the nausea took you, it feared and pleased you, made you sick with the thought of it even as the tears of joy spilled gently on to your cheeks in the box bed's dark from the wonder of it. You spoke then in your heart to the fiddler lad with the brown curls, sad that he would not know . . .

Lander Gregg turned in at the gate of the Procurator-Fiscal's house, one of a granite terrace in the better part of the town, square-fronted and douce; from such a background of respectability might a man send another to the gallows without fear of impeachment or the slightest twinge of conscience. Its only frivolity (maybe even the mason who biggit it had rebelled at such uncompromising conformity, Gregg thought) was the two gilt globes that sat on the peaks of its third-storey windows like balls on the snouts of performing seals. Gregg smiled to himself at the thought; he was relaxed and refreshed, and had come but an hour since from a well-kept house in a sinuous vennel on the far side of town that catered for the darker side of men's souls. He carried still, in the retinas of the mind, the gleam of warm candlelight on taut and glistening thighs. He soughed the notes of a merry reel quietly below his breath as he waited.

For all the lateness of the hour he was admitted almost at once and shown into the study where MacVie drowsed by the fire in a big winged chair. The Procurator-Fiscal strove to rouse himself as his visitor was announced.

'What brings you at this unGodly hour, Gregg?' His voice was tetchy at the intrusion.

'Urgent business, you may be sure,' Gregg lied easily. 'I would not have troubled you otherwise.' He smiled his apology. 'I'm but newly back from Hallerton House——'

'Hallerton's well?' MacVie was solicitous.

'Indeed. I——'

'And his l-lady herself is well?'

'Charming and well, I'm bound to say. What——'

'Her dinners always a delight to the pa-palate. That French johnnie a master of the culinary arts. It's not often we have the chance up here for such gastronomic odysseys.'

'No, to be sure,' Gregg said quickly. 'Like yourself, I am, as you know, privileged to sit at the Hallerton table from time to time.' A little ice crept into his tone. How long would the maudlin old fool be before he let him come round to his errand?

'A fine hostess, the lady of Hallerton,' MacVie nodded seriously. 'And, mind you, a remarkably well-preserved woman. Remarkable, eh Gregg?' MacVie peered over his eyeglass at the younger man, inviting agreement.

'I've always thought so,' Gregg said.

'Gentry to her very finger-ends,' MacVie said, pleased with such a summation and well-disposed to a world that contained such gems of the female gender, such paragons of taste and grace and every fine quality.

'You came to see me?' he said accusingly, surprising Gregg by his change to the authoritarian tone.

'I did.'

'And urgent you said?' MacVie adjusted his eyeglass so that he could see Gregg more clearly through it.

'Aye.'

'Pertaining to what?'

'Really, I suppose, you might say on a matter of some

concern to the lady of Hallerton.' With that quickness of mind, a mental adroitness that was the secret of his social elevation, Gregg saw his chance to change tack to his advantage.

'You d-don't tell me so!' MacVie's feelings were already enlisted, a victim at once of the other's manipulative skill. 'In what manner, may I speir?'

'In the matter of the estate's improvement policy. There's some little resistance to the development of the Croft Hill. Nothing of great consequence, ye understand. Just one or two of the tenants . . . Nothing organized so to speak, but still and all, causing the lady of Hallerton a little concern.'

'The rowdier elements, eh?' MacVie saw the situation wrongly at once, taking Gregg's silence as assent. 'Always trouble! The same thing when they had the improvements over in the West. Came the time for going aboard the ship in Loch Broom and more nor half of them had it suddenly in their minds to stay! Mutinous, some of them! Had to be draggit on to the boat, some of them. And keepit in chains till they were out of sight of the land in case they would try for the shore. Always trouble——'

'A handful, no more,' Gregg reminded him. There was hardly a parallel.

'Just so.'

'They will not pay the new rent, nor are they willing to quit it seems.'

'Causing impediment to the owner's title and enjoyment of his land. Interference with the rights of property.' MacVie bridled. Property was sacrosanct. 'That canna be allowed, Gregg.' MacVie peered imperiously through his eyeglass. 'Where would we be were the law not to protect it? The rabble would ruin the country!' He looked keenly at Gregg. 'You want them out? Evicted? Is that it?'

'Sadly . . .' Gregg shrugged unhappily. 'I see nothing else for it.'

'Save your sympathy for the lady of Hallerton that she has been so damnably vexed by these hooligans,' MacVie commanded, taking charge of the interview, angry about the whole business. 'If you will just give me their names . . .'

'I believe I have them . . .' Gregg made a fumbling pretence of combing through the contents of his pockets, coming at last, in a consummate performance, to the paper he had carefully crumpled and prepared. He handed it to the Procurator-Fiscal, who scanned down the listed names.

'MacGillivray, Maclean, MacCaskill . . .' he had difficulty with the last. 'Mac——'

'Morgan,' Gregg corrected. The deliberate illegibility absolved him from all premeditation.

'Morgan,' MacVie said, straightening the characters with the nib of a handy quill, so as to remember the name. 'Leave it be, with me,' he said. 'I'll be before the Sheriff myself first thing in the morning to seek writs of removal.'

'Ye really think that would be the best thing?' Gregg asked.

'The only thing!' MacVie said, his tone brooking no denial. 'If my years as this county's Procurator have taught me nothing else it is this: show a mad dog an ounce of mercy and he will be at your throat. No, no, Gregg . . .' he waved an expansive hand. 'Malcontents must be dealt with harshly. Otherwise they will upset the ordered structure of a society.'

'I suppose yer right, sir.' Gregg was servile, quiescent.

'Dammit, man, of course I am! There's one thing, though——' There was a sudden cloud on the sun of MacVie's self-importance.

'Aye?'

'In whose name will I be making the application? Hallerton's I suppose?'

'Eh—— Maybe no,' Gregg said. 'Gurney is more or less the owner now. The application could maybe go forrit in his name, wouldn't ye say?'

'Capital! Of course.' MacVie saw the point at once. 'No need to embarrass the House of Hallerton in the matter, eh?'

'None that I can see.' Gregg smiled hopefully. 'Unless——'

The Procurator's silencing hand was eloquent. 'Nor me,' he said, his firmness hardly concealing his relief that he would not besmirch the name of respected gentry in the common court of law.

So that was the move of events; with the spring work past, the rain had settled in to send squally skleets of showers across the Hill. It ran on the minister's brae, making it a sea of mud so that it took an effort of will as well as conquering energy to tackle it; it sat in muddied puddles round the Hallerton estate roads, dubbing the heels and toecaps of James Grant's spatted boots so that sin was allowed to flourish unmolested. It seeped into the bones with sciatic swiftness and stiffened the limbs to a rheumatoidal lethargy . . . Deepest of all, it seeped into the soul, eroding the spirit, sinking it deeper into despair.

They came now, those who would be moving away, for individual absolution; to Pringle's manse to be privately shriven: Kirsty Maglashan that had been Kirsty Morrison, no longer ungainly, asking for a blessing on her first-born; John Macpherson, seeking succour from the drink—he could afford it no longer; fleet little Duncan Ogilvy who once in the long-ago time had coveted his neighbour's daughter and had not been made unwelcome, the guilt of it lying on him all these years like a stone in his belly; Morris MacLoonan who had once stolen silver, his sister Shelagh of the Songs who said many men had had comfort of her; a woman who had let her baby die uncaring in its cradle; Kirsty Lorimer, repentant in that time of change, who once, to save John's face, had let a seedsman mount her. . . . Women with insoluble sorrows, guilty of fallible follies, men with black marks on their souls . . . They came all of them to see Pringle, to sit in the manse kitchen in the last of the day's light and relate in gentle, Sunday-genteel voices, the sum of their sinfulness, without rancour or real regret; to tell of their hopes (now in the past, forlorn), to speak of their lives. Closing a chapter . . .

Margaret among them, quietly before Mungo would come in for his Saturday supper; telling him simply, without excuse or adornment. 'It is not love, as I have known it, Father. Not a passion like——'

'Like Gordon?'

'You knew?'

'Not for sure.'

'That was——'

'A kind of fever in the blood.'

'Aye.'

'There was no peace in it?' How could he know? 'And Mungo?'

'Maybe I needed a companion of the soul, some siccan thing.

A schoolhouse is a lonely place, Father, a kind of outpost on the fringe of real life.'

'Like a manse.' And he smiled then, and they laughed thegither at that.

'Will your God forgive me?' she asked, serious again, the little girl he remembered.

'There are waur reasons for being in a man's bed.'

'He's an atheist.'

Pringle chuckled. 'Aye, well . . . We have only his ain word for that. It is maybe only that as a doctor he gets owre close to suffering at times to be able to equate it with God's will.'

'You like him?' She needed his approval.

'Always have done. He is a better man than he ever gives himsel' credit for.'

They laughed again at that, sharing a mood they had not shared since her childhood.

'You had better nae tell him so,' she said. 'He will be terribly offended.'

'I would not be so uncivil!' Patrick protested. A barrier had lifted between them. He turned for the kitchen door. 'I've my sermon to think on—cry me down when we're ready to eat.'

Tomorrow would be the last Sabbath in their kirk for the folk of the crofts flitting out at Whitsunday; the last time they would hear the Word from Pringle's lips in their old family kirk. It would be a day to test the steel in old Pringle's soul.

It had faired in the night as though God's hand had stayed the clouds. Pringle rose from the chair in which he had spent the sleepless silent hours, and laved his tired een, plashing water from the ewer into its companion basin and then cupping it up in his hands to his face. In himself he recognized all the bone-weariness he hid from the rest of the world. Standing mirror in hand at the window in the early light, he trimmed the grey bush of his beard. With a shameful awareness of his soul's despair he dressed, adorning himself as he did so in the ecclesiastical mien, assuming his minister's role like another skin—as always in recent years on Sabbath mornings.

There had been a time when Pringle believed in God; believed in Him implicitly. Believed that a righteous man set his hand to the plough and that the course of the furrow was of his own choosing; that with God's blessing he might stand on the last end-rig of life and look back on the straightness of the new-turned earth and feel safe in the rewards to come. The moment sunk him in deep reflection. Maybe the power of God had diminished. Or was it only that men's souls were chancy things?

Pringle sighed. In all his days, never had he been on such an unsure footing with the Almighty. The last months had shaken him deeply: now did he see men who had sown well unable to reap, men who had kept God's laws cozened and confounded by the guile of fellow men without scruple; men of courage robbed of their resolve. Strange indeed, were His ways . . .

Reminded, he looked across the still of the parks to the steekit doors of the croft biggins.

'God has betrayed us,' he said, soft and laich-in to himself, unable, quite, to acknowledge it.

'Aye.' His shoulders slackened with resignation. 'Aye, maybe that is it.' But he would not tell them; he owed them that.

Settled in his mind, he went down the manse stairs to the kitchen below and with practised deftness threw the dried kindling sticks at the fire's side into the grate. With the quick skill of his widower's years he teased them into a trellis and set flame to their tinder dryness. From the barrel he skulled water into his porridge pan and set it on the fire; he would be a poor servant, he reflected wryly, who unyoked the plough before he won to the furrow's end.

The kirk folk were early on the road, bonneted and shawled, coming in from the south of the strath and moving slow, beetle-black, down the flank of the Croft Hill to meet the main metalled vertebrae of the turnpike that ran like a spine through the howe, the artery of its existence. Along it Kilbirnie carried on its commerce with the world beyond the blue and distant hills; on it, its departing sons paused for a last look homeward before the world claimed them. It ran unwavering as the bone down a herring's back, until it disappeared round the rump of the hills, an avenue that many men travelled in their mind's eye to fame and fortune, that some in their time had walked shackled to the Sheriff Officer's horse on the road to a brittle justice and a board bunk in the Tolbooth.

Driving out from the gates of the big house, Hallerton, it was seen, was not without a sense of occasion: he was frock-coated and velveteen-collared as befitted a gentleman of refurbished means, and, if anything, more aloof than ever.

'Hallerton is haughty on it,' Rob Maglashan said, as the gig passed him. 'A dandy in his fine figured-silk waistcoat.' The rough humour with which he might once have greeted the laird's appearance had deserted him, lost in the slow stoon of his disillusionment.

'He is, to be sure,' Kirsty at his side, agreed, her progress now unimpeded and threatening to outpace them all.

'Better to him, surely, to have bidden from sight, you'd have thocht,' said Fiona MacGillivray, alone in her pilgrimage for Andra had declared he would embarrass neither God nor himself by running to Him *in extremis*. Not a bonnet, Fiona noted, was being lifted as Hallerton wheeled past.

'Bad cess to that bastard and all of his kind,' said John Macpherson; he spat in the road, a cloacal splatch on the toecap of the gentry. The lack of the siller for drink had improved neither his manners nor his temper.

Round by the kirk's west door, as always, Pringle watched them come down the Croft Hill and ben the strath, a strange calm on him now, a numbness he had not known before in all the years of his ministry. A warm morning sun slanted its yellow rays on the parks new-brairded in their tender green.

'Patrick.'

The voice startled him, turning him sharply.

'Mungo!'

The doctor's face creased wryly. 'You are surprised?'

Pringle nodded. 'I would be a liar gin I were to say otherwise.' And then quizzically: 'What brings you—Margaret?'

'You know?' Pringle nodded. There was quiet between them. 'Not just Margaret—but maybe life too, Patrick. When it gives you hostages, I find lately I have grown hellishly feared of it.'

'Aye,' Pringle said, his een distant, his gaze far off on the Hill. 'A peace in the heart can be worth a hosanna or two.' Dry on it Pringle, as once he had known him.

'There'll be a big kirking from the look of it,' Mungo said, reassured. Together they saw James MacCaskill stoop out from his dwelling on the Hill black-suited.

159

'James, I hear, is for sitting still and damn Hallerton,' Munro mused loudly.

'So I'm hearing.' Pringle was non-committal.

'But what can he gain—a bed in the Tolbooth?'

'What will he gain?' Pringle seemed puzzled, shaking his head. 'Maybe the knowledge, long years from now, that he once stood against injustice . . . Something like that. He's a proud man, Mungo, and we maun remember: gin it were not for his kind authority might never have to expose itself.'

They watched Campbell hirple ben the Mossgair road, unashamedly staffed (all pretence at wholeness gone), to meet the cruel metalling of the turnpike—like MacCaskill a man alone but, unlike the crofter, ill-suited to the burden of his loneliness.

'Poor Angus,' Pringle said. 'Aye, poor man!'

'Life is foreclosing on him. He's drinking himself into the grave.'

Pringle turned for a moment, his een keenly on the doctor's face. 'We are stock-takers, Mungo, you and me, in the world's most precious commodity.'

'And its most perishable,' Munro said.

Pringle pulled his black gown about his shoulders as though, suddenly, he too had felt the chill draught of mortality. Above them, strident, the first peal of the kirk's bell struck its tongued clangour, a stern rebuke on those who had lingered to put salt into the Sabbath broth and a spur to the step of those others who had set out later than they had intended (always the same ones, Pringle had noted over the years, sensing their reluctance). Its toll rang round the countryside, echoing faintly back from the Hill. 'Speir not for whom the bell tolls . . .' Mungo said. The thought, unguarded, had given itself utterance.

'It tolls for all of us, Mungo.' And then, lightly: 'I have always thought that Donne should have been a Scotsman—he understood sae weel the appeal of the Devil as well as the mercy of God.'

Strange Mungo thought it that a bell, in its plurality such a thing of joy, should carry in its single peal the knell of doom, the echoing measured tread of funeral feet . . .

So they came down from the hill, the folk who would move away, coming for their last kirking, to be pewed and shriven

160

in their little kirk for the last time. Slowly the kirk filled, its empty holy silence broken now by the steady shuffle of feet, the scrape of a boot on the plain floor, the rising hum of voices taking through-hand the week's work, quietly arranging a deal, binding in contract with solemn nod . . .

But at last they were all of them in. The door was deserted by the beadle John Slessor, who went out and came presently back, bringing Pringle, gowned and sombre, and shut him into the pulpit and syne retreated, head bowed, to the back of the kirk, his bootheels ringing an unholy echo from the flags of the floor.

Silence then.

And just for an instant it was fine; peace and melancholy gripped you, all the sadness of bitter-sweet and ephemeral things. You were lulled like a child, cocooned in holiness. Fine it was then with the grace of heaven around you. Fine then the lulling, somnolent drone of the harmonium washing your sins away, stilling the mind, lifting the heart in piety. Campbell contrite in his pew . . . Kirsty Maglashan fleetly into hers; all of them in and James MacCaskill last of all, steeking the door and walking straight-backed and alone as always to his seat, all eyes on him. Quiet then the hush of its holiness; in the shafted sunlight that spilled through its windows. Still and quiet the peace of it crept into your soul, its simple sanctity bringing a lump to the throat, the tear brushed surreptitiously away with the corner of a shawl.

And Pringle in his pulpit. 'Lay down your sorrow,' he told them, 'and let us pray,' slow, dark and dour as always they had known him, looking black-eyed down on them. 'Lay down your sorrows,' he said, so gently now, and the slow susurration of prayer filled the kirk as Pringle's hands gripped the pulpit, gripping where his hands over the years had worn thin the veneer. There were many of them who minded well that time when he had come among them, when he had stood first in that pulpit and glowered down on them. Well he had served them.

They sang an old psalm, well-loved, but its joy was muted, it stuck in their throats, stifled with sobs till it became a hirpling tune helped on only by the determined voice of Caroline

MacFarquhar and the heroic fingers of Margaret on the harmonium, playing blind through her tears. He had thought to preach them, knowingly, a hypocrite's sermon that would lift their hearts nearer to heaven. Instead, unrehearsed, unashamedly caught and moved by the mood of unreality, he began slowly to address them:

'Brethren—my friends'—for so they were, he knew that now—'we are at the end of an old song. You are the victims of a base persecution . . .' His voice faltered for a moment. 'A fiendish injustice . . .' Now the rich timbre of his voice grew stronger, and as suddenly drew into it all the homely words of his youth. 'Ye maun, many of ye, believe yersels to be the playicks of God. Let me assure ye, ye are but the pawns of men, men of little conscience, men willing to speculate in human misery. The world and the Devil have always kenned such men. But mair nor that: ye are the victims of greed—of men whose greed has soured this land . . . These men will answer on Judgement Day. Siller, now, will not prosper them then.'

He paused, looking round them.

'Ye are not innocent, for man is frail, man is fickle, man is easily misled. Still and all, I believe the sum of your sins is but a mote in God's eye compared with the wrang that has been done tae ye.'

Again his gaze swept round them.

'They will argue, these sillered folk, that they do all this to ye in the name of progress—that strange Being that gives his blessing tae the jingle of silver, the sheen of gold, the ring of the guinea-piece. God, I remind them, said: Thou shalt worship no other God.'

His voice softened. 'If it were otherwise, I wid tell ye.'

He rocked gently back on his heels, making the wood of the pulpit crack, his head nodding the surety of his words. 'But I tell ye this. These men—their wealth will be as ashes. They would bigg a new society upon the quicksands of quick profit and human suffering when what the warld needs is the brotherhood o' man.'

Pringle faltered, swaying in the pulpit, as if to gather his strength. 'If I had the words to comfort ye at this time, ye would be comforted; if I had the riches to buy your release from the bondage of landowning men, ye would be free. But I hae nane o' these things. But I can tell ye this . . .'

His voice rose on a note of anger.

'Mebbe not in our time, nor in the next generation, but soon, my brethren, there will come a time when men will be ashamed of what has been done here this summer, of what has been done in the name of progress, of so-called Improvement. There will come a time when men will feel shame that proud names could ivver hae been associated with these acts of pillage—this pillage of the pen more despicable in its way than the havoc of the sword. A man who will murder wi' steel maun face his victim, witness with his ain een the culpability of his deed. What has been done tae ye has been stealthily done by nameless men hiding behind the anonymity of advocates. These nameless men will sleep ill for all their wealth; their happiness will be a hollow thing. In God's name I promise ye so.'

Fine then the resonance of his words, the promise in them; fine their iron ring against the bare stone walls of the small kirk; the sweetness of God that danced in the iridescent dust of the barred sunlight, their dread in that moment all but stilled. The throaty notes of the harmonium distilling their drowse over them, laving the spirit, and Pringle rising to announce an old and hallowed hymn, invoking its number, and standing with them to sing.

The hymn ending and Pringle putting down his book.

'Now let us pray . . .'

Their heads going down then, their hearts quiet, stilled as yet with bewilderment for never had they heard Pringle like that before . . . The prayer ending in a rustle of petticoats along the hard pews and the men easing saliva quietly back into their dry-parched mouths so that you could near hear the relief flooding back into the kirk. It was like some stranger had been there and now gone away. Pringle waited for the absolute silence that was his due. He gave them the Benediction (in-the-name-of-the-Father-the-Son-and-the-Holy-Ghost-be-with-you-now-and-forever-amen-Amen) and came pale down from his pulpit, unfastening his gown.

Margaret with Mungo found him at the west door, looking up at the Croft Hill, at its folk already straggling their way homeward on it, singly and in groups. She put a hand on his arm and found he was trembling.

'Hallerton will not thank you,' she said simply, feeling a rush of tenderness for him, a pride she hadn't known before.

'Mebbe not.'

'It was courageous, Father.'

Awkwardly, he put a hand over hers. They had never been close: now he wished that it might have been so.

Sad you were, Old Woman, going home by your lone, minding still the lad who had walked the kirk road with you; bereft in the days that followed as the folk took their leave of the Hill and the dwellings that were the only ones they had known. Proud and stoical still they were the most of them, for life had long inured them to its griefs and bitter disappointments; tearful some at the last . . . They piled their few pitiful possessions, detritus of their bare lives and all that was left to them after their roups, on to the farm carts they had hired to take them where they were going, closing their dwelling doors for the last time to hand the key to a waiting Farquhar Douglass. Watching, lounging against a dyke at some distance as they cleared out their belongings, the ground steward rehearsed the last barbs of his spite:

'Peety yer hadnae the siller, John—she's a fine croft.'

'Yer leaving a fine placie, Tam.'

'Ye'll hae naething like sae muckle freedom aboot a cottar's hoose.' Each was a personal and private revenge, savoured with pleasure. His beating had scarred him; as his body healed, the natural malice of his nature had given way to deep-seated hate, to a festering bile within him. Waiting, he looked across the Hill at the croft steadings of MacGillivray, Morgan, Mac-Caskill—the handful who had not spared him their open contempt and who yet defied him. Whitsunday would come soon enough; in the darkest corners of his being he promised himself a quiet vengeance.

They came, cursing the clods of earth as they crumbled under their unaccustomed feet, slipping to a halt whiles as their legs all but went from under them. They were wet and angry enough by the time they won to MacGillivray's where they found Andra's door as free as his friendship. (He never barred it, he boasted whiles, except when he saw the factor coming.) They found Fiona seated by the ebbing warmth of last night's peats, keening gently, her een sightless on the grey ashes. She had not heard the latch. The een she lifted on the intruders were blank with incomprehension, the scream she might have uttered stillborn, stifled on her lips as one of them cupped a hand hard on her mouth.

'Sit you still,' the big man warned, noting the firm thrust of her belly, taut under the nightgown winceyette as she struggled, 'or you will get young Garrett here all excited.' He indicated, with a nod, the young man with an unsavoury complexion and the slackened lips of dolt idiocy who held her. Fiona did as she was bidden, fearful of the cruel light in the big man's een, and when he was sure of her silence he led the way quietly into the closet.

Four weights, thudding suddenly and simultaneously on to his shoulders and his legs, woke MacGillivray and in that same instant apprised him of the fact that he was pinned helplessly to the bed. And there was something else: an edge of sharpness lying across his larynx. Again, if he might have doubted either the sharpness of the weapon or the intent one glance at the face of the man who held it convinced him. As though reading his thoughts, the big man chuckled.

'He is a high-strung laddie that, Mister MacGillivray. Once in Nantucket I saw him open a man from the gut to the gullet. Keep your adam's apple still, I beseech you, or I will not vouch for it!'

'My wife——'

'Ach, safe enough,' the big man assured him. 'For the moment—— They say, MacGillivray, that you're a man without kirk or creed. But they say, too, that you're a man of your word.'

'Gin it be so, I promise you this: I will settle my account wi' ye for this.'

'Och now, I wouldnae be hasty with such promises, Mister MacGillivray. Not with your wife this minute in the close custody of a man on whom women have nivver smiled kindly.'

'If you lay hands——'

MacGillivray strained every limb but was forced to relax his struggle as the sharp blade at his throat nicked flesh.

'She is safe,' the big man said. 'I telt you so. And I am a man of my word no less than yerself.' He reached into one of the side pockets of his reefer. 'I have something here for ye—a present ye could say.' He drew a small velvet bag from his pocket and tipped ten gold guinea-pieces into his hand, holding them close so that MacGillivray could see. He jingled them. 'Yer word, MacGillivray, that you will make use of them! They could buy passage to Canada maybe . . . Get ye twa rooms in a city tenement certainly.'

'And why in hell should I give ye my word?' The veins of MacGillivray's neck bulged with anger.

'Come, Mister MacGillivray.' The big man was infinitely patient. 'I could give you a dozen good reasons. All of them imperative upon you to accept.'

'But I was raised on this land!' Andra's wrath exploded heedlessly. 'Raised from it, like the crops—raised from its earth. Why in hell should I willingly leave it?'

The big man shrugged, 'Oh, Mister MacGillivray, let's not be speaking of rights and heritages and sic things—they are surely nae mair than the loose cement of history.' The big man sighed, considering the world's ills. 'Speak of silver if you will, Mister MacGillivray, and the rights it buys. It buys me, Mister MacGillivray, and it is buying you. Speak of that if you must.' He held the new shining coins under MacGillivray's nose.

'Well?'

His een and his voice had hardened. His tight smile mocked Andra's predicament. 'I have nae wish to alarm you, I assure you, Mister MacGillivray, but, to put it in its crudest terms, I should maybe warn you that the man wi' yer wife is not a sophisticated man. I would be playing ye less than fair gin I were not to tell you so.'

'Aye, ye bastard!' Fury blazed along with the contempt in the pinioned crofter's een. 'Ye don't trade in honest threats, do ye?'

'No, Mister MacGillivray, not always.' The big man's features relaxed in a mirthless chuckle. 'No—— after all, look on it from my side. I am but a negotiator. I have tae trade in whatever commodity or condition is open to me. The weakest

166

thing about a man whiles, Mister MacGillivray, is his humanity. And in that he is, like yerself, damnably vulnerable . . . But again, he's maybe lucky forbye, when ye come to think on it. Take the likes of poor MacAllister noo—we have visited him this short time since—you'll likely have heard . . . Poor man, he had naething to trade with. Nothing! We hadnae a thing there to trade on, Mister MacGillivray. We had to threaten him most grievously——'

Andra nodded, understanding.

'Aye, yer a clever bastard and nae mistake, whoever ye might be . . . Bring my wife through to me then, so I can see her.'

'Surely.'

The big man turned. 'Garrett!'

'Aye.'

'Bring through yer captive.'

'Aye.'

A moment later Fiona MacGillivray was thrust into the closet, imprisoned by the thick arms of her loutish captor.

'There,' the big man said. 'Safe, like I telt ye. So——' He gazed quizzically at MacGillivray, enjoying the croft man's predicament, his impotence, his utter and complete inability to manoeuvre to any better bargaining standpoint. He savoured the moment.

'Ye will give me your word then?' he asked finally, softly menacing.

'Aye.' MacGillivray nodded. 'Ye clever bastard. Aye!'

What else was there.

They had the steady seep of the rain in their faces as they set away round the side of the Hill; it hung in their eyebrows, a momentary dampener to their jovial spirits; in the big man's beard, so that he brushed the wet from it impatiently as they pulled slow against the hanging slope of the ground, quiet now as the climb took the breath from them, the chill beginning to bite into their bones. They paused to rest limb and lung, and the big man pulled the bottle from his reefer pocket, taking a long swallow from it before passing it round.

Waiting on the raw edge of morning, he looked down the long flank of the Hill to the village below, sleep-silent as yet, and beyond it to the dim, square bulk of the manse, gaunt and bleak-windowed, granite-quiet as a mausoleum. A flitting thought lifted the corner of his mouth wryly: they had catched God with his een shut! But below them on the Hill now there was a stirring round the crofts, the darting of solitary figures followed by the quick assembly and sundering of groups, a fearful shadowed scurrying between the dark outline of one bigging and its neighbour.

'We've fair stirred them up,' he said, running the smirr rain off an eyebrow with a scrape of his thumbnail.

Pocketing the bottle, he set his step again to the Hill. 'Come, lads. There will be a goodly handful of silver atween us for this nicht's work . . . And the nicht after next, what say ye? We will maybe pay a visit on MacCaskill.'

'You needna fear for yer father, child. They will not find him.' Resting in the shadowed dark of the recessed bed in the ben end, Martha MacCaskill looked at the outline of her daughter's head, framed in the pewter light of the small window pane.

'They will not catch him,' she said, repeating the thought, this time to herself, something she had come to do through the recent months of her loneliness with Morag away and Jeemes himself out of the house. From beyond the runnelling wet on the window glass came the incessant murmur of the rain drumming on the earth; the steady seep of it as it dripped in patterned sound from the roof thatch. For Martha MacCaskill the murmur of it neither deepened nor lightened despair; it emphasized only the sad solitariness of her life.

'I wish tae God I were as sure of it,' Morag said, a maturity in her voice that her mother in no way resented. She had seen in the last month or two the strain in her daughter's face, the hardening lines. Life had made the only child of her womb a woman. So be it; it had bestowed on them a kind of equality, a freedom to speak. They were alone; in the kitchen Grandfather MacCaskill crooned by the hearth.

'Ye dinna sleep in a man's bed for nigh on twenty years without getting an insight into his soul, child,' she said, chiding gently. 'Without kenning what is in him—what it is in him to do. And I ken this aboot MacCaskill: there is a loneliness in him beyond loneliness, a self-sufficiency in him that is whiles uncanny. Oh, this land has broken men, lass! Guid men! Ye would hae seen it yerself in their faces, yon blank kind of look in their een like they werenae just sure where they were nor yet maybe wha they micht be . . . I've seen it! I've kenned what they would come to; kenned weeks aforehand when they were like to put an end to it all in the loch. For some it was the only way. They set their hopes owre high.'

Her speak from the shadows quieted for a moment so that the steady thrum-thrum of the rain again filled the house.

'I nivver had that to fear with MacCaskill.' Like all the croft women, she called her man always by his surname. Strange, Morag thought it. Strange and cold; strange-like to hear her say it so: had there been a love between them once, she wondered, a warmth, a draw and a destiny between them for all that? Or had it been but a cold bestraddling, no more than a duty done on the marriage sheet: the dour young MacCaskill unsmilingly doing God's will between chill thighs, chilled by their charity, offended by their sacrifice?

'No, nivver with young MacCaskill,' her mother said, startling her, as though she had read her thoughts. 'No, that was something I had no fear on.' She moved, rustling the chaff palliasse, as she raised herself on one elbow.

'Ye should have seen him then, lass, yer father! New home from the war, brown as a nut, a something about him, in his een . . . I canna explain it. Sitting straucht as a staff on the Sabbath in his father's pew, his moustaches curling . . . a rare macaroni. We set oor caps, I can tell ye, the young weemin among us that had not had an offer, or maybe if we had, saw now the chance to better it. The young MacCaskill would hae the croft. He fair excited us . . .'

Martha MacCaskill's voice trailed off, lost in some dwam of memory. When she continued it was in a sharper tone.

'We will speak as weemin, daughter, will we, eh?'

'What mean ye, Mither?'

Morag turned from the window, the skin tightening involuntarily over her cheekbones, the colour draining unseen from her cheeks.

'I'm meaning yerself and the young Carmichael, poor loon.'

'Ye ken?' Morag said dully, not wanting to deny it.

'I jaloused it. Tae be coorse-tongued about it, a wumman

aye kens when a young lass has been beddit—her ain especially. Mebbe it is herself she sees, that long time ago!' Then softly, compassionate: 'It is not aye something that can wait a preacher's word. Gin it could, I doubt it wid hae muckle value. My maidenheid God help me couldnae . . . And yer father, after all the carnage he had seen, was ripe for the softness of a woman. There wir some as wid hae teased him, tae first get the ring on their finger, but atween yer father and me it couldnae hae been like that. I had owre muckle care for him. I socht neither to haud nor bind him, God help me. I speired him nae promises.'

So, after all, she thought, it had been warm and fine, a wild and tender thing between them. Hard now to think of it so; hard now to think of MacCaskill the soft-voiced lover.

'His wee whoorie, he wid call me, not meaning it. That wis yer kirk-going father, lass, when he was young. Afore the croft took a hold on him. . . . Still and all, even then I kenned weel there was that iron in him that would not be bent like the spirits of some. When I was bairned wi' ye I telt him, so he would ken. "We will be marriet," he said. "It is not for that I am telling you," I says to him. It was the God's truth. "It is not for that I am marrying ye," says he, quiet-like, and I kenned the last word had been spoken on it. That was the temper of the man then. . . . If he now seems dour to you, lass, it is from the disappointment of the years, the struggle to sustain hope atween one season and the next. Each year, ilka disappointment, has honed away some more of the softness of him, sharpened the edges of him. God knows, he has reason enough for his bitterness, but there's a side to him noo that cuts friendship and more's the pity for I cannot believe it is only the weak that needs friends. But to come through the hell of the Crimea, and syne, now, to be robbed even of the very ground he is heir to, the ither men nae less! Ye will not see their like. They are the last of their kind . . .' Then gently, without condemnation: 'Are ye bairned by him?'

'It wid be a wonder gin I were not!'

'Just so.'

So the wheel turned. Martha MacCaskill nodded slowly. There was a kind of inevitability about life she had long ago accepted: the flesh didna listen to sermons.

'And Campbell? Will ye tell him? Or kens he? What says he? They said Carmichael was his ain blood, that he wid heir Mossgair.'

'Campbell? He sees little but the hobgoblins in his heid. What diet he needs noo he gets at Miller's.'

'Aye.' Martha MacCaskill sounded sorry. 'The world broke Angus. God knows how, but it broke him all the same. Like it breaks the most of us.'

In the quiet that fell between them the rain blattered on the window pane, drumming rhythms on the mind. Slowly, in some personal destiny, they had come full circle; their lives had locked in a continuity of experience; the wells at the world's end were full with the tears of women.

Near to dark, from his vantage point in the long gallery of Kynoch's Castle, where the driven rain had sent him, Mac-Caskill looked down through the canopied branches at the desolate countryside below him, his dyker's jacket upturned against the raindrops that showered down on him with every gust of the wind. For three nights now he had eluded his hunters, for such they were, lying low in the day in the deep bracken by the lochside that could bury a man dry on a bed of moss as easily as it concealed and cushioned lovers from the world, moving position always a little ahead of the men who sought him. He had no fear of the night, liking its cloak about him, the safety of its shadows: in the dark a man renewed acquaintance with his own soul; in its treacle black he could let the mantle of Christianity slip his shoulders and assume again the pagan pelt, think deep the thoughts that calmed and satisfied the darker recesses of the psyche. He was hollow-eyed from want of sleep, his features drawn with fatigue, and now hunger clawed at his belly, sharpening images in his mind. Into his thoughts there came the crystallization of another landscape and another night, a distant glen, the glen of his childhood. Hidden so, on such a night, a small bairn had watched, that bairn himself, the memory of it burning still in the mind . . .

First one and soon another of the dark-shrouded biggings taking light, the pattern repeating with a numbing and appalling rapidity, one flame begetting another, growing first from the speck of a spark, spreading slow, surely, into the dry under-thatch then bursting, all at once, into a sheet of ravening flame over the roof of the dwelling in a conflagration sending couples and the roof cabers crashing like torches on to the earthen floor below and leaving the rooftree a smoking, flame-lappered spit. Within the walls the dry wood of the box beds stoking the fires, making each bigging a seething cauldron of flame.

Round the periphery of each circle of leaping flame, some-times shadowed, whiles plainly seen, a pathetic bundle of belongings, thrown mercilessly into the night. And round each sad cairn of possessions, through the drifting reek, a glimpse of the cringing figures of the evicted, those without silver to buy passage to a new life: a weeping mother with her petrified bairns clutching her skirts, their faces buried in its tattered folds; there, a wailing widow body without menfolk; again, an old man without kin to comfort and care for him. Borne by the wind there had come to him that night the yapping of demented dogs, the whimpering pitiful cry of the homeless women, the drunken shouts and coarse laughter of the burners, their voices torn away from him by the wind as suddenly as it had brought them. And the acrid stench of soured thatch drifting up to him . . .

In the spreading light of the flames he had seen the torch-bearers busy about their devilish work. Like fiends from Hell, and primed with raw whisky, they had pranced between one pool of light and the next, sustaining their frenzy with fresh drink.

Pity that night had been a stranger. Old Angus Mackay who had sat in his dotage through nine summers or more, charting his remaining days through the course of the seasons from the first brave braids of barley to the ploughing-in of the stubble, had been seized like a common miscreant from his chair by the fire and put out to the cold with a suddenty that robbed him of speech, his sticks of furniture hurled after him. He had beaten his drum bravely, worn the King's red coat proudly. Fingal Clark's old mother, who'd lived by her lone in a little black house close to the moss, and hovering sickly and poor and near to death's door had but a few hours since set her een on her departing grandchildren for the last time in this life, had been taken from her bed and put callously into her barn outbye.

The destruction had gone on . . . relentless. Old work it was, its ritual long known to the Highlands, handed down in the memory from one generation to the next, a shadow always on the subconscious, a melancholy in the soft voices that told of it. A madness, it had spread from Farr and Kildonan, been seen in Assynt and in the parish of Rogart, in Cromdale and Cawdor, Kintail and Kilmartin. Nothing, it had seemed, could smoor it. A scene it had been to bedevil description, the cruelty of it all but unknown for long years after for the tell of it was in a language that was as foreign as Swahili to a Southern ear . . .

There would be no mercy, no compassion. Little it mattered then for both, to be sure, were strangers in the land, outlawed by the lairds so that you would wonder whiles did the old chiefs turn in their graves from the shame of it all, from the indignity heaped on the old clan names. Proud and fierce they had been; what had become of their kind? The tide of history had swept over them, swept them aside; crushed them forever. What were they now these lands but the sport of destiny, counters in the hands of men, won and lost by the throw of the dice in a London gaming salon; beggared by the money-itch of the new rich and the industrial age that had spawned them. Poor apologies for men they were, to be sure, some of these 'new men', striding the hillsides with mincing steps in their buttoned boots, the time gone, and that forever, when a man might with impunity shoot a moorcock for his pot, or lift a salmon from the river. All bye and done with now, the songs of the bards; bye and done with forever from that day when they had stood hungry and tattered in Drummossie's grey mist. More than a defeat that day had been, more than a profound humiliation; that day they had crushed a people. Broken them forever. And what Cumberland had not achieved—and that was but little—had been safely left to the lairds. Where Telford had biggit his stark grey kirks, as austere as the hills that girt them, silence now greeted the Sabbath morn; bye, forever, the uplift of joyous voices singing their succour in the Lord. Through the glens now the pulpits rotted from the want of men to listen to the Word; through the broken windows of these lonely kirks the wind sang now with a terrible lamenting; round them, and in them whiles where the decayed doors swung on twisted hinges, there was now but the cry of sheep . . .

And so the whisky had gone round and the work had gone on (remembrance came perfectly now) one spurred by the other, till the sweat ran on their faces, runnelling with the grease from the fatty flares that sputtered and spat at them. In their drunken state there was little they'd not been capable of. Fifteen, sixteen, seventeen, eighteen . . . terrible that night had been: the bairn numbed with fear had counted the biggings as they were given to the flames; had watched the thatch and rooftree of his father's dwelling crash into the shell of its familiar walls in a shower of sparks, lighting vividly for an instant the faces of the torch-carriers, grotesque and grease-smeared, their crooked smiles advancing, retreating, pirouetting, mocking him . . .

MacCaskill had never forgiven those men for that night; he knew that now. A quiet curse broke his lips, a soldier's oath long buried in the subconscious, exhumed now by the overwhelming rage that rose in him and uttered easily with a soldier's disregard. It was a curse on the men who had allowed it—that night and all the other nights like it that history had seen. Now he was driven again from his home. He looked down from the height of Kynoch's Crag to the Hill and the homes, now deserted and silent, of the folk who had gone, folk who had seen him go to war and been happy, the most of them, to see him come home. The stripling had come back a man, honed and hardened by the experience, a man needing the softness of women. And Martha, grown in these years from the bloom of girlhood, waiting. Known between them at a glance, that unspoken contract. Daft days, the two of them not able to bide away from each other, her hands finally, shamelessly, unbuttoning him, the moss a soft bed to them.

'I'm nae a whoor, Jeemes . . .'

Pulling the sark up from his belly. Her hands sweeping the breeks down his thighs . . . and pulling him down, down, whimpering like a whipped dog at the sight of her, sinking on to her, to the softness of her young belly, slipping into the liquid darkness of her, deep, deep, held for a moment by her gasp, broaching her at her bidding her smile thanking him, her

174

maidenhood gone and her een misted and veiled . . . Rocking
him in the cradle of her thighs till she told him . . .

'Slip your rein, my love! Slip your rein!' And he had burst
like a dam, spilling hapless into her. And again almost at once
from the pagan joy of it, the mindless, bewildering, stupefying
splendour of it, slipping sure and swift into her, the low
laughter breaking in her belly, her movements melting, her
voice soft-crooning in his ear.

'Spur yer steed, my love . . . MacCaskill, my love.'

So, so . . .

Long after they had lain in the concealing bracken till the
wild geese came back to the lochside from wherever they
wandered (she often had wondered), till the summer dusk and
then the dark settled around them and the day stilled down to
the slow throb and the cricket cry of the night, all the long
years gone between them, fine then to speak of all the things
they had thought on, and the young MacCaskill's manhood
slack upon him and she loose, loose in the belly, the knot of
the years broken so that in that joyful moment near any man
might have known her.

'Ye liked it?' she asked shyly. And his smile told her so.

'Aye and you?' His concern now that his roughness had hurt
her.

'Fine, my love, fine,' she assured him, and kissed him now
to thank him, gently on the mouth among his moustaches that
tickled and made her feel funny in her belly and she thought
Michty, not again, or he will think me a whoor right enough!

'I am well womaned,' she said . . . but aye, aye, gin he
wanted, gin he was sure, and so in the dark, like that, the cool
moss a pillow for her burning cheek. . . . That summer he
had taken a sodger's fill of her, quietened his mind with her,
down by the lochside. Fine it had been before the years soured
him . . .

Now the evening light masked the old stones of Kynoch's
Castle, softening its grim walls. MacCaskill counted the Hill's
empty croft dwellings, those biggings that had been the homes
of folk who had mirrored his own existence, some of them
friends. Not close, but friends all the same—closer, maybe, if
he had allowed it for he was aware of his own loneliness, of
the unease he congealed about him. Memory rekindled for a

175

moment a flicker of kindlier times; with an inner eye he retraced the steps, the road he had come, and a sudden sadness assailed him for all the promises of life he had left unfulfilled. For all his resilience, his whiplash toughness, life had beaten him, reduced him to this: a fugitive from his own dwelling, from his own wife and bairn. Maybe, he reasoned, it could not have been otherwise; maybe always a man was snared in the trap of his own destiny. He searched in his soul for the reason, but found none in that void of bleak despair. Doubt and indecision had gnawed away the taste of hunger in him as he paced the long gallery, even eclipsed his terrible weariness from lack of sleep. And there was the memory now of that distant sweet summer . . .

Now he ran. Slithering and sliding. Reeling like a drunk when the rain-slackened earth yielded under the smooth soles of his boots. Across the face of the Hill pasture, chancing the luckless encounter. A terrible rage spurred him on, a rage inflamed by every slip and stumble. A yapping dog spotted him and streaked after him, teeth bared. He paused only to crack the heel of his boot across its mouth and watch, warily, as it rolled whining on to its back, its ferocity changed in an instant to cringing fear. A swell in the ground, a fold of the Hill, threw a deeper shadow and MacCaskill used its cloak without thinking, already an outlaw by instinct, his pace unslackening. He came out of the shadow where his own biggings lay below him, heedless now of whether or not he was seen for he knew he could outrun them. But unspotted he slid safe into the shelter of his own barn gable and was glad to brace himself against it, as his legs, from his weakened state and the wild speed of his flight, threatened to give way under him.

In the barn's dark he groped for what he wanted: a hayfork with steel tines a foot long. He twirled it in his hand, feeling the work-smooth haft of it against his palm. The feel of it comforted him, calmed him, and he stood for a moment in the dark hearing the speak of women's voices—Morag's with her mother's, he supposed—through the wall behind him. He stepped out and round to the dwelling door, hammering with his fist.

'It's me Martha!'

176

'Father?'

The voice was Morag's.

'Aye—open the door, lass.'

She slid the bolt, letting the crofter in without ceremony, thrusting the door to behind him and ramming the bolt back in the staple. MacCaskill's appearance, even in the faint light thrown by the bedside candle, brought a gasp from Morag and from her mother; his days on the run had given the crofter man a fearful gauntness. It was as though they had honed him down to the skeletal MacCaskill. Yet his sleep-reddened een, dark in their sockets, glowed with a bright intensity.

'Ye'll be needing meat and a change of clothes, man,' Martha said, her matter-of-fact tone quickly establishing the immediate focus of their concern. 'An' quick too, or they will catch ye here.'

'I canna leave you here!'

'For God's sake, man, think of yourself! Think of the mischief they did to MacAllister!' Her voice begged him, sharp in its appeal. 'They could be here at any minute. Morag! Get yer father some oaten bannocks and a nubbin of cheese if we still have some. And bring him his heavy breeks and waistcoat. Quick now!'

She turned back to her man as Morag went to get him dry clothes. 'Gin ye be catched they will malagaroose ye like they did poor Sam. Maybe worse. I'd not put it past them!'

'Ye'll be thrown into the nicht, woman!'

'Aye, maybe so, and maybe no. But so have ithers afore me. Widows and bairns, without men to fend for them. We will fare no better nor worse than the rest. And besides, Morag's been telling me, we could go to Campbell's . . . He says he could do with mair labour.'

'I'll see,' he promised, his tone giving little weight to the idea. 'But forbye, how long will Campbell last? The way he's going?'

MacCaskill took the oat bannocks Morag had brought through, cramming them untidily into his mouth as he spoke. His other hand never for a moment relaxed his hold on the fork.

'Listen!' Martha MacCaskill's alarm brought them nervously alert. It was plain that flight for any of them was now

177

impossible; there was no doubt, from the approaching sounds of carousal, that men were coming the way of the croft house.

'Well,' Martha said, resigned to it, 'ye've lost yer chance, if you had one, MacCaskill.'

They waited, the laughter coming ever closer, the news of the men heich now, uncannily heich, bordering almost on the babblings of the demented, of dangerous simpletons. Above it, Douglass's shouts rose from time to time, uncharacteristically loud in their drunken authority. As they drew near, the light of their tarry flares threw a leery light into the ben end of the MacCaskill croft. The crofter man moved to the door, crouching behind it, his ear to the boards, listening. He turned to Morag.

'Ye say we can go tae Mossgair?'

'And welcome, Campbell says.'

'Tak' yer mither and grandfather there, lass.'

MacCaskill glanced at his daughter, her hair and een as dark as his own, seeing in her all the traits of himself, his own kind of loneliness. They had been strangers, one to the other. Maybe he had been too unbending, owre tied in his mind to the croft, too occupied with the brute facts of existence, of survival even. Maybe the struggle had stunted something in him, dried the juices of human response, stifled in him that ability to give and receive affection. Surely that was it? The croft life stunted the growth of men's souls as surely as it stilled the laughter in them. Och, to be sure, there were men whose spirits had retained their richness, men ready to laugh, to fill their lungs with the clear, cold air and give life a terse obscenity in riposte. MacGillivray was one, beyond doubt. Maybe that was the thing he had envied Andra most: his readiness whiles to spit in the eye of the gods and fart in the face of misfortune. Aye, MacGillivray had done that all right; he had liked him for it.

'So,' he smiled wanly, 'ye wad hae me gie up my freedom? Tae be what? A hired man?'

'Ye have nae freedom, man,' Martha spoke from the bed, chiding him gently. 'Nivver had.'

'I had a bit ground——' Smiling at the thought, a twist of the old reckless amusement shifting the corners of his mouth. Like the old days, Martha thought.

'That enslaved ye—as it did ithers afore ye.'

178

'Maybe it was a dream I had.' It seemed so now. He could examine his life with detachment.

'Aye,' Martha said dryly, softly. 'And they are damnably chancy, unsubstantial things.'

So that would be the way of it: memory and fealty would pass down and life would go on; the landscape would change but the contours of the soul would remain the same. Hope and dreams would pass down to the child unborn, absorbing even now in the womb-dark, a pattern and rhythm of life, that crofting sadness, a sense of injustice deep-grained. That much at least MacCaskill had bequeathed: that and a restless blood that time would dilute and diminish. . . . The seed of his young manhood bursting strong and free into the willing wetness of Martha Gibbons that soft summer night by the lochside had been but the thread of history. He understood that now. The thought lifted his heart, lightened his spirit. The heavy thunder of a fist on the door jarred his mind.

'Mistress MacCaskill?' It was Douglass, the thickness and uncertainty of drink discernible in his voice.

'Mistress MacCaskill? Ye'll have tae come oot. And Morag, gin she be wi' you. We are charged to teem the dwelling—the court's order of eviction, ye understand. But nae harm will be done ye.'

Douglass waited, his patience ebbing with the lack of a reply. 'Mistress MacCaskill——'

The sneck of the door was lifted lightly out the latch and the weight of a shoulder eased the door against the bolt. 'I will have tae ask ye to open the door Mistress MacCaskill or I will have to order it broken in.'

'Then let me tell you this, Douglass . . .' MacCaskill spoke close to a seam of the door-boards, 'the first man to come through it is in for a most painful surprise!' His words quietened, instantly, the high speak of the men outside. In the hush, a whispering was heard, a hurried consultation in which, although the words were inaudible, the tenor of their excitement was apparent.

'MacCaskill?' Douglass had advanced to the door again.

'Aye, Farquhar, it's me!'

The ground steward's steps withdrew again from outside the door, and again there was the sound of heated conversation in which the passion of the tones suggested violent disagreement. Douglass returned to the door, stood silent for a moment so close that the crofter man could hear his breathing on the other side of the boards.

'We think you should give yourself up, Jeemes.'

'Nae doubt.'

The voice, so close, made Douglass jump back from the door. When he continued a note of menace had entered his tone.

'There's enough of us to tak' care of you, MacCaskill, gin it come to it. Enough o's tae truss ye like a calf.'

'Nae doubt, Farquhar—just like ye took care o' MacAllister, eh?'

MacCaskill signalled to his daughter, his words now a whisper: 'Look frae the window. How many of them is there? Dinna lat them see you!'

Morag, her cheek pressed against the rough stone of the inside wall, looked out along the thin angle of vision towards the door. Her lips moved as she counted.

'Nine,' she whispered.

'Counting Douglass?'

'Counting Douglass,' she confirmed. 'He's forward by himself, just ootside the door.'

'And the others?' The crofter man's whisper was urgent.

'Back—well back. In a huddle thegither.'

'Douglass armed, can ye see? A stick? Staff? Onything?'

Morag shook her head. 'Nae that I see,' she said slowly. 'No I dinna think it.'

'Fine!' The crofter man chuckled.

'We could fire the roof owre ye head, MacCaskill, and be within oor rights,' Douglass said. The crofter wondered that it had taken him so long to think of it.

'Surely, ye could, Farquhar,' he said, speaking close and loud behind the door. 'Like ithers o' yer kind once did in Sutherland and Kildonan. And syne ye could add murder to all yer ither black deeds.' MacCaskill taunting him; cool now as he had been in that thin, thin line, waiting at Balaclava . . . 'Think you that Gregg, or even Hallerton himsel, will stand with you afore the judge in Aberdeen? It is damned unlikely, I'd say. Damned unlikely, Farquhar!'

'Yer forgetting, MacCaskill, that it is yourself that is agin the law.' But the ground steward's tone lacked conviction.

'And yer forgetting that my wife and my daughter hae nae crime to their name,' MacCaskill retorted.

'I ken that fine. But their safety maun be on yer ain heid. I canna answer for it.'

'Oh, but you can! And by God ye will . . .' MacCaskill said, allowing himself a burst of anger as he inched the bolt from its retaining staple, drawing it back slow, slow, holding his breath against the scrape of metal on metal that might betray him '. . . by God, you will, Douglass. You will——' The bolt, silently, finally, slid free. 'You will!'

If they had done nothing else, MacCaskill's furtive nights had sharpened his senses. In one swift, deft movement he flung open the door and with his free hand clutching the ground steward's waistcoat lapel swept the open-mouthed Douglass inside, slapping the door closed again and ramming home the bolt in its staple but an instant before the weight of two of his accomplices thudded against it. It was a damned close thing, and maybe none but a desperate and enraged man would have attempted it. All the same, the sheer audacity of it brought a gasp of delight from Morag as she watched Douglass flung sprawling on the floor.

'Noo look ye here, Jeemes——'

The surprised Douglass, when he had some collected his wits, started to pick himself off the floor and prepared to bluster, maybe even cajole.

'Bide ye still.' MacCaskill's command had a whiplash edge. The hayfork he had set against the wall was again in his hands and now one of its sharp shiny tines glinted against the ground steward's throat.

'Jeemes! Jeemes, for Christ's sake, man——'

'Wheesht!'

Douglass did as he was bidden, abject in his desire to comply.

'Back,' MacCaskill demanded. 'Lie on the floor.'

Douglass resisted momentarily, then thought better of it as the fork's tine indented the flesh of his neck and, unrelenting, forced him down till he lay on his back, spread-eagled.

'Think Jeemes,' he begged. 'This can dae ye nae good. What

good am I tae you?' There was terror now in the little man's een as they appealed in turn to Morag, then Martha.

'Stop him, lass . . .'

'Our bonnie bird is like to sing a different tune,' Martha said dryly.

'What good——' Douglass looked into the blank een of Martha MacCaskill and saw nothing there that could comfort him.

'Ye're my hostage, Farquhar,' the crofter said. 'Gin they burn the roof, then you can count on't: ye'll burn wi' the rest of us. Likewise, let me tell ye at once, were yer felon friends outside to make any sign of inviting themselves in, you will be a deid man, Farquhar. Deid! I promise ye! Gin I hang for it!'

It was raw rage born of the past days' strain that was sustaining MacCaskill now, rage and that savage bile of bitterness that had festered under his skin all these years, a blistering sore laid bare by the night's events. In Douglass he had not only a hostage but a scapegoat for all the injustices the men of the Hill crofts had endured not only at the ground steward's hands but from life itself. From Douglass's growing nervousness, it was evident that he believed him. Morag too now realized that the threat was real enough; that her father had been driven to the end of his tether.

There was commotion outside the door, some sign that the men beyond it, getting cold and restive in the chill air, were making preparation to break in. MacCaskill, keeping the fork still firmly against the ground steward's neck and one wary eye on his prisoner, half-turned his head to the door behind him, raising his voice.

'Listen, you oot there! And hae some heed for what I'm telling you. I have the tine of a fork resting on Douglass's jugular vein. Gin anybody sae much as breathes hard against that door, yer ground steward comes to a slow and bloody end. I'm warning ye!' MacCaskill rounded again on the prostrated Douglass, his tone quieter but laced with a menace that etched the words with crystal clarity. 'I wid say ye wid be well advised to tell them to give up any thocht they might have of rescuing you, Douglass.'

'Aye, aye.' Douglass gave the suggestion his anxious agreement, and MacCaskill withdrew the fork sufficiently to let the steward's adam's apple, dancing nervously in his neck like a ball on a string, the room it needed to function without injury. Even so, Douglass's fearful een never left the crofter man's face.

'It's true! It's richt what he says,' he shouted. 'For Christ's sake, Morgan, keep 'em back . . . Keep them back!' Terror welled in his appeal.

'Well back,' MacCaskill instructed.

'Well back!' Douglass shouted, spraying saliva over himself in his haste to have them comply.

'Away from the door——' MacCaskill demanded.

'Back from the door,' Douglass said, his words spilling out almost before the croft man himself had finished speaking.

MacCaskill nodded towards the window, a sign to Morag.

'They've moved awa', maybe a fifty feet or so.'

'All of them?'

'The whole drunken crew of them.'

'That's as weel, for oor friend's sake.'

'Get up.' MacCaskill turned back to Douglass, and, shortening his hold on the fork handle without easing it an inch from the little man's throat, drew him by the waistcoat lapel to the door.

'They're still back fae the door?'

'Aye.' Morag's look was puzzled as she watched her father edge Douglass to the door and feel behind him for the door bolt, shooting it suddenly free so that the door slapped back on its hinges and, in a continuation of the same movement, pinning Douglass savagely against the door jamb where his band of hooligans would see his predicament.

'Which of you is Morgan?' MacCaskill let the sharp tine of the fork dimple the ill-shaven skin under the ground steward's chin. The big man in the reefer jacket stepped forward, but without owning to the name.

'That's far enough—for Douglass's sake!' MacCaskill warned. The big man stopped.

'What I want . . .' the croft man gave him a quick, side-long glance, '. . . is safe convoy for my wife and father and daughter. You will let them go without hindrance. Gin it be otherwise— I'll warn ye noo—the tine of this fork will cut yer paymaster's

183

life in its prime. D'ye understand me?' MacCaskill let the fork's tine push dangerously deep into the ground steward's flesh.

'Perfectly. I understand ye,' the big man said; he seemed amused more than angered by Douglass's plight. 'But ye could get hanged for that,' he said, reasonably, in a manner that suggested it was a minor thing but that MacCaskill himself might possibly have overlooked it.

'Maybe I wouldnae much care,' MacCaskill answered. 'Syne I could watch him burn in Hell.'

'Ye're sure of his destination then?' The big man chuckled. 'Still, I would not say but you were right.'

'Well?' MacCaskill demanded. Was the big man buying time to think, to manoeuvre?

'They can leave whenever they're ready. They will not be hindered. Ye've my word. Yer conduct, I'm afraid, precludes me making yerself the same offer.'

MacCaskill nodded his head, indicating that he wanted the man to rejoin the ranks of his companions and the big man did so, melding again into the group.

'Morag, get yer mother and grandfather down to the Moss-gair.' MacCaskill's urgency underlined their precarious situation. 'And thank Campbell for his offer.'

'But yersel——'

'When I leave it will be in Douglass's protective company, have nae fear of it.'

'I will bide, MacCaskill,' Martha said.

'No, Wumman!' It was sharp, final, as though MacCaskill doubted his ability not to weaken in the face of further pleas. 'No!' And quietly. 'There is little time.'

'Maybe little for us both, I'm thinking, MacCaskill. For I feel it whiles.'

Black-shawled now, her thin figure swamped by the folds of a frock that had grown too large for her, she walked slowly toward him. By the door she paused to lay a hand gently on his shoulder. 'D'ye mind that summer, Jeemes? That summer by the lochanside?' It seemed for a moment that the light of amusement glinted in her een, that she was teasing him.

'Aye, I mind it,' he said quietly. No more than that, but Martha MacCaskill that had been Martha Gibbons smiled, a soft, secret smile to herself, to him, a silent winged recognition

184

between them that none could share. Her head nodded gently. Then she turned for the door and hirpled out to the night, a frail woman grown old before her time.

'Come ye, Morag. Yer arm. Grandfather . . .'

Soon they were swallowed in a grey roll of mist.

Hours it seemed now since the mist had taken them. MacCaskill stood, still, with the tine of the fork pocking the ground steward's neck, Douglass himself pale and frightened and not daring to speak for fear of what could befall him—drawing breath furtively, in case that alone should enrage the crofter man. The muscles in the ground steward's calves quivered, barely able to support him. Only terror kept him on his feet.

It was the man in the reefer who broke the long silence.

'Sooner or later ye will have to make up yer mind, Mac-Caskill, the one way or the other. If ye want my advice, it would be this: let Douglass go and come with us, quiet-like. We might be able to overlook the assault.'

'Gin I be in need of your advice I will speir for it,' MacCaskill said.

'All the same, I would take heed of it,' the big man replied, reasonably and without rancour. 'You're in no position to make conditions.'

'I hae Douglass.'

'To be sure,' the big man allowed, then added: 'But in that you have nothing, MacCaskill, for ye have only a pawn, hardly a principal. In fact, let me tell ye this, out of common kindness . . . It's the Hallertons and the Greggs of this world who drive the bargains. The likes of us, man, we bid for nothing. And as for yer prisoner . . .' he pointed to the cringing Douglass, 'like I was saying, he's a damned poor hostage. Live or die, I care little about it, for the truth of it is I care less about the wee bastard than maybe ye do yerself. So ye see, the end of this nicht is not the thing in doubt, only the time and the means of it. Stick yer fork in the wee man's throat gin it please ye, though ye've nothing to gain by it.'

'And damned little to lose!'

'Except yer life.'

'And after yer nicht's work, think you it will hae much value?'

'Ah-ha!' The big man's voice took on a new seriousness. 'There now, I would not attempt to advise ye. Ilka man has his ain measure of fulfilment, MacCaskill—that's as it should be.' He took two, three steps nearer, amiably and without menace.

'Ye're far enough!' MacCaskill warned.

The big man shrugged. 'As ye will . . . But ye've nothing to bargain with, MacCaskill. Not a damned thing! In fact, man, it is the tragedy of yer life that. That ye never had. That ye never will have. Life had ye by the ballocks from the day ye were born. It's as simple as that. Ye've nae assets, nothing negotiable. Nor Douglass either, gin it come to it. In fact, I would say he was a waur case, for he has deluded himself all these years, poor little bastard, that he was the master of his own destiny, that he was skilfully maintaining his balance on the tightrope atween the gentry and the croft folk, atween the idle rich and the indolent rabble.'

The big man sighed, his shrug eloquent.

'He is wrong about that though, hellishly wrong. Misguided, like so many. He is, whether he kens it or no', in that lonely no-man's-land atween the contempt of the one and the unconcern of the other. Look at him! Like a mitherless bairn! He will leave nae mark on life, unless it be a lingering odour— and his blood on your doorstep. He's no more nor a pimp for the land princelings, a procurer, and that not even in the purveyance of the sweet comfort of woman-flesh but in pursuit of the hollow tinkle of gold. Let him go, MacCaskill, he is worthless tae ye and his death would not be worthy of ye.'

The big man signalled with his arm, a sweeping gesture, the sign the men behind him had been waiting for. The group thinned into a semi-circle of grimy, pinched faces. 'Let him go,' the big man said, 'he's not our paymaster, just a pawn like I told ye.'

They came slowly, warily forward, encroaching stealthily upon the ground between them and MacCaskill, stealing a foot here, another there, keeping their een on the quarry they knew would bring them a bonus on that night's work. MacCaskill jabbed the fork-tine hard into Douglass's neck—dangerously hard, till the skin tightened like old elastic yet somehow remained unpunctured.

'Go on then.' The big man's tone lacked all concern. 'Stick

the bugger like a killing pig and be done with it. Good riddance at that!'

But he stayed the slowly advancing ring of figures that had now cut off all possibility of escape even if MacCaskill could have bartered with Douglass's life, something, he saw now, that was impossible. For the first time the spirit failed him, sapped by the cold, the wet of the clothes he had not had time to change, the hunger that had again become a deep pain in his gut. Terrifying, in a way he had not realized before, was the quiet menace of the faces, their blank and senseless vacancy.

'Go on,' the big man said, as if sensing his unspoken fear. 'This crew of cut-purses will watch murder as coolly as though it were but play-acting.' And then, feeling explanation necessary: 'There is something about the sea takes a man's wits from him, rubs the feelings out of him.'

He waited, and then, with another signal, allowed the net to close a little more.

'They are the scruff of the sea,' he said. It was a straight statement, without equivocation. Again his hand stayed the advancing faces. Silent, waiting, watching faces. 'I wid sooner ye come with us quiet-like, MacCaskill. That's my last offer to you, so make yer mind up. Ye've tae the count of ten. One . . . two . . .'

He watched the uncertainty, the indecision flit across the crofter's drawn face. He counted, unhurried. MacCaskill had not moved; the fork-tine remained at the ground steward's throat. But though the pressure it exerted had slackened, Douglass's terror had not.

'Haud yer hand, Morgan! Haud yer hand! For God's sake, man!'

The ground steward's voice was a plaintive, whining thing, issuing with difficulty from his nerve-contracted throat. His bowels threatened movement at any moment and against his will and it was only by the sternest discipline that he managed to control their trembling. So far had his control crumpled that he had also, and simultaneously, the desire to be sick and a compulsion—almost beyond all containment—to pass water. His een like a stricken spaniel's appealed to the reefered man: 'Wait! For God's sake, wait, Morgan——'

'Five.'

Finally the ground steward's nerves failed him; he could no longer make the wilful and deliberate anal contractions so necessary. The surprise lit his face briefly as consciousness slipped from him and he slid limply to the ground.

'Get him!' Morgan was too experienced to miss the chance.

His voice rapped its command and before the crofter man had time to gather his wits—even as he watched the senseless Douglass slip from his grasp—he was pinioned firmly by three pairs of arms. His strength, what was left of it, was no match against their brutal handling. As his futile struggles subsided, the big man pulled a flask from his inner pocket.

'Here, man. Sink this into your gut. It will make the taste of defeat less bitter.' He put the flask to MacCaskill's lips, holding it for him '. . . though in all conscience, man, ye have nothing with which to chide yerself. Yer only fault was to believe ye could stand alone. Nobody can.' He waited for MacCaskill to swallow and again put the flask to his lips.

'And yer other crime was to believe ye could tweak yer nose at the gentry.' A bitter, brittle smile of amusement lifted the corners of his mouth. 'Well, ye canna, and ye were a bloody fool to try it—though ye will have this consolation as ye lie cold in the Tolbooth: that ye may have brought nearer—by maybe a fraction of a second—the day when men can.'

The big man took a pull from the flask himself before ramming the cork back into its slim neck and pocketing it.

'We will take him down to Hallerton Hoose,' he said roughly, his brusqueness that of a man used to command and its responsibilities.

He watched MacCaskill's bent figure as he was marched away, a slender silhouette braced by the arms between the two tallest men of the gang and with the rest in attendance in front and behind him in a tight, watchful cordon.

'Wait!' His shout halted them, turning their faces in puzzlement as he stepped after them, searching the inside pockets of his reefer. 'I forgot tae give ye this—I've been looking for ye for three nights, Mister MacCaskill, to deliver it.' He stuffed the long buff envelope into the crofter man's side pocket. 'Yer writ of eviction, man.' There was a glint of wry amusement for a moment as his een met MacCaskill's. 'The law requires it.'

Low moaning behind him told him that the ground steward was regaining consciousness, and he walked back to where Douglass lay in the doorway. The ground steward's een had flicked open and now swivelled fearfully in his head.

The big man chuckled. 'Dinna excite yourself, man. Yer not in hell. Not yet anyway.' Their siege of the crofter man had, if anything, increased his intense loathing.

'Where's MacCaskill?' Douglass, glancing anxiously round him, straightened himself on tottery legs, clinging to the croft-house wall.

'We have him.'

Douglass's relief was audible. 'I will speak to Hallerton,' he promised. 'I'm sure he will see his way to——'

'Aye, just as ye wish.'

The ground steward tried a few steps out into the night and taking courage from that success, watched as the big man picked up a guttering flare abandoned on the ground and held it up for the wind to fan it again into flame.

'Fire the hoose!' Douglass's cry was near hysterical with hate.

'No,' the big man said bluntly. 'I've fulfilled my contract. Nae mair will I stand here and watch you dae it.'

'It'd be a warning to the likes of MacCaskill,' Douglass said. The thought pleased him.

'Me now . . .' the big man's voice was quiet, it was a thought spoken aloud rather than a reply. 'I'd say it was more likely to be a memorial to his martyrdom.'

Turning up his collar against the night air, he started after his captive with Douglass beside him. They walked in silence down the Croft Hill.

'I—— I hae to thank ye,' Douglass said, running to keep up with him, 'for saving my life.'

For a moment only, the big man shortened his stride to look down on Douglass. 'I didna,' he said quietly, 'I saved MacCaskill's.' Tomorrow, with daylight, he would return with his men to lift the crofter man's belongings and few sticks of furniture out at the dwelling door.

MacVie sat morose, desultory in his demolition of the syllabub, for he now kenned himself taken for a fool, manipulated by shrewder men and the victim of his own goodwill, which is always ill to bear. Indeed, dinner at Hallerton House that night had been miserable from the start, with MacVie not only immured in a brooding silence but by an unforgivable accident of seating sitting warty-nosed side to the mistress, thus equally out of humour. The Procurator-Fiscal had picked over his helping of pheasant as if he might yet find it guilty of some felony (or maybe saturated with arsenic) while the laird's own depression had deepened in proportion to the dosings of claret he had swilled down him. It was evident from the glaze of his een, if not from the slur of his voice, that he was no longer a candidate for enlightened conversation.

Poor beggars, Gregg thought them: the latter helpless in the matter of his own destiny, the legal worthy trapped as neat as you please, compromised completely. Neither of them with the stomach that leaders have need of, the mistress mused, noting with reluctant admiration Lander's remarkable appetite, the way his teeth had savaged mouthfuls of pheasant. He ate like a man with a hunger for life, a quiet smile on his face, but a hand's stretch under the table linen from her satined thigh. She herself dined sedately but in subdued mood, unable to hide her fury at the failure of the occasion. Her frustration had garred the cutlery ring on her plate.

'The pheasant was not much to your taste, Andrew?' she speired of MacVie, unable to keep the brittleness out of her tone.

The Procurator-Fiscal smiled weakly, apologetically. 'Ach, it is the stomach, the stomach. It is not as it was.'

No, she thought to herself, it was not. He had once tried a timid hand on her.

'A pity,' she said, and then, finding the barb irresistible. 'And me thinking, Andrew, that you were a man with a liking for all the fine things of life, a ripe bird among them.'

MacVie smiled again, sheepishly, recognizing the allusion. He seemed a poor Don Juan for all they said of him. She turned to James Grant, clerically intactus in Pringle's absence. 'And you, minister?'

'O-oh,' Grant stammered, discomfited by the surprise of the attack. 'Eh-excellent, to be sure.' He stabbed a loosely-held spoon into the syllabub and reddened with embarrassment as it sprang from his hand taking its contents with it to the floor.

'Leave it,' the mistress of Hallerton advised, and added with malice and a glance at the laird, 'Margaret can have the pleasure of cleaning it up and giving it to the dogs. They will appreciate it.'

She turned her gaze on young Gregg, her een smiling into his, a smile of complicity, savouring the direct, transparent delight with which he at least methodically cleared his plate. 'And what of you Lander?' Ill-bred upstart that he was, his appreciation was unsullied by the social sophistries.

'Truly superb,' he said, smiling broadly back at her but without letting his spoon pause in mid-air. His free hand slid on to her thigh.

'And the wine?' she cozened. 'A fine liaison, wouldn't you say?'

Gregg nodded anxious agreement, his heart and his mouth too full for the moment to give coherent reply. 'Almost——' he swallowed quickly. 'Almost, I would say, amounting to the ecstasy of misconduct.'

Glancing quickly again towards Hallerton's end of the table, she knew at once from his dulled look that his mind was too far into befuddlement to follow the drift of their conversation, and emboldened, and in gratitude for her body's excitement, she now bantered lightly:

'Is it your experience, Mister Gregg, that leads you to that comparison?'

'Alas——' The bold Lander blandly denied it, his smile one of self-mockery. 'It is an observation that I must make at second hand. For the truth of it,' he lied. 'I would have to refer you elsewhere.' He hesitated only for an instant, savouring their conspiracy: 'Maybe the Procurator will know?'

'What say you, Andrew?' Her gaze swung again with amusement to the unhappy face of MacVie (*the old ram: they said he battered his kitchen maid against the wall whenever he had a mind to and paid her a shilling for the privilege*).

'Eh, well——' Reluctantly, MacVie allowed himself to be inveigled. 'They say, don't they, that stolen kisses are aye the sweetest?'

The mistress twirled the stem of her claret glass, watched

the light spangle on the cuts of its crystal. 'I think, Andrew, what Mister Gregg has in mind is more than stolen kisses. My distinct impression is that he is suggesting a comparison with the carnal joys of a more unbridled passion.'

Talk ceased as Margit Taylor flitted deftly round the table with a phantom skill, clearing their places—and Grant's lost syllabub.

That silence continued, as though the lappering flames from the larch logs, spewing their dull, deadening heat into the room, had suddenly stifled thought and speech and concentration; a silence in which the mistress of Hallerton savoured the sensual abrasion of crisp under-linen on a thigh she had allowed Gregg to slacken to a languorous lassitude: a silence in which Hallerton himself slipped suddenly into the stupor of a drunken sleep so that Margit again had to be rung for.

No apology was given; none, it seemed, was expected in that night of unease in that house of shuttered silence; eerie, MacVie thought it, as distant doors opened and shut on their invisible occupants, like the doors of the cells in an asylum he once had visited (or the doors of Hell that now he dreaded), and distant footfalls hurried on mysterious errands. They heightened his nervousness, his guilt. Now, in a pique of conscience he had taken vigil with his glass at the window, staring sourly into the deepening dusk.

His cry drew Gregg quickly to his side, his gaze following the pointing finger to the shadows of the tall beeches that tossed in the wind at the end of the wide Hallerton lawn.

'Where, man?'

'Th-there, there . . . Alow the beeches. Co-coming out from under them now!'

Gregg's een separated substance from the shadow and saw now the huddled group of men emerging from under the trees, their halting progress explained by the struggling figure at their centre: a tall man, bonnetless, and, as he came out from the rim of dark shed by the trees, seemingly badly dishevelled.

'Ye have visitors!' MacVie said, turning to his hostess.

'At this hour of the night?' The mistress of Hallerton's thigh mourned the loss of the importunate young Lander's hand with regret.

'I doubt it's a social visit,' MacVie said, taking a malicious enjoyment from the moment. 'More like a deputation, I'd say.'

His tone drew her quickly to Gregg's side, at the window. 'It's Farquhar Douglass, your ground officer,' he said.

'What can be his errand?' Her een sought Gregg's, and the lawyer's smile at once quieted her concern. 'He is acting, gin I be not mistaken, as escort to the man we have been scouring the country for.'

'MacCaskill?'

'None ither.'

The Procurator-Fiscal drew back from the window as the raggle-taggle group passed it, a thin glaze of speculation hazing his een. 'I would not say ye were wrong, Gregg,' he said cautiously. 'But *why* in God's name? The man could have been miles away by now!'

'No, not MacCaskill.' Gregg was serious now, quiet in his conviction. 'His kind are trapped aye by their own loyalties. Some folk would say even strangled by them.'

'Ah well, maybe there are worse cr-crimes?'

'But hardly stupider ones.' Gregg's anger surprised even himself. He felt disconcerted by it, unable to say why.

'There are men that canna betray their class, Lander.' The Procurator's wily barb stung.

'They need the comfort of the herd.' The mistress's tone was icy. 'And you are forgetting, surely, the two of you, that this man has defied the law. He is an agitator. I'd have thought that you, Andrew, would have been more jealous of the duties society has conferred on you.'

'And you, Ma'am,' MacVie lashed back, 'more careful about creating martyrs!'

It was an old anger that flared between them then; private and deep, a resentment in him that she used him like a pawn in the affairs of the Hallerton estate; in her, a residual scorn that in all the years he had been a guest at her table he had not thought her worth cozening into a convenient bed—had preferred, instead, to cup his hands round the dowps of his common kitchen maids.

'You are forgetting, surely Andrew, the events of this very decade in Paris——'

'The Communards?'

'The city reduced to terror, the Louvre all but destroyed by fire, the poor Archbishop shot . . . The revolutionaries even holding concerts in the Tuileries gardens——'

'They had the decency, I hear, to play Mozart,' MacVie said waspishly, 'though for the life of me, I canna see the connection you're driving at—MacCaskill's hardly a revolutionary!' In all truth, the Procurator-Fiscal was sickened by the entire business, sickened, too, at MacCaskill (as well as for him) that he had not had the good sense to put distance between him and the men whose duty it was to evict him. The arrest of a man for flouting the law was one thing; hounding folk from their homes, quite another.

'I'd like to see him,' she said suddenly, leaving them all flabbergasted by the suddenness of her decision. 'Have them bring him in.'

'But——' Lander Gregg glanced urgently to his adversary for support and MacVie in turn, intercepting his startled, disbelieving stare, protested: 'I would advise you most strongly against it. I'm sure James, gin he were here, would say with me.'

'I'm sure he would Andrew, but since he's not and since he is hardly this moment in a condition to handle his own affairs, I feel that that responsibility devolves to me. Will you have him brought in? Or will I be forced into the night to look at him?'

The Procurator made little effort to hide his displeasure. He shrugged his defeat. 'Gin it please you . . . Gin it please you.'

So they faced each other, in the gilded splendour of the Hallerton's dining room: the Big House's fine lady and the evicted crofter. She minded him now: an unbending figure on the kirk road, his bonnet lifting as she passed in the high Hallerton gig, but out of politeness never servility, his gaze cool across the gulf of their separated lives. Even now, she saw, his black-ringed een showed no humility, were unnerving in their cool intensity. He had been brought into the room behind MacVie, escorted uncomfortably by Douglass, some recovered from his experience, and held by the big man in the reefer.

'You're a fool, MacCaskill!' Her tone was shrill, betraying the nervousness he stirred in her.

The crofter man was silent.

'A fool.'

His continued silence angered her for she knew it for contempt of her kind. She had a sudden desire to hurt and humiliate him—to physically brawl with him. 'Your kind are dangerous—dangerous to the society we live in MacCaskill, forever nibbling at its established structures, whittling away the fabric, undermining it—— Like the sewer rats that work below the foundations of our cathedrals. Society needs protection against your kind—— If I be not sorely mistaken you will be wearing prison hoddy for the next twelve-month and breaking stones.'

She swung round to MacVie. 'What will his sentence be, Andrew?'

'You will be charged, MacCaskill, on Douglass's testimony.' MacVie addressed the crofter directly and not unkindly. 'From what I've already heard, likely with assault and breach of the peace in resisting lawful eviction.'

'And the sentence, Andrew? The sentence?'

The mistress was beside herself.

'He has first to be found guilty.'

'Surely you cannot be in doubt of it?'

'The burden of proof must sustain it. It is nae for me to anticipate the court's proceedings,' MacVie said, coolly rebellious, defying his hostess who now swung sharply back on MacCaskill, making no attempt to conceal her hatred.

'You'll have this comfort in the Tolbooth, MacCaskill,' she said tauntingly. 'You will be getting no writs of removal in there. It will make a fine story in the newssheets: an elder of the Free Kirk arraigned as a common rabble-rouser. I must say, I fail completely to see what you're to gain by it!'

The coolness of the crofter's dark, penetrating gaze humiliated her.

'What will he get, Andrew?' His hostess's voice was strident.

'A chance to speak, if nothing else,' said MacVie. The Procurator's voice was dismal.

You would mind on that night for all of your days. Telling me of it, you drew your shawl about you Old Woman, as though feeling still the chill and anger of that time, all the ill-will there had been: your father taken like a common thief to the Big Hoose to be mauled by her ladyship's tongue and you not knowing it till Margit Taylor had sneaked away to come late to Mossgair to tell you. It was kind of her that. Bitter you felt that men should have so little regard one for the other: what was it that drove them? You thanked Margit—poor Margit that let the laird into her bed it was said and was trapped atween her twa worlds, in flight whiles from one and then the other. Hardly a soul but spoke ill of her: a harlot they said that took the laird's guinea (*Weel, weel, it'll aye help tae keep her auld mither*) but you had known, sad and weary like yourself, she had done no more than love a man, not able to help it.

So there, in the grey hours of morning in the old Campbell kitchen you had sat the two of you to drink tea and you saw the tired lines of her face and the greying streaks in her thick black hair that had brushed and warmed Hallerton's cheek and brought him a kind of comfort he had not known. It was not himself, she told you, even now in her misery begging forgiveness for him. *It is that bitch herself, that was never a mistress to the hoose nor a wife to her man. And the likes of Gregg that helps her. Himself is but a helpless breet, hardly kenning noo what's happening.* Fine you liked her, the two of you cowered over the peats while they began to throw out their warmth on a new day, two souls that the world and men had soiled, your mother and grandfather asleep in the attics and Campbell asleep God knows where for he had not come home, lying snug in some ditch like as not . . . *You will bide on?* you had speired, aware of her terrible dilemma. *When he leaves for the South?* Her een hazed with hurt had looked deep into the woman's heart of you. *Wi' Gurney? I s'pose so, gin I be speired tae stay.* And syne, kenning clear that you knew, or maybe wanting just for once to acknowledge what she had hidden all those years: *He would take me wi' him, I ken, gin I asked. And I'd gang with him but . . .* In the rosy glow of the peats a tear crept on to her cheek and ran slow to the trembling edge of her mouth . . . *it's my mither, ye see. I have her to think on.*

Aye, you had said, quiet and still the two of you as the day began to break owre the parks.

★

The manse quill poised hesitantly over the vellum of Pringle's daybook, and when it began to write, it was with a languid, desultory grace that reflected the writer's inner melancholy. For once Patrick's hand seemed unwilling to do his bidding, recording without relish an entry that had to be made, a thing that had to be said. The quill trembled slightly, reflecting his anguish. He wrote sporadically, marooned for long moments in bitter introspection.

June 1, 1880.
Saw this morning from my study window a sight I had never thought to see: the figure of my most senior and respected elder, a pillar of the community and a man with a fine war record in the Crimea, led out cuffed like a common miscreant from the inn and put into the Aberdeen carter's gig under escort of a constable from Alford. It is said he will be charged with the assault of Hallerton's ground officer the-streen in resisting eviction from the croft dwelling that has been his home these last forty years. The croft bigging of his youth is this nicht empty for the first time since his father biggit it, clogging cold clay with rubble stones for its walls and roofing it with heather. This nicht there is no smoke from its thatch, no fire in its hearth where the peat was reisted from one day to the next, no glimmer of licht in its small square window pane. This morning almost ere daylicht was upon us it was repossessed for the estate by strangers—men brought from outwith the parish boundaries, men without fealty here—and his family's belongings set out at the door in a careless pile. In its quiet this nicht the house is neither better nor waur nor the many others that stand now so empty of folk, for the Croft Hill this month or two bypast has shed its people, those lives that had dominion there. It is become a desolate place that was once for its folk a fresh beginning. That James MacCaskill is guilty as they say of the crime laid against him I would not doubt. In committing it he broke the law, maybe in the greater cause of exposing injustice, who can say, for he is become a dour man that keeps his own counsel. But that he should have been driven to such straits lies at the door of society and the greed of men. It is an ill thing that sets one man against his

neighbour and the laird against his tenant. The heart is heavy that it is so.

So that was the way of it, Old Woman: with the morning licht the man with the reefer jacket and his unsavoury crew returned to the Hill to set your family's possessions out to the open air, a cluttered mass that mixed furnishing and crofting gear, the dresser plates with the dung graip from the byre, the beasts led out and tethered where they could get a bite of grass by the big man himself (a strange kindness that, you thought, as you watched from Mossgair). Out at the door they set all the worldly possessions of the MacCaskills, collected and cherished over the generations, the trivia of a lifetime, last of all the Bible that your father had read to you every Sabbath nicht wet or fair and sometimes between-times. Thrown open on top of the heap, its pages riffled in the wind, verse and chapter sought by restless, flurrying fingers. It had been your home that old bigging where the smell of the beasts in the abutting byre had regularly filtered through the wall into the ben-end. It had been your home, the centre of your life . . .

Late on in the afternoon, maybe moved by pity or by compassion for the lass who now ran his house, old Campbell rose out of his stupor by the fire and ordered Chae Skene home from the neep-sowing (late, late though they were) to yoke his pair into their carts and bring your gear down to the barn at Mossgair. You thankit him for that, for a kindness unexpected that could do him no good in the factor's een but Campbell, sober at his supper, smoored all further gratitude with an authoritarian wave of his hand.

Nonsense, lassie! It will be fine in there gin it come weet as it may. We will throw a cover owre't tae haud oot the worst o' the thrashing stew and not a thing will come owre't. And gin yer time come . . . for by now the burden of your belly could be no longer hidden even by the voluminous folds of your grey wincey frock . . . *Gin yer time come, ye'll hae the bairn here and maybe yer mither will fa' tae wi' the housewark till ye're weel again.*

I'm sure she will be pleased to, Mister Campbell, you had said, *And she will milk the kye forbye till I'm able.*

Then what mair need we say, lass. There was no censure in his een, only the question he had long wanted to speir. *It will* be *Carmichael's bairn?* Colour swept your cheeks, hot and bewildering. But for his unexpected kindness you could have brazened it out uncaring.

Aye, Mister Campbell, it is Ewan's.

God rest him.

He'd hae marriet me——

I'm sure, lass, for I nivver saw twa folk sae taken up, ane with the tither. He nodded, as though wondering even now at the strange forces that propelled folk through life. *He was Campbell blood, ye ken.* He stirred the cream carefully into his kail brose, looking up at her. *It will mebbe be a laddie.*

Aye, Mister Campbell . . . Blithely you spoke of it now. *Aye, it might be. It would be fine gin't were.*

Aye. Campbell nodded solemnly. *It would be fine.*

That night, in Aberdeen, as the douce townsfolk slept, Lander Gregg turned late down a side vennel and was immediately swallowed in its dark. Worsened with drink though he was, the unfaltering ring of his footsteps on the causey stones betokened an old familiarity, and he paused presently in the deepened dark by a door that gave no chink of light to passing feet, knocked, and in a moment was answered from within.

'Wha is it at this hour o' the nicht? This is a respectable tavern. Gang ye hame tae yer wife like decent folk.'

'It's Lander Gregg.'

'By yersel?'

'As far's I can tell, though in truth it's sae damned dark out here that for all I ken Auld Nick himsel micht be standing at my elbow.'

'Wait!'

Behind the door Gregg heard his interrogator shuffle away to return accompanied by a lighter step. The voice now was a woman's and Gregg recognized it.

'Gregg?'

'Aye, Ma. Are ye letting me in, or am I tae die of double pneumonia oot here?'

Muttering behind the door was followed by the sound of bolts slipping quietly from their sockets. Well-oiled hinges gave not a squeak to betray his admittance as he stepped in from the cold of the smelly vennel to the fetid warmth of Ma

Gordon's howff and swept Ma's ample shoulders into a good-humoured embrace.

'Ye've been drinking, Lander,' she upbraided, ill-pleased with his appearance so late. 'And forbye, it's awa' beyond midnicht. What brings ye at siccan an hour?'

'I was wondering if maybe my good friend the mate of *The Falcon* micht be with ye?'

'And always supposing he is, what business is't of yours?'

'Ye would oblige me, Ma, by telling him I'd like a word with him.'

'This is a decent house, Lander, I nivver interrupt——'

'Which one?'

'The negress, gin ye wish to ken.'

Gregg smiled. 'Ah—— How long?'

'This past hour or mair.'

'Then his account must surely be rendered, eh?' The jovial Gregg cozened a smile to the landlady's face. Yet still she demurred.

'The man is awa' tae sea these next twa months, he was telling me,' she protested, her humour restored.

'All the same, Ma, *please* will ye speir at him will he be long?'

'Gin it please ye, Lander.' Ma Gordon shrugged, resigned to his request, to the breaking of her house rule. 'I'll see,' she said, leaving him.

'Gin ye would,' Gregg encouraged, 'and when ye come back we will broach atween us a bottle of yer most excellent Bordeaux.' He settled himself at a table beside the ingle-neuk, where a hanging paraffin lamp threw down on him the soft beneficence of its yellow light, enjoying its oily odour and its guttering shadows after the frosty crystal and gleaming brass of Hallerton House. He was, he reasoned with that equable ease that comes when drink has dulled the stings of even the mildest self-criticism, a most fortunate man, able to move without embarrassment through the whole spectrum of society, as much at home in the drawing-room as in a whorehouse. A classless man without allegiance, a man hamstrung by no loyalties.

The landlady's return broke his reverie of self-adulation.

'I telt him ye wis here.'

'What said he?'

'That his account has been settled——'

'Ah, well——'

Ma Gordon silenced him with an admonitory finger. 'But that he was much in arrears.'

'But he can spare me a minute, surely?'

'I doubt it. He was, he bade me tell you, putting to sea again directly.'

'The dog, he is!' Gregg shook his head in disbelief, convulsing with laughter. 'Then bring ye the Bordeaux, Ma, and twa glasses and we will toast the mate soon into a quieter harbour.'

Ma Gordon did as she was bidden for Gregg, she knew, was by way of being an important man in some quarters of the town, and while she cared little about losing his custom she was not anxious to gain his ill-will. She brought a bottle and the glasses, and before long, the seaman's appearance allowed her to excuse herself. Bringing a fresh glass for the mate, she left the two men to have out their speak.

Gregg filled his companion's glass. 'I hear that *The Falcon* is near ready to take the tide.'

'Twa nights from now.' The big man nodded his agreement.

Gregg might have said more but was discouraged from further banter by the mate's dour countenance. A touchy devil, to be sure, he thought, raising his glass.

'Well, I have this to say: the laird of Hallerton, like myself, is beholden to ye.'

'Just so, Mister Gregg. There will be tangible tokens nae doubt.' The mate allowed himself a tight, sour smile.

'You are damnably direct, man,' Gregg said, discomfited by the seaman's bluntness. 'But there will be, as you say.'

'There is not much time for sophistry on the sea, Mister Gregg.'

'I suppose not.' Gregg shrugged, accepting it. 'Well, tangible tokens—indeed, indeed. The purpose of my errand here this nicht is none ither.'

Gregg looked expectantly at the seaman over the rim of his glass. 'There will be a purse of fifty sovereigns waiting ye tomorrow morning at my office in Bridge Street.'

'As agreed,' the mate said, reducing at once Lander's bag of swagman's gold to payment for services rendered. 'A small enough fee for selling men into slavery.'

'As agreed.' Gregg was unable to hide his disappointment with a man who took silver with so little enthusiasm. It was time he was home.

'Well,' he rose, hand outstretched. 'I will bid ye a safe voyage.'

'Wish me and the poor bastards I carry with me a fair wind.' The big man rose, taking the lawyer's hand.

'One thing I forgot,' Gregg paused on his way to the door. 'When ye call at my office tomorrow ye can pick up a smaller, special purse, a ten extra sovereigns, addressed to Morgan Keller—if that be your name?'

The big man smiled, buttoning his reefer.

'It will do, Mister Gregg. I hae mony names.'

Campbell's good foot slid on the wet ground, sending him slithering. It was near to morning and had come on to rain, a steady drizzle that fell softly on to his face refreshing him, some clearing his senses but steadily dampening his clothes. He lay where he fell, all desire to move again stilled. Fine and comforting just to lie there, to lie and let it end there; he detected in himself no regrets. He no longer felt his limbs. They had been numbed long since into utter exhaustion like the pain in his heart—his, certainly, but somehow unable to respond to his will, extremities away and beyond the immediate focus of his semi-consciousness. For an instant in the grey light his een drew into vision the low, jagged spur of a gorse-bush beside his head and his brain marvelled at the perfect, jewelled clarity of the raindrops on it, their symmetrical precision, their distance one from the other and their equal proportion a work beyond human accomplishment. Beyond them, as far as his vision extended, was brown, wind-blasted grass, a featureless waste, an endless world stretching to a grey infinity, an unknowable dimension without pain, a nothingness comforting and sucking him into a deeper oblivion.

He felt sleep overtaking him, let his head sag on to the hill grass and allowed it to lie there, smiling slightly. Slowly, the drizzle started silting up his vision, narrowing the aperture of recognition till, so it seemed to him, he looked down a long clear tunnel whose diameter diminished as he watched. At its centre, blurred in a spectral mist but recognizable now on the retina of the mind was something that intrigued him: a grey-slated house with tall windows in the far, far distance, and, in their protective quadrangle, the traditional structures of barn and byre. Its shape and outline nagged at him, reawakening bewilderment, engaging the memory, etching an irritation on the membranes of the mind; restoring consciousness and will. Slowly, methodically, he sifted the memories, sorting shape and circumstance, without sequence, jumping from boyhood to young manhood, to his own farming years in a fleeting stream of impressions that barely crystallized before floating away in the mists enfolding him. The effort was taking him again to the very edge of unconsciousness, but he persisted; tantalizing him, the answer swam behind the veil of immediate recollection. Then, with a triumph that drew from him a low moan of delight, his mind catalogued the image: Mossgair! It was Mossgair!

So close and so far.

Its location and significance lingered for a moment longer on the frayed edges of memory, then haphazardly, piecemeal, in spiky unrelated succession, knowledge began to accrue and agglomerate, each ingot inviting the next:

The Campbell place . . . Poor Angus Campbell, a frail man among even frailer mortals, born fatally without the landsman's power to subdue intractable nature and breathe in her heartbeats. A man who tilled parks should stride like a conquerer: Angus Campbell had been condemned to hirple like a crone over his acres—a man with a staff, forever at odds with the landscape in which he moved, broken even before he was born . . .

On such slender scaffolding, his mind began now to erect more substantial planks of introspection: more than most he'd had a need of laughter and been denied it, the need of some strong single, solitary attachment to another human soul as a kind of consolation for the failure in himself. There had been none.

Even at that distance, as his vision sharpened, Campbell could discern the Mossgair's air of decay. Let it stand, he thought, cavalier in his impatience, as a monument to the Campbells, the whole damned race of them, from his Campbell great-grandfather who had builded its first crude steading with his own hands: little more had it been than a rickle of stones cemented by gour and cold clay.

But now, too, there flowed back into Campbell's memory the bitter recollection of where he was, a sudden clarified understanding of why he was lying there. He was in a shallow gully far out on the hillside, and lifting his head saw its lip a few feet above him. Summoning every reserve of will, every ounce of strength left in him, he watched the outspread fingers on a hand close and clench round a tussock of grass. Simultaneously, he dragged a leg, made seemingly of lead, up under him and gouging earth with his boot-heel, drew himself upwards.

Time passed, and was endless; time flew, evaporating from him with a terrifying swiftness. He inched his way to the rim of the gully with a single-mindedness that excluded all other thoughts: the drenching rain, the remembered faces of the past. Such remembrance debilitated his will, and sapped his physical strength, what was left of it . . .

Slowly, as he watched, the tussock rent its root from the rim of the ditch. He slid slowly backwards. He watched dispassionately, shuddering a little as the slime of the gully's bed inched and rose between his spread fingers, covering them slowly. There was no pain now, only a lightening of the spirit, a light-heartedness. It was fitting it should be so: all his life he had been alone . . .

It was two days before they found him so far out on the Hill; before his low moans drew a truant schoolbairn to the ditch in which he lay. Terrified, the bairn ran owre the fields for his father and Campbell was carried home to the Mossgair and laid into the bed in which he had been born.

He never rose again.

He lingered through the first nicht, rallied with the morning licht and spoke muddled about the ploughing needing to be done before sinking again into a dwan broken by bouts of translucent consciousness in which he castigated the government for the falling price of oats and brought a blush of black burning shame to the cheek of Chae Skene's wife, come to nurse him, by trying to cajole her into his bed.

Doctor Munro came—and came out to the close, shaking

his head. Pringle came, too, to sit by the bedside. And the rhythm of the work dachled at Mossgair while a Campbell cousin was sent for to the Drum of Wartle, and came, a great gurly gurk of a cheil ill-suited to his fine sark and his Sabbath breeks. Ill at ease he was in both, and damned ill-humoured he was too at old Campbell for choosing the time of the neep-hyowing to quit.

So the men of the howe, of the village, and the lonely farmtouns and the few crofts that remained took an afternoon off from the on-ding of that summer's work to take Campbell to meet his implacable God, all differences forgotten in death. They came down to the Gair in their black jackets and their bell-bottomed breeks, their necks hankit stiff in their Sabbath collars. Sorry they were that Campbell had died. Sorry, too, in themselves that they had not liked him more but honest enough not to repent it. So it had been; so it would be. They stood quietly round the door of the Mossgair house, doffing their cloth bonnets as the coffin appeared, carried in front by John Lorimer and the Campbell cousin, at the rear by Banker MacFarquhar and Hillhead, and set out behind it, slow-stepping men, down to the lochside. They took stock of the work, behindhand as it was, and the portents for harvest.

Now and then a man would go forward to put his shoulder under the coffin and give one of the bearers a rest. Only John Lorimer brushed their offers aside, impatience in the wave of his hand as he set the pace, calm and unhurried.

From the small gable window of the Mossgair kitchen Morag watched the cortège, a caterpillar of black-coated men wending ben through the howe to the kirkyard, passing into the after noon dark under the yew trees. . . . Away to the south, where the Grampians lurked in the blue-distanced haze of a clear day, angry clouds had begun to pile in the sky.

'There's a storm coming,' she said without turning.

'Tchech, tchech!' Grandfather MacCaskill stirred himself by the fire. His blood was cold; he wanted to warm it.

'Tchech, tchech. It's been threatening for days . . . Been threatening for days.' He turned back to the fire, seeking reassuring warmth for his bones.

Morag stood still by the window. If he had died, she thought, I'd have had a grave to go to. I'd have gone to put flowers on it, taken his bairn to see it maybe. . . . Madness it was to be thinking so, of all the dreams you'd once had. . . . She turned back to her house chores, changing the blankets and linen of the box-bed in which Campbell had lain and knew that the time was come for herself to lie into it.

Doctor Munro, in folded shirt sleeves and embroidered waistcoat, pulled the blankets up from the bottom of the bed where they had lain throughout his examination. He smiled down at Morag's white face.

'Not yet, lass—but soon,' he promised.

His gaze was not unkindly; it held no condemnation and for that she was grateful. His face, she noted, was strangely unweathered, smooth and pale, unlike the farmtoun men's. His een though twinkled with an earthy amusement.

'As ye sow, lass, so shall ye reap . . . We'll deliver it the way that ye got it, eh?'

'Aye.' She flushed red, nodding her understanding. It was an ill-like speak from a doctor, she thought, to a lass like herself.

'Rest a little now—till it come time.' There was a comfort in him that reassured her.

Munro, turning away, checked his watch with the mantel clock, soughed a tune low, low, below his breath and wandered over to the kitchen's window. Beyond the panes, the midsummer evening was dissolving into a liquid lilac dusk. The breeze that had fanned in the faces of Hector and himself had died; a peace had fallen on the countryside, the beasts in the parks quiet and still. They lay chewing rhythmic cuds, their contentment begetting beef. His mind brooded reflectively: so maybe, in the end of the day—at the centre of creation—there existed such a core of peace, somewhere in the pattern, a reason. It was not a week since he had closed Campbell's een on the world for the last time; now from the same bed, he waited for the curtain to rise on new life, a bastard bairn denied a name by the caprice of fate . . . He had speired the father and finally, ill-willing, she had told him. Was life as simple as that, he wondered: a timetable scheduled by some heavenly stationmaster, our destinations and diversions already determined? Along the howe where his gaze lingered, he watched the schoolhouse light blink out behind its screening trees, abruptly snapping the thread of reflection. A stoon of tenderness tingled through him, a warmth for the thing that had entered his lonely clinical life.

Behind him, Mistress Wilson, uplifted in his bygoing from the toun of Kingsmyre, filled the kitchen with her presence. Like himself, she kept vigil with birth and death, midwife and layer-out-of-the-dead, and seemed remarkably undisturbed by it. A dominating woman, she bustled about now, washing the kitchen table-top, laying out sheets and towels, a tin wash-basin with soap and towel; kettles and pots of water boiled and hottered on bink and swey-hook above the peats. Methodically, Munro's gaze checked and double-checked her preparations as he marvelled yet again at her unfailing efficiency. At the table's end he swilled his hands in the basin of warm water she had provided, laving them carefully through the water as she watched: bonnie delicate hands for a man she thought them, smooth on your dowp.

'Nae complications, Doctor?' Her concern was professionally sotto voce; they were, after all, the two of them actors in life's most sacred drama, its most magical and primitive moment.

'None, Jess—she's young and healthy. At that age nature does her own work. You'll be back into your own bed by three o'clock at the latest.'

'Time for a wink o' sleep afore the milking, eh?' She was a sonsie wife with massive thighs and a sweet rounded face.

'I'd wager on it.'

'Will ye hae tea, Doctor?'

'That would be fine, Jess. What, by the way, have you done with the lass's mither and old grandfather?'

'Packed them ben to the ben-end and warned them weel tac stay there.'

'Oh——' Munro nodded, letting out a low chuckle. It never ceased to amaze him the audacity with which John Wilson's wife ordered folk out of their own kitchens—out of their hoose, gin need be—to give him freedom to do the job he had been summoned for. Waiting for his tea, he quietly unpacked his instruments from the battered black bag he took everywhere with him and laid them out along the edge of the table.

'Doctor——' The voice, diffident from the bed, held a panicky urgency. 'Doctor——'

'I'm here, lass.' He was at the bedside in an instant, coolly appraising.

'I think maybe——' The dark een, widened with bewilderment, beseeched him and simultaneously drew comfort from his smile.

'You're not going to let me have my tea, then?'

'I'm sorry, I——' The pains cut her breath.

'Easy, lass. Easy!' Munro wiped her glistening forehead and pulled down the blankets, nodding to his helper. 'Light, Jess. Please.'

'Aye, Doctor.' For her size Jess Wilson had more speed than you might have supposed. She disappeared through the kitchen door to reappear in an instant with a large paraffin lamp already lit and glowing brightly behind its opaque glass bowl.

Munro's eyes lit with approval, with admiration even. 'Splendid, Jess!' He glanced up for a moment, the question on his lips already redundant.

'From the ben end. I've had my eye on it since ivver I came in, in case we should have need of it.'

'And we have!' Munro affirmed strongly. Below his breath he cursed the awkwardness of his situation and the shadowed dark of box-beds, the imbecility of a nation so devoted to them that all birth was left-handed, and, as the need became apparent not for the first time in his medical career for him to clamber on to it on his knees, the necessity for its country physicians to be part-time mountaineers.

'Push, lass!' It was brutal command.

'Aye, dae whit the Doctor says. Dinna haud back, Morag.' Holding the lamp aloft to let Munro see his work, Jess Wilson wiped the crofter's daughter's brow. 'Push now!'

'Aye.' Morag nodded, gasping deeply, urgently between the contractions that rent her, one following fast in the wake of the other, the pain now limitless, a blurring moil of bruising, tearing turmoil in her body that took her to the teetering edge of unconsciousness and in its faintly relenting moments allowed her, just, to regird herself against it. Finally, a cry, half-sob, half-rage, burst from her . . .

'Push hard, lass!' Munro's voice was sharp and unheeding in its stridency.

'Birss!' Jess Wilson's as urgent.

In her anger, her mind thrust hatred at the pair of her tormentors—and felt her tortured body slacken as its burden began to slip from her. Kneeling patiently on the bed, Munro took the baby's head in his hands and waited for nature . . .

Munro, laving his hands gently in the soapy water, hardly heard the knock at the kitchen's inner door. It came again, timidly, aware of its intrusion. Jess Wilson, washing Morag's face, read the irritation in the doctor's gaze.

'Martha MacCaskill likely,' she said quickly.

'God, yes—I'd forgotten,' Munro sighed, shrugging off tiredness. 'Let her in.'

'Come ben, Martha.'

The door opened tentatively, a fear in its hesitancy, and Munro looked into the worry of the croft wife's weather-lined face. He noted the tired een, the listless grey of her hair and saw what the last months had done to her; how her man's arrest had affected her.

'She's a' richt, Doctor?'

'Right as rain, Mistress MacCaskill. As fine a delivery as ever I've seen. No problems. Both well.'

'And the bairnie?'

The sacredness of life he thought transcended all commandments. 'A boy, Mistress MacCaskill.'

'An' weel?' her voice was anxious.

'As I said: a fine sturdy specimen.'

'A fine loon, Martha,' Jess Wilson's friendly brogue confirmed, in sisterly feeling for this woman whom life had lately used so ill. 'Come see for yersel!'

She guided the older woman to the bed and for a moment Martha MacCaskill looked down on the two heads pillowed there.

'Godbethankit!' The tears trickled on her cheeks, hot and uncontrolled as Munro packed his bag, pretending preoccupation and prolonging the task.

'She has the milk, Mistress MacCaskill,' he said finally, brusquely. 'See that she feeds the child correctly, won't you?' His bag snapped shut.

'Aye, Doctor. I will.' The crofter's wife dried her tears with the corner of her apron. 'I will that.'

'Get it tae sook,' Jess Wilson said. 'Gin it dinna be like tae, come for me.'

Munro shrugged into his coat. 'And keep her to her bed. I'll be back some time tomorrow.'

'Aye, Doctor.'

He walked over to the bed where Morag drifted already on the verge of sleep. 'I hope,' he said smiling, 'it will be the first of many.' Then, turning to his midwife, 'If you're ready, Jess, I'll drop you home.'

Outside they found a night soft as velvet, balmy and still. Gallantly in the half-dark Hector took the road in a canter, his hooves ringing through the still air.

'Another son for the soil, eh Doctor?' Jess's voice as always was bright despite the hour.

Munro was thoughtful.

'Another lad, Jess, to roam the farmtouns and their damp unsavoury bothies, all his treadmill days.'

It seemed, on the face of it, a predictable future for the bastard bairn they had just brought into the world.

There was a rakish streak in the psyche of Sinclair MacFarquhar that squared ill with his position as Kilbirnie's banker and man of affairs and manifested itself in the kind of tweed suits he insisted on wearing. Ill they sat on him too, for his was a slighter figure than should have entertained their earthy sartorial image, making him seem at times more like a dubious auction-eer or a fugitive from some travelling fair. Since his arrival about the place the cautious men of the farmtouns had quietly, surreptitiously and in small doses shifted their little siller from his care because of it and it showed, as his wife said, an unfortunate contagion of the blood that came through in the behaviour of his daughter, with her reckless ways: it was a disgust (his wife again said for, poor man, he got little peace from her tongue) the way she threw herself at every man that came her way and treated poor young Davidson so badly.

'Just so,' MacFarquhar always said. 'Just so,' for he was a man full of all the bland phrases and responses of life (as befitted his position) who could turn his remarks and his coat to any occasion. On the credit side, he could always be relied on to interject a leavening of calm between heated conversationalists and to fill the overwhelming silences of any social event with the state of the weather, the government, the crops . . . He was in short a man who moved effortlessly in any vacuum, and indeed, was deeply afraid of the silences of life and unable to endure them. Yet now, in the bare room at the back of the house that was his bank and business office, words had failed him utterly. He sat in the profoundest dumb-founded silence he had yet endured. His een, he considered—it was the only conclusion—were undoubtedly deceiving him.

His composure returned sufficiently for him to re-read the letter he had torn from the envelope but a minute or two before—the sealed envelope that his long-time client Angus Campbell of the Mossgair had deposited with him a mere three weeks before for safe-keeping and against the day of his death. A great gasp escaped the banker, of disbelief and incredulity—never had there been the like of it in Kilbirnie, he was sure—but there was indeed no doubt of it and Sinclair MacFarquhar eased his collar stud with a trembling hand. He scrutinized every word on the white parchment in his shaking fist, each scrawl in the outline of what he recognized as Campbell's own hand:

I, Angus Macqueen Campbell, these many years, like my father before me, farmer of the Mossgair, a toun of one hundred and twenty acres or thereby, being this day of sound mind and will and having no direct heir nor close kin belonging or known to me, bequeath the said toun of Mossgair with all stock, implements, appurtenances and equipment thereon to the child to be born of my servant maid, Morag MacCaskill, it being the issue of the said person and my second ploughman, Ewan Carmichael, who passed from this earth in the terrible tragedy of the Tay Bridge.

I have no doubt but that had he lived, the child of their union would have been countenanced and provided for by him and that he would have acknowledged it as his own. Carmichael was of my own blood, though but distantly related. In that he is no longer able to do so, it behoves me to implement what I know would have been his wish.

As to Morag MacCaskill, since my wife's passing she has run my house and kitchen uncomplaining and without help and kept kindness with me when I might have deserved otherwise. In the circumstances it is meet that the bairn— bastard alas though it will be—should inherit what would have been the father's portion had he lived. So being it be a male child, it is my wish that he should grow into the occupancy of the Mossgair at his twenty-first birthday, the farmtoun to be worked and so managed the meanwhile as his mother deems fit. In the event that the child be a female, it is to be the mother's free choice as to how the farmtoun be employed to secure the bairn a comfortable future.

Campbell's undisputed signature gave authority to his words, his witnesses two of the smaller savers of the Shorthorn Bank, Margaret Pringle (schoolteacher of the parish) and Patrick Pringle (minister of the same).

'Well, dammit!'

MacFarquhar finally swore loudly in his surprise, a mark of how deeply the whole thing had thrown his careful world out of kilter, for ordinarily he would have considered 'Dash it' expletive enough and it would have caused hardly a ripple in his blood pressure. He considered the letter again, peering closely, as though he might yet find the code that would counter what it was that it said to him. Alas, there was none. MacFarquhar sighed deeply. He had to accept it; his duty was clear.

There was just one thing more.

After a substantial lunch had soothed his stomach, Sinclair MacFarquhar gave his brown brogues a rub with one of the maid's dusters and set off up the village the way of the Doctor's house. It was not his health that took him there, though in all conscience he felt a sickness in his stomach at the thought of siller going where it was not well acquainted and so sadly outwith the control of those who normally circulated it, but the most elementary of precautions that his office demanded of him.

Munro was at home: he'd made up a few drugs for collection and now took a moment of ease in his book-lined parlour. The unexpectedness of the visit surprised him.

'I'm not for the debtor's prison, surely, Sinclair?' he said affably as the banker was shown in. 'My affairs cannot be in that bad state, ill though they be.'

MacFarquhar smiled, a condescending benison on a man whose affairs were never in good order and who cared so little for his siller that he seldom speired after it. To MacFarquhar that was incomprehensible.

'No, no, Doctor. It's not that.'

'Ye're not ailing then, Sinclair?'

'I'm fine, Mungo. Fine! It's a more delicate matter that brings me.'

'Oh?' Mungo's curiosity was whetted. MacFarquhar surely was too wary for intrigue.

'MacCaskill's lassie, Mungo——'

'Aye.'

'She's had a child, they say.'

'They say right, Sinclair, though what business it is of theirs——'

The banker held a staying hand. 'Business of mine though, Mungo. Confeedential, you'll understand.'

'So——' Munro nodded his understanding.

'A boy child, Mungo?'

'Yes, since ye ask.'

'She's unmarried?'

'So's plenty more, Sinclair, in the same way—but the bairn's a bastard if that's what you mean.'

'Aye.' The banker looked at his brown shoes, a fine film of Kilbirnie's summer dust now lying across their polished toe-caps. 'They say the father is—was—the toun's second horse-man, Carmichael.'

'She told me as much.'

'Ye believed her?'

Munro was getting impatient. 'Why not, it's a remarkably common phenomenon in our farming countryside, Sinclair.' Surely the man was aware of that.

'There's nae doubt then?'

'None, I'd say, but——'

MacFarquhar again stayed the conversation with an admonitory hand. 'Confeedential, Mungo. Ye understand.' There was no doubt in his mind now but that he had to accept it.

★

So, maybe, it had been: the bold MacFarquhar stepping slow ben the howe in the late afternoon to tell you the news: the Mossgair to be yours. I cannot say how it was, one way or the other. I work only from memories faded by time, the nuances of sighs, the fragments of your reflective silences, mere echoes in the wind. Strange you thought it, no doubt, that it should be so, the bairn at your breist as he stepped in so you'd had hurriedly to lift the nipple from that warm, milk-wet bud of a mouth and slip the pap back into your frock . . .

So maybe that was the story of your days, Old Woman, the days when the bloom was on you, young and blithe you had been in that long-ago time, the heat of youth in your blood in those nichts in the loft and Campbell gone from the toun. And the loft in the soft summer nicht a fairy place of licht and shadow and once the red disc of a moon that shone down through the skylicht, turning the shadows to crimson and just the two of you there in that loft-warm nicht. . . . Had that been the nicht, you wondered, close and close, as though the heat of a hundred hairsts was in you, his lips on you maddening you till *pyach*! demented you tore the sark from his back and slid from your own inmost petticoat, the first time he'd seen you, for so long you had wanted—you gasped at his wonderment there in the shadows where his melodies lingered. The dreich dull toil of the day slipped from you then and you had floated that nicht in a fey kingdom of dream and fantasy, lapped by the whisper of restless tides and tossed in the tumult of unstayable storms. Near to morning you brushed your bruised lips on his and felt the blood in them and letting him sleep, slid from him . . .

Maybe that was the way of it: I cannot say for we did not speak of it. Yet I know in my blood that was your blood and was his blood the fires that bide and smoulder there; that bright, flichtering flame of life that burns unseen, that rouses whiles in the blood. Maybe you would wonder, Old Woman, the two of us by the ingle-neuk, at your blood on three continents, your pain carried and felt still in those moments when we venture beyond the comfortable limits into the emotional wastelands, as unbearable now as yours once was. Children you have not seen know your name and something of your story; they too have heired your legacy of love and sorrow and stoic endurance. They will know the pain of loving in a careful world. It is your spirit that will succour them: that indomitable song that sings in the heart . . . But these were the things unsaid between us; they came in the blood, sure and fine; we did not speak of them for there was a shyness in you Old Woman, that kept you still in that world before mine . . .

From his study window Patrick Pringle looked out to the Croft Hill where the old squat dwellings of the crofter men were fading into the late July dusk. Clouds lowered, scudding hosts fleeing across the sky, menacing, foreboding. Gusts of an angry wind buffeted the window, rattling it in its frame. It was a night for treachery and rape and unspeakable deeds, for settling old and festering scores, for slaking unslakable lusts. Along the howe, he saw the light in the schoolhouse. Behind him on the desk, unhasped and waiting, the quill across its open page, his journal awaited his thoughts. In the tumult of his mind their pattern formed and dissolved, grouped and regrouped, forming sequences of words so fleetingly that they were gone before they had been examined. For once, Pringle found words difficult—poor, stinting, inadequate cyphers with which to convey all that had occurred, oddly incapable of expressing the harsh and damning indictment, of conveying the betrayal, the treason of the blood that had lately afflicted his countryside. He turned wearily: yet he must record. Let others judge how deep was the hurt, how cynical the betrayal. His quill began its task, that hand-of-write with its surge and sweep and flow from the pages of earlier years slower now, carving jagged, spiky characters as though chiselling them in stone.

July 26, 1880
This year bypast has seen much change in the Howe of Kilbirnie and in its Croft Hill in particular for the fifty families or thereabouts that once had their small kingdoms there. Folk, some of them washed here like debris forty or so years ago from the ill-famed Clearances of the West, find their lives again cruelly interrupted. Again they are folk in flight for no longer can they afford the punitive rents that are being asked of them. Their siller will not run to it supposing they were to hunger themselves to the bone. They

are the victims of progress and maybe of their own natures. Their folly was to believe that they could have a kind of freedom beyond the reach of other men's greeds. In my thirty years in the parish I have watched the slow death of their dream; their hopes fading with every fall in the price of a stirk or a quarter of corn. For the crofter man, alas, cuts but a poor figure at the very edge of our rural economy: the farmer, grazier and butcher well ken it, that he is a man without the freedom of financial manoeuvre; that he of all folk cannot afford to return home the way he came with the beast for sale still behind him on the tether. He maun sell; in that he is the victim of his own independence for the world has deemed it meet that no man can now stand alone, sufficient unto himself. He is a lamb shorn short to the wind. Lord, have pity on him . . .

Pringle's hand paused and hovered over what he had written. *Lord, have pity* . . . He had written it unthinking, from the heart. It had been a simple cry, like a child's. Slowly, a quiet glow of elation took hold of him, a gratitude welled in him. He put down his quill to clasp his hands over the open pages of the journal and spoke softly for himself the words of a hallowed prayer.

Long after, alone in the manse's night-quiet he took the lamp from his desk and carrying it with him, went downstairs to the bite of oat bannock and cheese that Margaret had earlier laid ready for him. There was nothing now that he could add to the Croft Hill's story that would not colour it with bitterness; nothing more that he wanted to add. Seated at the manse table, he hesitated for an instant, then scorning the plate Margaret had set, broke the oatcake on the tablecloth in the pressure between fingers and thumb and mealed-down the blue-veined crofter's cheese to chimbles. It was something his old crofting father had always done; he had been a simple man with a love of the parks and nature who had brought little into this life with him and taken as little out of it. Quietly, Pringle realized: his action was a kind of sacramental gesture, keeping faith with the past. Maybe for him it was a necessary thing: patent boots, after all, did not make you one of the gentry.

★

216

So they went that year from the Hill, the most of them; selling up their pitiful possessions, roupit out at their doors, their beasts from their byres, their dung middens sold where they stood at the steadings' end fermenting their essences, the strongly-stenched juices of an ongoing fertility. Grogan Faulkner came back time and again, the unwilling agent of their destruction. As the Whitsunday term drew on the market for his patter and his guile sadly diminished with every performance. As he said dejectedly to Davie his clerk, he was suffering from over-exposure though it was not pity for himself that troubled him but for the folk whose life-gear had suddenly lost value in that dismal glut. That year there was a surfeit of hayrakes and hairst forks, bee-skeps and trump-picks, shovels, spades, corn riddles and flails, harrows and battered shelts' harness in every farmtoun of the parish as their folk in turn took in tow possessions they little had need of and would never have use for. In their bare and functional kitchens there had appeared an embarrassing sufficiency of chairs (that nobody had time to sit on) and of milking utensils. For some of the old croft folk it would seem incomprehensible that they would not have a cow to drive in from the parks or the milking to do. It would create an unaccountable gap in their day they never would get used to. With their suppers taken there would in future be womenfolk who would not know what to do with their evenings let alone with their days without butter to churn or cheese to chessel, their work aprons hung over the end of the bed long before noon and the afternoon stretching an infinity before them. It was a paucity of life they had never expected, could never have contemplated.

As the croft biggings were emptied they were locked by the laird's men and left to sit. Here and there a new tenant or two—incomers all—moved in, confident men, cocky in their stride, disdainful of the men before them whiles as they stepped into Miller's bar or the emporium of Robert S. Scroggie. Their wives congregated together, as though sensing the howe's hostility. Young they were mostly, those new men and their womenfolk, untried by life. Strive as they might in the years to come—though some in time might step from the tenancy of a lowly croft to that of a small farmtoun—they would not be able to catch the spirit of the old crofter men or imbibe that all-consuming fire that had driven men like MacGillivray and Morrison and Maglashan and those unfortunates like John Glennie, who had so feared failure he could no longer face his bairns. They would not light again that torch of freedom that made a man take a bit of the moor or the hillside and pit his skill against raw nature, his life against a long tomorrow . . .

With the years, the last of the old croft folk would go, giving up their leases, unable to make them pay, not able to deceive themselves longer, lonely now and all but destitute. The wide world would claim them, cold and uncaring; they would don the compliant yoke that society demanded of them, fit in, conform. They had buried a dream, the dream that had once been John Glennie's and Maglashan's and MacGillivray's and James MacCaskill's, the dream that had justified their lives as they broke their roadmender's stones, biggit other men's dykes and drained other men's ditches. They had invested themselves heavily, muscle and brawn, body and will. Now destiny would cast them adrift, empty of spirit, a dreadful bankruptcy in their souls. Now and then, while his wife was at the evening milking, a man beset by his own despair would fill his pipe and walk down to the loch. So still the green water; just the lap of the ripples dying slowly away . . .

They went from the Hill those folk of the crofts who once stitched the small seams of history, the fight and the tyaave of their days behind them, a drift of folk aware that the land too had betrayed them. When they had gone from the lower crofts the farmtouns of the howe would set their head-dykes higher on the hill and take in the land that had been theirs and throw their small parks into wide brae-set fields: the reaper and binder would reign where the crofter's scythe and the sickle had swung, swinging through the long days of harvest; the corn would stand tall in the golden sunlight. Here and there on the Hill a dwelling better than its neighbours would be saved to house the poor wandering cottars of that far countryside with their sorely-pressed wives and their broods of raggy-arsed bairns, folk as unburdened by this world's gear as the Hill folk who had left it. But mainly the old biggings stood till time outwore them, till their old roofs fell in, till the frosts loosened their feeble clay-mortared stones and their old walls toppled into the nettles that now enfolded them. You can find them still, a birn of stones on the bleak hillside, a sad lichened memorial to those who once had their lives there. These clustered stones are all that remain . . . or almost all, for there is something else. There is a haunting sorrow still on the Croft Hill for all the things that died there. Harken for a moment and laich on the wind comes the sound of the old speak of the hill-folk, couthy and kind with a rough warmth, a sly, wry humour. It was rich and strong and it spoke to the heart, for it was the voice of the folk who were your own. But the old track now is grass-grown, all but obliterated by the years; once it was the way the cadger came and the packman and the dark-glowering tinker and folk known and unknown who passed in the night from whence to God knows where, silent unchancy folk who inhabited neither this world nor the next. Their ghosts wander still where the head-dykes and the whins and the broom begin.

Memory gathers here down by the lochside, here in the kirkyard where the rain beats down on the back-tilting tomb-stones: green moss on the stones hiding their legends and dreams in the kirkyard under the sod. It was here they once brought them, those hardy folk of the Hill and the howe when their day was done, free at last of laird and factor. They are quiet now with their griefs behind them. Here in the mirk they step briefly from the shadows, their faces lit for an instant in the infinitude of eternity before darkness swallows them again. It is one stone that draws me: a tablet of red granite that the years have faded and the rains eroded. It was here that they brought you Old Woman when your long day ended. Death did not fear you: you had lived long and had not had your sorrows to seek. But the man you came to lie with was not the young ploughboy of your girlhood years, not the one magical love of your life, but a good man all the same. He gave you love and children and took your fatherless bairn as his own. You cared for him in your way and he did not ask for more. Now in the evening gloam the wandering wind tugs the grass and the bracken encroaches; by day buttercups dance in the sunlight where the gravedigger's boot has not set foot this many a year.

I am a stranger here . . .

Yet still the heart has hurts it cannot speak. Greet soft for the dreams of men.